The Senses of Touch

DAVID LEARY
10/09

The Senses of Touch

Haptics, Affects and Technologies

Mark Paterson

Oxford • New York

First published in 2007 by
Berg
Editorial offices:
1st Floor, Angel Court, 81 St Clements Street, Oxford, OX4 1AW, UK
175 Fifth Avenue, New York, NY 10010, USA

Berg is the imprint of Oxford International Publishers Ltd.

Library of Congress Cataloging-in-Publication Data

Paterson, Mark, 1972-
    The senses of touch : haptics, affects, and technologies / Mark
Paterson.
        p. cm.
    Includes bibliographical references (p.) and index.
    ISBN-13: 978-1-84520-478-5 (cloth)
    ISBN-10: 1-84520-478-6 (cloth)
    ISBN-13: 978-1-84520-479-2 (pbk.)
    ISBN-10: 1-84520-479-4 (pbk.)
  1. Touch. I. Title.

    BF275.P38 2007
    152.1'82—dc22

                                                        2007028371

British Library Cataloguing-in-Publication Data

A catalogue record for this book is available from the British Library.

ISBN 978 1 84520 478 5 (Cloth)
ISBN 978 1 84520 479 2 (Paper)

Typeset by JS Typesetting Ltd, Porthcawl, Mid Glamorgan
Printed in the United Kingdom by Biddles Ltd, King's Lynn

www.bergpublishers.com

Contents

Acknowledgements

This project was completed with a year's Research Leave generously enabled by the Arts and Humanities Research Council (AHRC) of the United Kingdom, and supported by the School of Cultural Studies at the University of the West of England, Bristol, during 2005/06. A great deal of the book was written in Australia as a Visiting Scholar with the Department of Critical and Cultural Studies, Macquarie University, Sydney. I am grateful to both staff and postgraduate students there.

At Berg, Hannah Shakespeare has been extremely supportive of the project from the beginning. Thanks go to her tireless efficiency and enthusiasm. Emily Medcalfe has made sure the cover remained as envisaged. Thanks also go to Giselle Arteaga-Johnson at The Norton Simon Foundation of Philadelphia for allowing the reproduction of José de Ribera's painting *The Sense of Touch* as a cover image. Not only is the title appropriate, but the relationship of touch and vision in the blind man's tactile exploration is a central theme in this book.

A few of the chapters have previously been published in various incarnations, although each has been modified extensively.

Chapter 3, 'Seeing with the hands', is based on research conducted for the article 'Seeing with the hands, touching with the eyes: Vision, touch and the Enlightenment spatial imaginary' published in *The Senses and Society* 1(2), 2006, pp 224–42.

Chapter 4, 'The forgetting of touch' is adapted from an article originally published as 'The Forgetting of Touch: Re-membering Geometry with Eyes and Hands', in *Angelaki: Journal of the Theoretical Humanities* 10(3), 2005, pp 115–31.

For chapter 7, 'Feel the Presence', I must acknowledge my great debt to researchers Calle Sjöström and Kirsten Rassmus-Gröhn at CERTEC in Lund, Sweden; Stephen Furner at BT Research Labs, Martlesham Heath, UK; The ReachIn Technologies AB team in Stockholm, Sweden; and Dr. Mandayam Srinivasan at MIT TouchLabs. Without exception they were welcoming and generous, with both time and ideas. A version of this chapter was published as 'Feel the Presence: the technologies of touch', in *Environment and Planning D: Society and Space* 24(5), 2006, pp. 691–708.

For chapter 8, 'Affecting touch', my thanks to two Reiki practitioners, 'Louis' and 'Rachel', in Bristol. Material from the research originally appeared as a chapter in J. Davidson, L. Bondi and M. Smith (eds), *Emotional Geographies* (Aldershot: Ashgate). The version in this book has been extensively modified, and I am grateful to Ruth Barcan and Jay Johnston at the Department of Gender Studies, University of Sydney, for their insights.

For related content, illustrations to accompany the text and helpful internet links, please visit **www.sensesoftouch.co.uk**

Glossary

Haptics terminology used throughout the book.

Haptic   Relating to the sense of touch in all its forms, including those below.

Proprioception Perception of the position, state and movement of the body and limbs in space. Includes *cutaneous*, *kinaesthetic*, and *vestibular* sensations.

Vestibular   Pertaining to the perception of balance, head position, acceleration and deceleration. Information obtained from semi-circular canals in the inner ear.

Kinaesthesia   The sensation of movement of body and limbs. Relating to sensations originating in muscles, tendons and joints.

Cutaneous   Pertaining to the skin itself or the skin as a sense organ. Includes sensation of pressure, temperature and pain.

Tactile   Pertaining to the cutaneous sense, but more specifically the sensation of pressure (from mechanoreceptors) rather than temperature (thermoceptors) or pain (nociceptors).

Force Feedback Relating to the mechanical production of information sensed by the human kinaesthetic system. Devices provide cutaneous and kinaesthetic feedback that usually correlates to the visual display.

Compiled from numerous sources, including Cole (1995:xix–xx) and Oakley et al. (2000:416)

–1–

The Primacy of Touch

The Manifold Senses of Touch

> And I found that of all the senses the eye was the most superficial, the ear the most haughty, smell the most voluptuous, taste the most superstitious and inconstant, touch the most profound and philosophical.
>
> Diderot, 'Letter on the Blind,' 1749

While we might agree with the sentiments of Diderot, we usually think of touch in more prosaic terms. A hand brushing or stroking a piece of exposed skin, perhaps. The immediacy of cutaneous contact with the skin surface. But if we scratch that surface, if we dig deeper into the physiology, psychology and the fleshy philosophy of the body, the manifold meanings of touch start to reveal themselves. Sight, sound and the body in general have been studied extensively in the humanities, the social sciences and the natural sciences. But within an academic climate that celebrates visual cultures, and the popular media's infatuation with visuality, touch remains largely neglected, forgotten. Looking at the cultural, historical and philosophical treatment of touch, we can see why. We have an enduring cultural assumption, present in Plato and compounded in the Enlightenment, of the primacy of vision. In Aristotle's famous hierarchy of the five senses in *De Anima* of *c*.350 BC, sight is the superior sense while touch is relegated to the lowest, basest position. He reserves contempt for the 'bestial' pleasures of taste but especially erotic touch in his *Ethics* (1118a24–25).[1] The Neoplatonic philosopher Ficino was not untypical in equating touch with the baser, more carnal forms of love, contrasting it with the 'higher' or spiritual love associated with vision (Johnson 2002:62). Yet touch is crucial to embodied existence. The lowly position of touch in the hierarchy belies its complex constitution, being a singular sense that corresponds to no single organ. Physiologically, touch is a modality resulting from the combined information of innumerable receptors and nerve endings concerned with pressure, temperature, pain and movement. But there is more to touch. It is a sense of communication. It is receptive, expressive, can communicate empathy. It can bring distant objects and people into proximity.

More than a series of physiological explanations, this book is about the manifold senses of touch, from the quotidian and everyday to the abstract and rarefied. Since Diderot regards touch as the most profound and philosophical of the senses, accordingly we pursue several historical debates and philosophical problems that concern the relationship between touch and vision, hands and eyes. Less abstractly, unless we have an extremely rare neurological condition, touch is present within every single interaction with objects, and a considerable amount of interaction with people. Within waking consciousness, and sometimes within dreaming, it is undeniably present. As a reprehensibly under-examined component of everyday, embodied experience touch is everywhere, yet almost nowhere is it discussed. The submissive position it is accorded historically, plus the complexly articulated world that it allows us to have, means that indeed, to quote Klatzky et al. (1987), 'There's more to touch than meets the eye'.

Doubting Thomas, embedded in the Christian heritage, is so-called for not believing what he saw, having to physically touch Christ's wounds to ensure certainty, to find proof. The popular expression 'seeing's believing, but feeling's the truth' reflects this, as Bronner reminds us (1982:352). Yet our current cultural perspective has favoured one side of the equation, and 'seeing is believing' is the oft-remembered and rehearsed part of the phrase. At least in Western industrialized cultures, such attitudes maintain the sensory stereotype whereby vision is predominant, is distanced and even deceitful, whereas touch seems more intimate, reassuring and proximal. As in Doubting Thomas, touch is associated with verification, the connotations of tangibility being solid, foundational, undeceiving. And, as in Aristotle, touch in its immediacy is base or bestial. But elsewhere Aristotle does celebrate the aesthetic pleasures that touch affords, decoupling valid sensory pleasure from more bestial or carnal appetites. This is the case only with humans, who have the most finely discriminating powers of touch in the animal kingdom, and he sees this discriminatory power as indicative of superior intelligence (*De Anima* 421a22–26). So touch, like vision, articulates an equally rich, complex world, a world of movement and exploration, of non-verbal social communication. It is a carnal world, with its pleasures of feeling and being felt, of tasting and touching the textures of flesh and of food. And equally it is a profound world of philosophical verification, of the communication of presence and empathy with others, of the co-implication of body, flesh and world. That tension between the quotidian immediacy of cutaneous contact and the philosophical profundity of touch, between 'immediate' and 'deep' metaphorical touching, is present throughout this book.

Let us pursue further the distinction between 'immediate' and 'deep' or metaphorical touching. On the one hand, to write about touch is to consider the immediacy of our everyday, embodied tactile-spatial experience. The feeling of cutaneous touch when an object brushes our skin is simultaneously an awareness of the materiality of the object and an awareness of the spatial limits and sensations of our lived body. Reaching out to touch and caress an animate object, such as a familiar cat or a warm-cheeked lover, the immediacy of sensation is affirmatory and comforting, involving a mutual co-implication of one's own body and another's presence. On the other hand, touch can cement an empathic or affective bond, opening an entirely new channel of communication. Rather than immediate and embodied, this touch shifts toward the metaphorical, the alternative emotional connotation of 'touching' (e.g. 'I was touched by her speech'). Since the senses of touch are themselves plural, we similarly encompass a number of accounts and approaches that range from the literary, historical and philosophical to the psychological, physiological and technological. So, as the book progresses, the seeming immediacy of touch on the skin surface unfolds into deeper, more distanced, even metaphorical senses of touch. Like Merleau-Ponty's project in his *Primacy of Perception* (1964a) this is something like an archaeology of perception, attempting the understanding of the social, cultural and psychological mechanisms of the manifold forms of touching. I term this the remembering of touch in chapter 4, an attempt to recover the hidden histories of touch. Edith Wyschogrod has similarly called for a recovery of the meanings of tactility:

> The meaning of tactility has however been hidden both in the classical philosophical tradition, which forces touch into conformity with a general theory of sensation, and in the physiological reductionism of contemporary psychology, which interprets tactility as the complex of interactions among afferent receptors and kinaesthetic acts. If we are to recover the meaning of tactility we must search in familiar analyses of sensibility for the trace, *for the break with the conventional schematization of tactility as a species of the genus sensation.* (1981:193; emphasis added)

This is not to disregard the straightforward data of the psychology of touch, nor the importance of kinaesthesia or the other under-examined somatic (bodily) senses. Indeed, rediscovering these somatic sensations is imperative in understanding the manifold senses of touch and their integration. As such, the measurable certainty of cutaneous contact unfolds into other forms of touch, such as the somatic senses interior to the body and their role in quotidian embodied experience. But Wyschogrod suggests something stronger, the decoupling of 'touch' from mere 'sensation', whereby something more abstract and barely articulable arises within touching experiences. Touching thereby encompasses the affective, the emotional (the notion of touching as feeling) or, toward the end of the present volume, more metaphorical meanings of touch.

But to return momentarily to the immediacy of the skin surface. Despite the inescapable nature of everyday touching and tactile experience, it is astonishing how under-theorized even the immediacy of tactile sensation remains. Since Aristotle's time we commonly refer to the five senses, these senses being exteroceptive (outward-oriented). Even in its immediacy, the brushing of object against the skin implies not only cutaneous receptivity but also a spatial awareness that derives from interoceptive (inward-oriented) senses of bodily position, movement and balance. Tracing shapes or letters onto the skin, as the deaf-blind sometimes do to communicate, involves a form of sense-specific tactile-spatial memory. Walking through a building, for example, involves not simply a correlation between vision and touch but also combined somatic senses, the modalities of *proprioception* (the body's position felt as muscular tension), *kinaesthesia* (the sense of the movement of body and limbs) and the *vestibular sense* (a sense of balance derived from information in the inner ear).[2] A BBC *Horizon* documentary (1997) about the loss of proprioception, for example, stated that it was 'so basic to our sense of being in the world that most of us are unaware we have it'. The same might be said for touch and the somatic sensations in general. These interoceptive sensations combine in a felt coherence of bodily perception of the spatial environment, a synergic interaction of the somatic senses sometimes referred to as 'haptic', often contrasted with the 'optic' or visual system (see for example Gibson 1968, 1979; Bloomer and Moore 1978; Paterson 2002).

Haptic, from the Greek word *haptesthai*, means 'Of, pertaining to, or relating to the sense of touch or tactile sensations' (OED 1989, 2nd edn). Aristotle uses the term *haptesthai* to refer to tactile sensations in both *De Anima* (*On The Soul*) and *De Sensu et Sensibilibus* (*On Sense and the Sensible*). But a more contemporary psychology would treat those somatic senses of proprioception, kinaesthesia and the vestibular sense as working synergistically, as the inwardly-oriented sensations necessary for feelings of embodiment. 'Haptic' could therefore effectively encompass these somatic senses of touch. The term is deployed in various contexts such as art history, aesthetics and architecture, although most frequently in the psychology of perception and engineering, especially the technologies of touch. The utility of the term 'haptic' lies more in scientific, psychological and engineering concerns about embodied tactile or somatic perception, and there are obvious implications for dealing with problems of spatial access and mobility for those with sensory or motor impairments, especially the blind and visually impaired. But while 'haptic' commendably expands the reach of touch from cutaneous surface to more inwardly-oriented senses, as the chapters unfold and the book progresses we move away from the psychological orientation of individual bodily experience to consider other bodies and more metaphorical senses of touch.

Despite the theoretical paucity of treatments there is a philosophical and historical tradition of the primacy of touch, wherein touch is the first sense prior to the differentiation into other sensory modalities. It also works as a model of perception in general. This tradition, spanning from Ancient Greek philosophy to recent Russian linguistic expressions, classifies all senses as variations of touch. Writing around 350BC, in *De Sensu et Sensibilibus* Aristotle reports Democritus and his followers sharing this view, as 'they represent all objects of sense as objects of touch', and so 'it clearly follows that each of the other senses is a mode of touch' (442a–b). Aristotle himself hastily dismisses this treatment of sense perception as irrational, conceding only that taste and touch are related as they share the necessity for contact (423b). Yet touch as a universal sensory model persists in some popular conceptions and folk knowledges. A Russian émigré writing for an influential collection of anthropology essays as recently as 1953 employs exactly this notion of touch as first sense, for example:

> The dictionary of the Russian language ... defines the sense of touch as follows: 'In reality all five senses can be reduced to one – the sense of touch. The tongue and palate sense the food; the ear, sound waves; the nose, emanations; the eyes, rays of light.' That is why in all textbooks the sense of touch is always mentioned first. It means to ascertain, to perceive, by body, hand or fingers. (Anon., in Howes 2003:12)

Themes of flesh and feeling, of touch as communication and the relation between bodies, are revisited throughout the course of this book. The primacy of touch and the celebration of the ambiguities of touching and feeling are also present in the work of figures such as Luce Irigaray and Edith Wyschogrod, as we shall see, and an essay by Wyschogrod is even subtitled 'On the Primacy of Touch' (1980). While touch is, indeed, the first sense to develop in the human embryo (Rice 2001, Montagu 1986:4), the primacy of touch lies not in its sometimes proposed status as a model for all senses. Instead, in our next chapter we return to Aristotle to consider why the sense of touch is exceptional, not fulfilling the supposed requirements he believes should underlie all sensation: a sense organ, a medium and an object (Wyschogrod 1980:193). This is an appropriate point at which to commence a project for a reconsideration of the importance of tactility and touching, of the significance of tactile experience. If touch and the non-visual senses are largely forgotten or ignored in Western industrialized cultures, this book follows recent sensuous scholarship (e.g. Classen 1993, 1997; Stoller 1997; Geurts 2002, 2005; Howes 2003, 2005; Feld 2005; Drobnick 2006) in attempting to repatriate and reconsider non-visual experience, within the wide focus of cultural history as well as the narrower focus of individual experience. So, alongside this significant acknowledgement of the senses in cultural history and ethnography, I also stress the relevance of some existing phenomenological work in this area that can help advance sensuous scholarship.

Unfolding Touch: the Shape of the Book

For the reader to come to terms with the scope and themes of this book, we can see how it is comparable with, and complements, other works. Most significantly, Constance Classen's *Book of Touch* (2005) is a valuable literary, sociological and cultural-historical resource, collating diverse writing and scholarship on touch. As should already be apparent, *The Senses of Touch* is more philosophical and psychological in its approach, and usefully complements that volume. Further, and as alluded to previously, the term 'ocularcentrism' is coined by Martin Jay in his *Downcast Eyes* (1994), an intellectual history of the gaze. This book adopts a comparable intellectual and historical scope in terms of tactility. But my purpose in surveying and deploying historical and philosophical treatments of touch and its relationship with vision concerns the development of a 'felt' phenomenology, stating and developing theoretical, philosophical and ethnographic concerns along the way.

So the senses of touch are multiple, complex and intertwining, and the chapter-by-chapter description that follows marks out the trajectory and the various 'senses' of touch encountered along the way. It provides an overview of how these various senses and conceptions of touch are folded into each other, how certain tactile themes recur and develop throughout the book. Here is an opportunity to summarize the central arguments developed and revisited throughout the book, to provide a succinct schema for understanding the different 'senses' of touch to be examined. While cutaneous contact is the most immediate and obvious form of touch, the book progressively departs from this particular sense in order to consider other, less literal senses of touch. Accordingly, by departing from the literal touch of immediate sensation, each chapter unfolds some of the manifold senses of touch, eventually revealing forms of 'deep' touch that invoke more affective and metaphorical forms of touching. All of these senses of touch are loosely framed in terms of a phenomenology of touch and touching, what I call a 'felt' phenomenology.

Stated simply, some recurrent themes that emerge and develop throughout the chapters, although not exhaustive, will aid the understanding of the whole. First, the Western cultural and historical bias of opticism, what Jay (1994) terms 'ocularcentrism', recognizing the primacy of the visual image and the privileging of ocular observation as a path to certainty and knowledge whereby touch is routinely debased and ignored. Secondly, the long-running philosophical and psychological debates concerning the relationship between vision and touch, being periodically referred to through the synecdoche of eyes (denoting vision) and hands (denoting touch). This complex relationship between vision and touch, eyes and hands is sometimes cast in terms of the optic and the haptic. Although these are not equivalent terms, the fundamental relationship between vision and touch invariably underlies each chapter. Thirdly, the historical conception of blindness and visual impairment, and a consequent foregrounding of touch as the most significant sense for perceiving and interacting with the world. Fourthly, the role of touch within everyday, embodied experience for sightless and sighted alike that goes largely unacknowledged, including the lesser-articulated forms of bodily or somatic sensation concerning movement, position and balance. Fifthly, the more philosophical notion of touch as a sense of proximity or distance, where immediate cutaneous touch is popularly conceived to be a sense of nearness and proximity, and vision as a distance sense. The various technologies, affects and aesthetics of touch will considerably complicate this division, as we shall see. And, finally, the conceptual slippage between touching and feeling, between touch as cutaneous contact and a more metaphorical notion of being affected emotionally, being 'touched'. Appropriately enough, as we move ever further from the identification of touch with skin surface, this relationship between literal touching and more metaphorical and emotive forms of being touched finds its most direct treatment in the final chapter.

If the trajectory of this book is partly described by the movement from the immediacy of cutaneous touch on the skin surface to more metaphorical and affective conceptualizations of touch, then in the first chapter, 'Learning How to See, Describing How to Feel: a "Felt" Phenomenology', we start to develop an examination of the more inwardly-directed senses. Being relatively easy to recognize and quantify patterns of cutaneous sensation, we complicate this by invoking other receptors and the more somatic (or bodily) senses that constitute the background of everyday embodied perception. Often these sensations are vague, barely articulable or easily confused. But bodily sensations such as kinaesthesia and proprioception are the subject of phenomenological analyses by both Husserl and Merleau-Ponty, and phenomenology is thereby shown to be a suitable mode of analysis of these more interior senses of touch. But before launching into detailed phenomenological discussion we establish some of the intellectual legacy to thinking about the body and its various senses. By returning to Aristotle we therefore determine some of the conceptual underpinnings and historical assumptions behind such experiences. If, historically, scholarship has neglected the role of the senses and even actively exercised scepticism toward their veracity, in several works Aristotle does treat the senses as philosophically important, and touch is singled out. In fact, Aristotle's fairly detailed discussions in *De Anima* and *De Sensu et Sensibilibus* of *c.*350BC both argue that touch is simultaneously the most base yet most primary sense, and references to his postulations help frame later phenomenological considerations of touch throughout the book.

The opportunity arises here for a brief historical overview of the phenomenological method, and for beginning to formulate a 'felt' phenomenology, marrying up Aristotle's reflections on *aesthesis* (the sensory faculty) with more contemporary discussions of the hidden somatic sensations and their presence in everyday embodiment. In that overview we introduce the later work of Husserl on the 'aesthetic body' and Merleau-Ponty's discussion of touch, but focus especially on their treatment of the hitherto under-examined somatic sensations of kinaesthesia and proprioception, seeing these as integral to a phenomenological project concerning the sensations of touch. Although the heart of the project starts here, the phenomenological treatment of touch is developed throughout the book, being augmented by historical philosophy in the following chapter, then by considerations of touch and technology, of play and performance, of a haptic aesthetics and, finally, by therapeutic touching between bodies in later chapters, as we shall see.

'Seeing with the Hands, Touching with the Eyes' takes the ideas of blindness that began the previous chapter and focuses on how blindness was conceived historically and philosophically, stemming from Descartes' idea of 'seeing with the hands' in his *Dioptrique* of 1637. This analogy, interpreting sensory data from one modality (touch) in terms of another (vision) was to be pervasive, informing successive philosophical debates and thought experiments throughout the Enlightenment. Indeed, much of the formative thinking concerning blindness and visual impairment, especially the imagination of blindness by the sighted, stems from this historical moment, the historical formation of the legacy of the relationship between vision and touch. This is one of the core themes running throughout the book, but finds explicitly historical, philosophical and psychological treatment here.

The centrality of the so-called 'Molyneux problem' at this time explicitly raises such questions concerning vision and touch in terms of the visual and tactile experience of the blind. Beginning as a purely speculative philosophical thought experiment, before ophthalmic operations could be performed, the debate continued and is examined in this chapter in relation to current work in psychology and neuropsychology. From debates and correspondence in the seventeenth century and onward, sparked by this hypothetical question, first-person accounts of the blind were sought to verify these abstract speculations. Molyneux's question is therefore crucial in Enlightenment philosophy and informs a series of subsequent dialogues between philosophers including Locke, Berkeley, Voltaire and Condillac, receiving especial treatment in the *Letter on the Blind* (1749) by the *Encyclopédiste* Denis Diderot. The problem concentrated on the interaction of hands and eyes, the visual and the tactile, and their role in producing a sense of space. Revisiting and developing the theme of 'learning how to see' from the previous chapter, and allied with those philosophical debates and speculations, we then look to evidence from actual historical case studies of post-operative vision to inform these long-running debates. This key historical and philosophical period, fusing as it does post-operative evidence with abstract philosophical speculation, forms something of the historical background to later phenomenological considerations of touch and tactile experience. Furthermore, the legacy of those debates concerning an imagination of blindness by the sighted remains pertinent to this day, exerting a fascination for the public as even recent newspapers, magazines and films attest.

'The Forgetting of Touch: Geometry with Eyes and Hands' hits another important theme of this book, the historical bias toward the optic and ocularcentrism in Western cultural history, and a concomitant neglect of the haptic. This tendency I characterize broadly as the 'forgetting of touch', in contrast to the celebration of visual culture that currently prevails. This chapter establishes a robust theoretical and historical context for this forgetting of touch, acting as a conceptual framework for more empirical investigations conducted in subsequent chapters. Directly addressing the way that tactility has been purposefully forgotten in our culture in favour of the 'nobility of sight' (Jonas 1954), some archival work and philosophical excavations are conducted in order to redress this balance. A prime historical exemplar of this forgetting of touch is the supposedly distanced, abstracted visualism of geometry and the history of measurement. Being two-dimensional, the products of measurement such as hard-copy charts, historical records and field-surveying manuals seem to obscure the actual bodily processes of measurement and fieldwork which presuppose their production. Through historical and philosophical analysis I then attempt to re-inscribe the body within these conventional histories of measurement. By redressing the optical bias and trying to 'remember' touch, I therefore reintroduce the concepts of embodied, haptic perception into geometry and field surveying. By adding hands (and feet, indeed) to the experience of the eye, this is as much a literal re-membering as a remembering of the body, that is, adding once again the concrete experience of hands and feet to the abstracted visualism of the eye.

In order to achieve this philosophically and historically I look at two things. First, Derrida's first published work was a deconstruction of Husserl's history of geometry, and reading Husserl with Derrida gives some sense of what a phenomeno-logical geometry could do. Referring back to the major theme of ocularcentrism, Husserl looks at the assumptions of what he calls the 'geometric spirit', or what Bachelard (1994) later terms 'geometrism', the emphasis on the detached eye rather than the embodied hand. That forms the philosophical basis for interpretation and a method for thinking through geometry. Secondly, I examine through secondary historical sources the way that geometry was disseminated in the Middle Ages, through practical methods such as field-surveying manuals and architectural discourse. These historical texts reintroduced practical, embodied ways of meas-uring alongside mathematical treatises, serving as an entry point into a critique of ocularcentrism or abstract visualism, again reinscribing the haptic and the tactile into historic accounts. Within this chapter, alongside that to Husserl and Derrida, reference is made to other figures who argue the relative merits of the haptic over the optic, of the significance of the hands and tactility, including psychologist Géza Révész and art historian William Ivins. Ivins noted for example that the Greeks adopted a tactile geometry, and such observations are further developed in the following chapter concerning aesthetic experience and the significance of the optic and the haptic in art history. Overall, the theme of the *forgetting* of touch and the rise of visual culture is therefore addressed through detailed philosophical and historical means, enabling a *remembering* and a rediscovery of haptic experience in different ways.

After remembering touch and the reaching-out of the body in measurement of the previous chapter, conversely '"How the World Touches Us": Haptic Aesthetics', looks indeed at 'how the world touches us', in Merleau-Ponty's words (1969:244), the alteration of sensibility and affects within aesthetic experience. As such, this is to advance a so-called 'haptic aesthetics', concerned less with touching than with being touched. Starting from Walter Benjamin's observations on the 'tactile properties' of art, which invoke the affective impact achievable through aesthetic experience, we consider examples of painting, sculpture and architecture, and use Merleau-Ponty's (1964a; 1969) arguments about the evocation of tactility in Cézanne as one route to achieve this. Merleau-Ponty's argument about the two-dimensional canvas, I claim, is eminently suitable to three-dimensional aesthetic encounters with sculpture and the built environment. This argument in fact has relevant precursors in aesthetics and art history, including Riegl's (1995 [1901]) distinction between the 'haptic' and the 'optic' in late Roman art, considerations of the role of touch in Renaissance art, and the nineteenth-century philosophical interest in empathy or *Einfühlung* of Vischer and Lipps, for example, involving empathic feeling in aesthetic appreciation.

But the role of tactility within aesthetic experience, and its empathic qualities, are exemplified much earlier than Merleau-Ponty and Riegl through the eighteenth-century philosophical approach of Johann Gottfried Herder. His seminal work *Sculpture* (2002 [1778]) is supremely aware of tactility and acknowledges the significance of touch for that medium. Herder himself refers to the classical Greek myth of the sculptor Pygmalion who, having crafted a beautiful form of a woman in marble, promptly fell in love with his creation. The goddess Aphrodite noticed this unwholesome affinity and, taking pity, granted life to the statue. The marble figure then becomes flesh, and a significant moment occurs when the statue responds to Pygmalion's erotic touch. The myth is explored in an early section of chapter 5 as the narrative of the discovery of the senses, and the significance of touch in becoming flesh is a useful way of conceptualizing the unfolding of tactility within increasingly spatial art forms, from painting to sculpture and architecture. The narrative therefore neatly maps onto the consideration of the unfolding aesthetic (that is, sensing, feeling) body, since by imaginatively inhabiting the statue's becoming-flesh we too start with the two-dimensionality of vision, opening our eyes, and subsequently start to correlate other senses with movement, becoming increasingly spatially aware. This is a similar trajectory to chapter 3's discussion of Richard Gregory's blind patient 'learning how to see'. The progressive dimensionality of space and sensation therefore maps onto the three sections that comprise the aesthetic 'body' of the chapter, that of skin (painting, surface), flesh (sculpture, volume) and body (architecture, space). Throughout chapter 5, and continually building on the theme of the relationship between touch and vision explored in earlier chapters, is the distinction between optic and haptic, eye and hand, in these increasingly spatial art forms. As a result the embodied, affective nature of aesthetic experience runs throughout, underlying the specificity of the art forms examined. We therefore return to the etymological and historical origins of *aesthesis*, as sensing and feeling, and employ this derivation of the aesthetic to better articulate the two-way process of touching and being touched.

CH.1

'Tangible Play, Prosthetic Performance' applies insights from the historical approach to a haptic aesthetics developed in the previous chapter, but here focuses on how touch is mediated and literally brought into play in recent art installations and performances.

Touch and the sensorium (the organization of the senses) is literally mani*fold* in the sense of folding parts of the body into others, re-mapping the topography of the body and its sensory properties, from one mode of mediation to another. Three digital artist/performers who play with different folds of body and sensation through different media will be introduced in three corresponding, thematically appropriate 'tangents' or cuts of the body, consistent with the structure of the previous chapter on haptic aesthetics. In *cosmetics: folding skin*, then *prosthetics: folding flesh*, and finally *aesthetics: folding body*, different approaches to sensation corresponding to these three 'tangents' are traced, revealing how touching and feeling are enfolded within each medium. Although each performance of *skin*, of *flesh*, and of *body* fold and unfold into each other, the loose tangents or sections are illustrated through an appropriate art work or performance.

The works explore, first, the cutaneous touch of the *skin* on the screen, being used as a play of presence at a distance; secondly, the mutability of *flesh* and the viscerality of touch in a live-performance setting; and thirdly, the exploration of the aesthetic *body* through a multisensory virtual environment, altering the digital sensorium and the spatial apprehension of 'inside' and 'outside'. So, to the corresponding works. In terms of *skin*, the self-styled 'performance surgery' of the French feminist artist Orlan is pursued as she continually undergoes cosmetic surgery, morphing her skin and therefore playing with ideas of feminine beauty. These performances are transmitted across the internet and by video feed into art galleries. The continual reshaping of *skin* represents both the cosmetic and the cutaneous aspect of touch, how it is mediated through different technologies from skin to screen. The second theme, *flesh*, is exemplified in the performance art of Stelarc, who modifies and appends his body with a prosthetic, tactile hand, and shows the inside of his stomach via a remote-controlled robotic creature. The transmutability of flesh, another aspect of a haptic aesthetics, is given active, visceral demonstration. Finally, the *body* is exemplified in the virtual environments of Char Davies, who has constructed painterly but interactive multisensory virtual environments that play with ideas of fluidity, and which seek to problematize the boundaries of inside and outside the body – going beyond the skin and flesh, extending the felt body. Through various technologies involving bodysuits and an unusual interface, she therefore achieves an altered sensorium. All these works are variously subject to notions of 'affect', 'immersion' and 'presence', offering a series of visceral, multisensory experiences that play with tactility and the digital sensorium. The different mediations and remediations of skin, of fleshy viscerality and of the layered, folding-unfolding of the body through technologies have implications for the affects and felt reactions of the audience, their own visceral, fleshly feelings. Supporting my observations of the works with past interviews, meetings and personal communications with the artists, we further establish a haptic aesthetics that clarifies the links between touch and affect, a playful 'felt' phenomenology, or play with tangibility, through technologies and mediations of the body.

CH.7

'Feel the Presence: the Technologies of Touch' takes up a theme from Walter Benjamin about machines of mimesis, and engages directly with some of the technologies of touch raised in the previous chapter. Here we focus on the engineering of supposedly realistic feelings of touch. Haptic technologies, known in engineering terminology simply as 'haptics', aim to reproduce tactile sensations and engage the user with 'force feedback' in a range of contexts, from the coarse rumbles and vibrations in gadgets and domestic technologies such as mobile phones and videogame controllers, to the more refined and specialized design and engineering interfaces such as the PHANToM (Personal Haptic iNTerface Mechanism), which more accurately models the surfaces and textures of materials used in computer-aided design and manufacture (CAD/CAM). Furthermore, included within an increasing array of consumer technologies, haptics are reaching near ubiquity by being included in everything from vibrating mobile phones, rumbling controllers for videogame consoles, the distribution of touchscreens throughout our urban environments, and even within the cybersex industry. On the other hand, more specialized haptic technologies are refining the human-computer interface and changing the way that virtual sculpting and virtual prototyping is achieved simply by offering more intuitive, tactile engagement with the computer. Returning to a major theme of the book, the relationship between vision and touch, these more naturalistic interactions are achieved through technology by the collocation of vision and touch, the coordination of a visual model on the screen (eye) and a textured model through the haptic interface (hand).

So after a brief overview of the history of haptic technologies, a detailed analysis of the first transatlantic 'virtual handshake' between PHANToM haptic devices at MIT (Boston) and UCL (London) in 2002 serves as a more sustained introduction to some implications of these new technologies of touch. A device stemming originally from rehabilitation engineering for the blind and visually impaired and from early telerobotics experiments, the accumulated effect is to remould the human-computer interface from being primarily audio-visual to being more truly multisensory, involving more sophisticated input and feedback through touch. As the technology advances, the fidelity of feeling – the sophistication of sensations – increases so that the creation of virtual objects and prototypes can be modelled through touch as well as sight, becoming available to the hand as well as the eye. By using the results of interviews with key figures in haptics research, engineering and marketing, and detailed investigation into selected haptic technologies, I build up a picture of how the discourse of 'presence' and the right kind of 'feel' are guiding the design, prototyping and marketing of various products, for example, the type of 'clunk' that a car door should produce when closed at Saab-Scania automotive. Haptics devices therefore help to engender and, indeed, engineer both tangible and intangible feelings, and detailed examination of the 'virtual handshake' example shows how touch and the feeling of presence can be performed over a distance. Some of the various spatial effects of touching, and the fostering of feelings of presence at a distance, help inform current debates concerning technology and space. In a section I call 'Bringing distance to life' we return to Merleau-Ponty's phenomenology via Hubert Dreyfus' notion of 'skilful coping' (2000) to consider this further.

Finally, there is a conceptual and empirical investigation in 'Affecting Touch: Flesh and Feeling-with', of the way touch is used within therapeutic practices. While the previous chapter examined touch and presence at a distance through technology, haptics as the proximal touch of the human-computer interface, this chapter focuses on touching between bodies and the sense of a 'felt proximity' that results. If earlier chapters concentrate more on experiences of individualized sensation, the touching between bodies exemplified in therapeutic touching further extends the scope of tactility to become explicitly interpersonal and deeply affective. At various stages of the book I have deliberately played on the conceptual slip between *touching* and *feeling* in order to positively foreground the manifestly affective content of sensuous experience, particularly the 'touching' nature of touch. However, this conceptual slippage or productive oscillation reaches its peak within this chapter, since therapeutic touching provides a suitable context for the consideration of touch as empathetic, as 'feeling-with' another.

The significance of forms of therapeutic touching such as Swedish massage, Reiki, Shiatsu and hapto-therapy lies in their intercorporeal nature and the way they restore tactility and the somatic senses into prominence. According to Jütte (2005), this is symptomatic of the rediscovery of the 'new pleasure in the body' in late capitalism. After some contextualizing remarks that place different forms of therapeutic touching within historical perspective, seeing this as symptomatic of the commoditization of touch, we narrow the focus to examine the touching and, significantly, *non*-touching of Reiki massage. Acknowledging that larger forces of energy and life force (*ki*) are central to this practice, my study concentrates on the relation between touch and affect in therapeutic encounters, and the use of touch for both practitioner and recipient in channelling or facilitating flows of energy, empathy and affect. In other words, touch as not only *feeling* but as *feeling-with*. Through a range of encounters with the therapy and its practitioners we discuss the affective power of touch, its empathic qualities, and its capacity to reach beyond the individual toward other bodies, effectively drawing them into proximity. The sensations and affects experienced within these encounters are then framed within a discussion of flesh and phenomenology, returning briefly to Aristotle in order to develop Merleau-Ponty's notion of 'intercorporeity' (2000), and employing some insights from the Levinas-influenced philosopher Edith Wyschogrod (1980; 1981) to articulate more metaphorical notions of touching. Aptly for a final chapter, the conceptual arc of the book is furthest away from the initial, immediate conception of touch as merely cutaneous contact, and the more metaphorical considerations of touching enrich and further diversify the 'senses' of touch. One empirically informed section dwells on an affective, cathartic experience within a particular therapy session which helps to clarify this relationship between physical and metaphorical touching, explores the felt proximities of touch, and further elaborates upon the notion of a 'felt' phenomenology established toward the beginning of the book. Some of the historical and conceptual insights from earlier chapters are therefore applied here to ethnographic encounters with therapeutic touch, and to both physical and metaphorical touching experiences. As such, these empirical observations and interview data help support the interpretation of therapeutic touch as a sense of felt proximity in two ways. First, as a felt emotional proximity, of empathy and feeling-with, bringing persons into nearness. And secondly, as a felt cosmological proximity, of collapsing distance, bringing forces and energies into nearness.

More generally, some of the somatic sensations and tactile experiences raised and discussed have previously been barely articulated, or perhaps articulated barely, since there is a lack of explicit recognition of this content in everyday embodied experience. Due to a linguistic shortfall, the poverty of our Anglo-American sensory lexicon, such somatic experiences are therefore apparently incoherent or seemingly ineffable. But new ways of articulating touch, feeling and moving are emerging because of recent interdisciplinary and cross-cultural research within areas such as anthropology, neuropsychology, cultural geography, dance, performance studies and others, and are referenced at various points throughout the book, most pointedly in the consideration of haptic aesthetics, the under-examined somatic sensations, and the engineering of feeling at a distance. This final chapter is the culmination of several of these concerns then, revisiting affects and a fleshly, 'felt' phenomenology, and reflecting more generally on methodological concerns of how to write, represent or evoke such tactile, embodied, experiential encounters.

–2–

Learning How to See, Describing How to Feel: a 'Felt' Phenomenology

> The perceiving mind is an incarnated mind.
>
> Merleau-Ponty 1964a:3

The 'Trick' of Perception

Having briefly introduced the under-explored somatic senses of proprioception, kinaesthesia and the vestibular sense previously, this wider notion of the 'haptic' as cutaneous touch working in conjunction with these bodily senses is the concern here. If cutaneous touch remains for the most part immediate and instantly recognizable, the deeper, more inwardly oriented somatic senses are more difficult to determine and threfore to articulate. If exteroception is outwardly-oriented perception, the interoception of bodily states has been treated for example by Leder (1990), himself influenced by the later Husserl (especially 1970a; 1989a) and Merleau-Ponty (1992; 2000). Both these phenomenologists conceive of a kind of kinaesthetic background within everyday embodied consciousness, part of our anticipative orientation to the world. So this is an opportunity to engage with relevant phenomenological debates, to directly address some of these vague and ill-defined somatic states, and to articulate something akin to a 'felt' phenomenology.

   This chapter attempts two things. First, to establish philosophical context for these phenomenological investigations we turn to Aristotle's treatment of touch and the senses in *De Anima* (On the Soul), and *De Sensu et Sensibilibus* (On Sense and Sensibilia), which have been influential in the separation and classification of the senses.[1] *De Anima* (especially Book II, 11) deals expressly with touch, and reveals a number of initial statements and problematics concerning tactility that figure throughout this book – for example the primacy of touch, the ambiguity of touching and feeling, the hierarchies of the senses, the role of touch and blindness in later Enlightenment philosophy, and the position of tactile experience in more recent phenomenology. Secondly, after some succinct preliminaries concerning phenomenology, a branch of philosophy which is unusually open to the interpretation of sensory experience, I develop Husserl's departure point from Brentano of phenomenology as a 'descriptive psychology', highlighting the need for a rich description of embodied processes and somatosensory events. Phenomenological methods have long been imported into the social sciences through such figures as Schutz (e.g. 1967; 1970), Garfinkel's ethnomethodology (e.g. 1967) and Luckmann (e.g. 1973), since Husserl's concept of the lifeworld (*Lebenswelt*) is amenable to sociological analysis. Attempting to bracket or temporarily suspend the lifeworld, the immediate social arena of embodied perception and action, it is possible to focus on how members co-creatively construct recognizable and 'real' elements of their social world, for example the self-regulation of queuing, or emergent forms of behaviour. More recently, figures such as Rodaway (1994), Classen (1997), Gell (1999), Howes (2003), and Geurts (2005) have explored the significances of embodied sensation within cultural theory and anthropology through ethnographic reflection. Like their work, my project is not interested in the mere facticity of embodiment, or the problematization of the 'body' per se. Instead, the need to articulate somatic sensations not simply as ecstatic presentments to consciousness but as ongoing, processual, non-representational but incarnated, co-constitutive entanglements of body and world, perception and action is a form of sensuous scholarship but also a recognizably phenomenological project. In terms of the significance of touch and somatic sensation, a framework for the interpretation of such experience can be traced from Husserl's notion of kinaesthesia in *The Crisis of European Sciences and Transcendental Phenomenology* (1970a, henceforth *Crisis*) and *Ideas Pertaining to a Pure Phenomenology and a Phenomenological Philosophy* (1989a, henceforth *Ideas*). We may consider its bearing on Merleau-Ponty's conception of touching and of 'body-schema' in *The Primacy of Perception* (1964a) and *Phenomenology of Perception* (1992). Finally, bringing these strands together, we consider the kinaesthetic background to embodied experience in the actual process of touching, with its emphasis on presence, immediacy and the relation to others through the hands.

Aristotle and Aesthesis

No one in the history of philosophy has ever conducted 'a more radical and patient investigation of touch' than Aristotle, remarks French phenomenologist Jean-Louis Chrétien (2004:102). Yet few of his contemporaries treated the senses as an object worthy of sustained philosophical enquiry, and Plato famously discredits the role of the senses as illusory and deceptive, revealing only appearances rather than universal truths (especially *Republic* 479b). Aristotle's treatment of the senses arises within the framework of his interest in biological ideas, the need to classify human and non-human perceptions, to survey the function and physiology of the sense organs. To contextualize this, in *De Anima* he proves there cannot be more than five senses for humans (424b), a legacy challenged relatively recently in psychology (e.g. Gibson 1968; see also Durie 2005). His texts remark variously on the exceptional nature of touch, its primacy, yet also its base nature. If touch is the most basic of the senses in the hierarchy (413b4–10), it is also the most necessary, for fundamentally an animal is unable to survive without it (422b). If this is true, then progressing toward more complex organisms, additional senses exist more for the animal's well-being than out of necessity (434b23–5). What distinguishes the most primitive animals like sponges from plants, which they undeniably resemble, is their capacity to touch (*Historia Animalium* 588b4–22).[2] Without touch, in consequence, 'no other sense is possible' (Sorabji 1992:216) for an organism. Touch is acknowledged not only as indispensable (*De Anima* 434b11–14), but as prior to the other sensory modalities.

In terms of Aristotle's sensory hierarchy, sight is the supreme sense, the ultimate perfection of sensoriality (*De Anima* 429a4–5; *De Sensu* 437a4–9). His sensory hierarchy mirrors his characterization of the sensory pleasures, as depicted in *Ethics* (X, 5), where 'the pleasures of sight are at the top, superior 'in purity' to those of touch' (Freeland 1992:239). Hearing and smell, thinks Aristotle, are purer than taste, so similarly superior, and touch remains at the base (*Ethics* 1176a1–2). Now, as sound is to hearing, and light is to sight, it is difficult to discern the 'single underlying thing common to touch' (422b). And because there is no obvious single organ to which it corresponds, unlike sight (the eye) or hearing (the ear), touch is distinct since flesh is the *medium*, rather than the organ, of touch. Indeed, if the sense of touch corresponds to any particular organ it would be the heart, as he claims in *De Sensu* (439a); and certainly 'the sense-faculty of touch is within', like internal organs, rather than 'without' (*De Anima* 423b), like eyeballs or ears. This Aristotelian separation of touch as a unified and independent sense remained unquestioned until much later, according to Jütte (2005:42). Crucially, in perceiving through our other senses we are conscious that the medium (light, sound) has an effect on us (423b). Yet in the case of touch, our contact with things is erroneously perceived as direct, as unmediated. When perceiving textural qualities of roughness or smoothness, for example, in reality we perceive through an intermediary, our flesh and additionally our clothes, but simply fail to notice this. With tactility we are not affected or altered by the sense-object itself, nor simply through the medium (flesh), but actually *in synchrony with* the medium (423b). Wearing a glove, we may still stroke an animal or imprecisely sense an object's texture; similarly, when walking with a stick we apprehend the roughness of the ground. The fleshy medium is corporeal then, and extendable through prosthetic means: 'so it is necessary that the body be the ongrown medium of the touch-faculty and that the sensations (which are indeed many) take place *through* it' (423a, original emphasis).

The particularity of touch, as treated by Aristotle, is augmented in both *De Anima* and *De Sensu* by a consideration of how the senses work together. There are few objects that are perceptible by one sense alone, and so sense-objects are available to a variety of senses incidentally. Various properties of objects such as size, shape, number and movement are perceived incidentally by a number of senses (425a23) working together. Thus, rather than positing a distinct, unifying 'common sense' that stands outside the five sensory modalities, nevertheless there is a unity (*koine*) to the sense faculty (*aesthesis*) as a whole. What Aristotle meant by *aesthesis koine* or 'common sense' has been disputed (see e.g. Hamlyn 1959; Lawson-Tancred in Aristotle, 1984:81). Is there a 'sense' that different sense-organs refer to, for example, where what is perceived by touch and sight alike cohere? In the case of size, visual information and tactile information corroborate each other so that we both see and feel the size and spatial dimensions of the object. Aristotle posits therefore a common sense for the common sensibles, a concept still disputed in current psychological debates, as we discover in the next chapter.

Although obviously a simplistic model of perception, and a crude account of how our potential perceptual capacity becomes actual, it should be clear that Aristotle's language opens up the pathway to consider the manifold senses of touch, including the somatic senses and the affective aspect of touching, each amenable to a phenomenological framework. The notion of *aesthesis* is therefore an important first step in conceptualizing sensation, movement and affect (e.g. Deleuze's reading of Spinoza, 1988, and Massumi, 2002), of thinking of the ambiguity of touching and feeling, and of expanding the notion of the 'aesthetic'. Prevalent since Baumgarten, philosophical 'aesthetics' is understood as the philosophy of art and the development of criteria for the judgement of taste (see e.g. Dixon 1995). Yet it is from *aesthesis* that Husserl for example talks of the 'aesthetic body' (e.g. 1999:11), Merleau-Ponty of the 'aesthesiological body' (2000:154), relating 'aesthetic' to the sensory body. In fact, in both *De Anima* and *De Sensu* can be seen the seeds of phenomenological thinking, and a statement of Aristotle's case in making touch a special case (*De Sensu* 418a) is a useful point of entry into the phenomenology of touch.

Aesthesis, Affects and Touch

At the heart of *De Anima*, and recurring throughout several of his other texts is the notion of *aesthesis* as the sensory faculty, or the 'psychic faculty of perception' (Lawson-Tancred, in Aristotle 1986:76). Consequently *aesthesis* is interpretable as a broad-spectrum 'sense-faculty', covering both perception and sensation. Whereas we now commonly distinguish between perception and sensation, perception being concerned with the correlation of mental activity and the processing of 'raw' sensation, Aristotle and his contemporaries often conflated the two. Linguistically, ordinary Greek makes the distinction difficult, notes Hamlyn (1959:11). And, reminding us that to perceive is not simply to have sensations, Hamlyn clarifies the definition of *aesthesis*: 'The faculty of sense-perception is that faculty by means of which we are able to characterize or identify things as a result of the use of our senses' (1959:6).

Before discussing each of the five senses in turn in Book II of *De Anima*, Aristotle devotes two chapters to a general discussion of sensations and sense objects. Here he defines perception as an organism's 'being moved and affected', an alteration (*alloiosis*) of the sense faculty (415b32) whereby perception is both potential and actual (417a). An 'alteration' of the sensory faculty by an external object therefore causes sensations. For example, sight moves from potentiality to actuality by the effect of sensible form, a specific colour, acting on the sense organ and causing it to see (*De Anima* II, 12). This alteration model is reiterated in a passage concerning the general problems of perception, where he states: 'For in just the way that both action and affection are in the thing that is affected not in that which acts, the activity of the sense-object and the sense faculty are in the sense faculty' (426a12–15). It is not the activity of the objects themselves, then, but the way the sense faculty (*aesthesis*) is affected or altered; and hence the sensory faculty allows both actual and potential activity, and furthermore has the capacity to be receptive. However, later he explicitly denies the initial characterization of *aesthesis* as *alloiosis* in Book III (431a5) as a result of the intervening discussion, as Hamlyn (1959:6) details.

Elsewhere, Aristotle refers to *aesthesis* as a form of change using the word *paschein* (424a1), which Freeland confusingly translates as 'some kind of suffering' (1992:233). However, the literal translation of *paschein* lends itself to an ambiguity of feeling, as an active undergoing rather than the passive experience of pain. Furthermore, there is an emotional component, as pathos (suffering, experience, emotion) is derived from *paschein*. Whichever, *aesthesis* involves a form of change, a necessary (but not sufficient) condition of perception, and in particular this form of change is *to paschein* (*De Anima* 415b24, 416b34; in Hamlyn 1959:8). The central ambiguity of touching and feeling, then, the emotional component of feeling complemented by the perceptual component of touching, finds its support in Aristotle through both *alloiosis* (alteration, being affected by) and *paschein* as both active and passive, the active undergoing of experience. Aristotle's attempt to explain how *aesthesis* is a form of change via *paschein* fails, thinks Hamlyn (1959:11), due partly to lacunae in physiological knowledge, and partly Aristotle's naive model of perception whereby the sense-organ becomes like the sense-object. While medical knowledge and psychological research has inevitably advanced since Aristotle's time, a generous attitude to this core framework of *aesthesis* as alteration (*alloiosis*) and change by active undergoing (*paschein*) might be rewarded in discussions of the contingency and contiguity of touching and feeling as this book progresses.

Aristotle's use of Greek underlines another ambiguity of feeling however, described by Freeland. Momentarily disregarding the emotional content of feeling, our perceiving organs can be affected by tangible objects in two distinct ways. For example, we can interpret 'feeling dry' as either the more generalized bodily feeling of dehydration, or the more literal interpretation of touching something withered and wilted, such as dry leaves:

This ambiguity is reflected in Aristotle's Greek by sentences using the word *haptesthai* or 'to touch': my tongue, say, and skin have been literally affected by what is touching them, the dry air, but nevertheless my feeling of being 'dried-out' is not what I sense when I touch dry objects. The latter sort of the phenomenon is the one Aristotle intends to address, and should focus on, in giving his account of sense-perception as a 'kind of being affected by' tangible objects (in parallel with other modalities of sense-perception). (Freeland 1992:233)

This will be another useful distinction that arises from Aristotle: feeling as tactual perception (*haptesthai*, hence 'haptic') as opposed to feeling as generalized bodily feeling, perhaps better reflected by the active undergoing of *paschein*. It is correct that Aristotle focuses more on touching and feeling as straightforward tactile perception in *De Anima* and *De Sensu*. Freeland herself allows a larger biological context for Aristotelian touch to be considered, wherein touch functions in more complex behavioural processes, as haptic interactions: 'In most instances the relevant sort of touch would be what contemporary scientists term 'haptic', active or exploratory touch: the digging and rooting performed by the pig's snout, the collecting of pollen and honey by the bee's legs, etc.' (1992:236). This wider definition of haptic confirms the earlier observations concerning its use in more contemporary psychological contexts which also accommodate the somatic senses. Nevertheless, we depart from Freeland's conclusion, that sense perception (*aesthesis*) as a 'kind of being affected by' (*alloiosis*) should concentrate solely on the psychological phenomena of tactile perception (*haptesthai*). Instead, it is fruitful to celebrate the manifold ambiguities of touching, to consider other ways of feeling, of being affected by, of touching and being touched, periodically revisiting and repatriating Aristotelian terminology in order to do so.

The Felt Unity of the Body

Since Aristotle's discussion in *De Anima* (424b), our five senses are thought of as separate, providing independent information. In the twentieth century, psychologists such as Sherrington (1947 [1906]) and Gibson (1968) started to distinguish other senses, and current wisdom posits anything between eight and twenty-one (see e.g. Durie 2005). Jablonski details the five different receptors within the skin, all responsible for providing what we think of as straightforwardly cutaneous touch, consisting of receptors responding to warmth, pain and different pressures (2006:97). Further, apart from the familiar, outwardly directed (exteroceptive) senses of sight, touch, taste, smell and hearing, some psychologists proposed the inwardly directed (interoceptive) senses of proprioception, kinaesthesia and the vestibular sense, as previously outlined. These three somatic senses work in synergy, complicating the previous belief in the distinctness and separation of the senses. Proprioception refers generally to the awareness of our body's position in space, using information derived from nerve endings in the muscles. It includes an awareness of movement and position through tactility as well as kinaesthesia, that is, through surface as well as internal events. It also includes a sense of gravitational orientation through the vestibular (balance) system in the inner ear. Likewise, kinaesthesia is defined as a sense of movement through muscular effort. Briefly, Benjamin Lee Whorf defines kinaesthesia as the 'sensing of muscular movement' (1956). Etymologically it is derived from *kinein* (to move), movement being the key process that integrates the senses in embodied perception, as we shall see. These three bodily senses are therefore interrelated and co-dependent, in Merleau-Ponty's words, working as a 'synergic totality' (1992:316).

Unlike other areas of philosophy which are hostile to the senses, phenomenology takes our sensory presentations to consciousness seriously. Finding ourselves caught within a continuous stream of sensations, we are always *in medias res*. The significance of tactility is shown in our lived embodiment, the 'natural attitude' (e.g. Merleau-Ponty 1992; Husserl 1970a; Schutz 1970) which is the everyday interpretive stance, a taken-for-granted orientation to the world. For the majority of sighted people, for example, vision and touch are unproblematically unified through the lived body, as Merleau-Ponty has written (1992:150). It seems unproblematic since the active work of perceptual and cognitive synthesis between the senses, the active correlations between the data of vision and that of touch, comes to form a habituated perceptual background. Such a habituated background of bodily experience becomes disrupted in cases of sudden blindness, or those rarer cases where surgery restores sight, the subject of the following chapter. Cases of sensory loss or restoration, both being equally a dehabituation of perception, highlight what Merleau-Ponty more generally calls our task 'to rediscover phenomena', revealing some of the processes that form everyday habituated perception, and so 'reawaken perception and foil its trick of allowing us to forget it as a fact and as perception' (1992:57).

The 'trick' of perception then obfuscates its very processes. It makes the varieties of sensations that constitute embodied experience opaque, and necessitates new approaches or modes of analysis in order to render these sensations more transparent. After all, the uncertainty we have concerning our own perceptual ability means we cannot even recognize whether we have five, eight or even twenty-one senses. Indeed, the taxonomy of the senses might literally be a senseless enterprise, since it is clear that the whole body is implicated in perceiving what Merleau-Ponty terms 'the thickness of the world' (1992:297). Film theorist Vivian Sobchack takes up an almost throwaway moment of doubt concerning the discreteness of the senses (1992:217), and baldly postulates: 'The lived body does not have senses', as this would require prior separation and codification of sensory experience. 'It is, rather, sensible' (in Marks 2000:151).

The following section addresses the 'trick' of perception, that is, how unprob- lematic, everyday tactile experience becomes thematic, and how this might be articulable, through phenomenological methods.

From a 'Descriptive Psychology' to a 'Felt' Phenomenology

A particularly significant and graceful passage from *The Primacy of Perception* stands out, demonstrating the remedial work necessary to comprehend the sensory, motor and affective structures of everyday, embodied perception:

> We grasp space through our bodily situation. A 'corporeal or postural schema' gives us at every moment a global, practical, and implicit notion of the relation between our body and things, of our hold on them. A system of possible movements, or 'motor projects,' radiates from us to our environment. Our body is not in space like things; it inhabits or haunts space. It applies itself to space like a hand to an instrument, and when we wish to move about we do not move the body as we move an object...

Almost as a summary statement of the project of the phenomenology of perception, he continues,

> Now if perception is thus the common act of all our motor and affective functions, no less than the sensory, we must rediscover the structure of the perceived world through a process similar to that of an archaeologist. (Merleau-Ponty 1964:5)

To expand on this assertion of the multisensory immediacy of embodied consciousness is to speak of what constitutes the background of everyday embodied experience. Concentrating on phenomenology's initial method of psychological description, previous insights from fiction, autobiography and the psychology of blind experience can be called upon to facilitate this archaeology of perception, recombining kinaesthetic or motor elements with the lived, sensory body. Merleau-Ponty's notion of the 'body schema' consists in a system of possible movements, bearings and comportments which effectively unite the sensory and motor aspects of the body. It is 'the crux or reference point that establishes a stable perceptual background against which I perceive and respond to changes and movements in my environment', as Carman (1999:220) explains. As a background to immediate embodied perception, the body schema also has an orientation to future action, anticipating future events and interactions with objects – that is, having 'intentionality'. Merleau-Ponty's body schema can benefit from some archaeology of its own, since he acknowledges a debt to Husserl, the originator of phenomenology. Later, these notions of body schema, kinaesthesia and subjective sensation will come together through the figure of hands touching, in both Husserl and Merleau-Ponty.

Phenomenology as Description

In terms of their suitability for the analysis of tactility then, phenomenological methods offer rich descriptions of the manifold contents of sensory experience, and the different senses of touch. In particular, the phenomenology of perception derived through Husserl and Merleau-Ponty provides a framework and a language through which the immediacy of embodied sensations may be articulated in their presence and absence, described and analysed. Furthermore, it shows the role of the somatic senses in our anticipative stance toward the world. So, to return to the beginning.

The objective of phenomenology, which had its origin in Edmund Husserl, is broadly-speaking 'the enlarging and deepening of the range of our immediate experience', as Spiegelberg summarizes, and therefore 'the emancipation from preconceptions' (1982:679, 680). At the same time as early phenomenologists stressed the radical nature of its enquiry, they also stressed a 'return to *concrete*, lived experience in all its richness' (Moran 2000:5, original emphasis). Husserl intended phenomenology to be a rigorous science of pure human conscious experience, a *transcendental* phenomenology through the rigorous development of phenomenology as 'the science of pure consciousness' (1981). Departing from the immanent domain of subjective consciousness, the transcendental component involves discovering the underlying relationships among essences, the essential structures of subjective phenomena through philosophical reflection, through what he terms the 'phenomenological reduction'. He emphasized the departure of this method from a merely subjective psychology. By extending and universalizing claims that are latent in descriptions of subjective phenomena, as Ihde helpfully summarizes, he thereby 'moves phenomenology from a regional method and claim (descriptive psychology) to a philosophy' (1986:42).

In this transcendental move the body becomes problematic for Husserl, being neither internal to our consciousness nor external to us in our environment. He describes it as an awkward anomaly, 'a thing 'inserted' between the rest of the material world and the subjective sphere' (1989a:161). Contrast this with the centrality of embodiment within Merleau-Ponty's phenomenological enterprise, where the body is conceived not as object but 'as the horizon latent in all our experience and itself ever-present and anterior to every determining thought' (1992:91). But Husserl's later work, along with recent translations from his copious notebooks, acknowledge the centrality of the body in the 'constitutive operations through which the objects of experience are endowed with meaning' (Petit 2003:284). He therefore approaches the themes, if not the style, of Merleau-Ponty's phenomenology of embodied perception, as both examine the role of the tactile and the kinaesthetic in our perceptual stance toward the world and, indeed, its constitutive role in basic intentionality (e.g. Mulligan 1995; Carman 1999; Petit 2003). The transcendental movement in Husserl's project, which seeks to universalize human experience, prompts huge reservations from those who wish to attend to the particularity of bodies and their sensations. Yet the psychological phenomenology of Merleau-Ponty has inspired fine-grained analyses that have taken account of the lived particularity of certain bodies, be they gendered or pregnant (see e.g. Iris Marion Young's work on female embodiment and pregnancy, 1990; 1999) or in disability studies (e.g. Rod Michalko's work on visual impairment, 2002).

So, to the question 'What is a phenomenological analysis?' Solokowski replies 'it describes the manifold proper to a given kind of object' (2000:31). Whether the object is an art work, a sensory experience or a memory, an appropriate phenomenological analysis can be applied wherein different manifolds and different contexts are described and analysed. In terms of touch, a phenomenological analysis may describe the manifold contents, intentions and relations inherent in the experience of touching, and as Solokowski explains elsewhere, 'list the forms of presence and absence that are possible for the object in question' (1985:16). Presence, through the immediacy of sensory experience, and absence, through memory, forgetfulness and longing, are continually interwoven within analyses of tactility.

A large part of this is therefore *descriptive* in nature, and what Husserl took from Franz Brentano was an initial formulation of phenomenology as a 'descriptive psychology' (1970b:262; also see Natanson, 1985). Rather than attempting causal explanation, then, for phenomenologists like Husserl and Merleau-Ponty the role of description is fundamental. For Merleau-Ponty phenomenology 'is a matter of describing, not of explaining or analysing' (1992:viii), the description of perceptual events being the gateway to understanding the relation between our body and the objects that it interacts with.[3] Phenomenology becomes description, the exercise of intuition, part of a wider critique of reason (and therefore simultaneously sympathetic and antithetical to philosophical modernity), relying on what is *given* or presented to us in our intuition rather than logically deduced. Whereas Descartes is alert to the deceptive power of the senses, trusting rationality over sensory experience, phenomenology is instigated within the flow of sensory presence, in analysing what is given to us. 'Givenness' (*Gegebenheit*), says Husserl, is the way that all experience is experience *to someone* (1989a:36; *Ideas* I, §19). Indeed, etymologically 'intuition' derives from the Greek 'to look upon'. Thus it is tempting and rather Cartesian to consider such given experience as a clear and distinct intuition, as if projected in sharp relief against a clear background. This could occur whether the intuition has the clarity of a simple mathematical calculation (2+2=4), or that of a complex set of sensorimotor activities. Yet against accusations of being merely 'subjective', simply being the study of private phenomena, Spiegelberg defends this view of phenomenology:

> its descriptions deal not only with the subject's side of experience, with his acts and dispositions which can become thematic only in a reflective return upon himself, but at least as much with those contents of his acts which confront him as the objects of his experience and which do not require any reflective turn. Thus colors, melodies, and specifically *those 'forces' which we experience in our own lived body appear in front of us, as it were.* (Spiegelberg 1982:688–9, emphasis added)

Conceiving of various sensations as appearing 'in front of us', as if projected on a screen, is clearly erroneous and simplistic, redolent of a Cartesian theatre of consciousness (e.g. Damasio 2000:9–11; and Geurts' critique, 2005:169–170). Yet Spiegelberg rightly emphasizes the way that such sensations, forces, presentments 'appear' or disclose themselves to consciousness in a meaningful way, rather than as discrete sense-data or qualia. We hear the melody rather than a sequence of resonant tones; we experience kinaesthetic feelings when learning and practising a dance move; and we are emotionally and physically moved when manipulated by a Reiki master. Clearly, some forces and perceptions are distinct and intuitable. But equally there are movements, sensations and combinations of these that are indistinct, processual, which arise from interactions with objects or people yet do not actually 'appear in front of us' as if purely mental phenomena. Merleau-Ponty insists instead that thoughts and sensations as such occur 'only against a background of perceptual activity that we always already understand in bodily terms, by engaging in it' in the words of Carman (1999:206). Unfamiliar combinations of sensorimotor feelings, compounded by the omission of a suitable lexicon with which to describe them adequately, means that our descriptive method cannot simply describe the forces and sensations that appear in front of us. Instead, a rich descriptive analysis must develop based on learning to see (and feel) such novel sensations, without descending too deeply into Cartesian introspection or subjective psychology. This is indeed one aim in proposing a 'felt' phenomenology.

Description and the 'Natural Attitude'

If phenomenology starts from descriptive psychology, this is not to say that descriptions operate merely at the empirical level. There is a clear difference between description of immediate sensation and experience, and the epistemological truths that can supposedly be derived through philosophical analysis: 'For pure description is merely a preparatory step towards theory, not theory itself' Husserl argues (1970b:263). This distinction between description and theorization highlights a crucial difference between descriptions of our everyday experiences (the 'natural attitude') and the ability to reflect and philosophically analyse those experiences (the 'phenomenological attitude'). It is only in the latter case that phenomenology is actually performed.

So it is that the 'natural attitude' or 'natural life', for both Husserl and Merleau-Ponty, is a key phenomenological term. For Husserl 'natural' refers to what is original or naive, prior to any conscious philosophical reflection, which he terms the 'phenomenological attitude'. In his last work *Crisis*, 'natural' means something pretheoretical; what is 'natural' to life itself, our waking consciousness. For this phase of Husserl's thought, what is 'natural' can be characterized as a life naively, straightforwardly directed at the world, the world being always in a certain sense consciously present as a universal horizon without, however, being 'thematic' as such:

> What is thematic is whatever one is directed toward. Waking life is always a directedness toward this or that, being directed toward it as an end or as means, toward the private or public, toward what is daily required or obtrusively new. (1970a:181)

This is a naive, pretheoretical life for Husserl that is *engaged in the world*, 'the milieu and horizon of its activity' in the words of his translator Carr (1970a:xl). It is the *Lebenswelt*, the 'lifeworld' of Husserl's *Crisis*, the world of immediate experience, before predication and theorization can begin. Husserl describes the lifeworld as 'the world in which we are always already living and which furnishes the ground for all cognitive performance and all scientific determination' (*Experience and Judgement* §10 p.38). And as embodied beings we dwell unproblematically in this arena. For example, in the normal or 'natural' attitude we are unaware of the functioning body as an object that takes its place among a world of objects (i.e. *Körper*), but as an everyday living, functioning, kinaesthetic body (*Leib*): 'The body is that underlying ground of sensuousness upon which subjectivity depends inasmuch as it is sensuous and corporeal', explains Landgrebe (1981:44). In contrast to the natural attitude, the phenomenological attitude steps back from (Latin *re-ducere,* 'leading back') this lived everydayness, instead making it 'thematic', becoming distinctly problematized. Although this is known technically as the 'phenomenological reduction', it does not diminish or demean the everyday experiences of the natural attitude. Actually it focuses upon and preserves those natural intentions and concerns, while distancing us in order to contemplate them. Despite the negative connotations to the word 'reduction', then, as Solokowski summarizes 'it amplifies and does not deprive' (2000:54).

With both the starting point of phenomenology as descriptive psychology, and the distinction between the 'natural' and the 'phenomenological' attitudes, the suitability of phenomenology as a method for the analysis of the manifold experiences of touch within the lifeworld, as a lived, kinaesthetic body (*Leib*) should be clear. Solokowski defines phenomenology ultimately as the 'art and science of evidencing evidence', in other words consistent with Merleau-Ponty's notion of the primacy of perception as an archaeology, bringing forth what is significant and non-obvious within everyday experiences and sensations within the natural attitude. Solokowski goes on to explain:

> [Phenomenology] stands back from rational involvement with things and marvels at the fact that there is disclosure, that things do appear, that the world can be understood, and that we in our life of thinking serve as datives for the manifestation of things. (2000:185)

Something of the wonder of the rediscovery of phenomena, of revealing the background of habituated perception, echoes Merleau-Ponty's discussion of the 'trick' of perception. Certainly, to consider examples of sudden sensory loss or impairment, or neuropsychological case studies of phantom-limb phenomena (e.g. in Merleau-Ponty 1992; Sacks 1996; Ramachandran and Blakeslee 1999; Goldstein 1995), is similarly to temporarily suspend or bracket the 'lifeworld' or 'natural attitude'. We can bracket the natural attitude of the lived, sensible body in order to observe the way that the senses co-depend and interact, giving us a sense of spatiality, of objecthood and suchlike. Now, whereas some sensory experiences are familiar and easily articulable, especially those exteroceptive senses defined previously, certain difficulties arise when considering the somatic senses since their mechanisms and interrelations are less familiar, the presentation of such sensory information to consciousness being unclear. In fact, uncertainty arises because of the unfamiliar interaction between our habitual methods of perception and our internal organs, and interoception is often vague due to the lack of nerve endings and can easily be mistaken. Cramps, indigestion or heartburn? There is something ineffable, something barely articulable about internal bodily states and somatic sensations. Unlike Husserl's thinking of the body, then, Merleau-Ponty explores the possibility that our embodied perception need not involve interior mental contents nor objective external events, but is a 'precognitive bodily engagement with the world' (Carman 1999:218) which is part of our bodily bearing, the 'body schema'. Hence the suitability of the phenomenological method, enhanced by rich description and the disruption of habituated perception, in order to make somatic sensations and interoception thematic or examinable.

Kinaesthesia: 'I Think' vs 'I Can'

We remarked previously on Aristotle's observation that, unlike seeing or hearing, touch has no singular organ to which it corresponds. Touch being a manifold of sensations, 'feeling' involves not only perception by touch, as we have seen, but also perception of our whole bodily state, involving interoception and somatic sensations. In a rare philosophical engagement with this area David Armstrong terms them 'bodily sense-impressions' in his book *Bodily Sensations* (1962:36). Thus part of the background receptivity of embodied sensations, or bodily bearing, are perceptions of our own bodily state that arise from what I term the 'somatic sensations'. This term is more specific than Armstrong's 'bodily sense-impressions', grouping the experiences of kinaesthesia, proprioception and the vestibular sense. Armstrong similarly notes the relatedness of tactual perception and bodily sensations, conceiving of them both as forms of bodily perception. Tactual perception he defines as a 'transitive bodily sensation', and involves perceiving a relationship between our body and a material object, whereas the immediate bodily or somatic sensations he distinguishes as 'intransitive bodily sensation' (ibid.:41–2), as in the case of kinaesthesia for example where no material object is required, the sensation being experienced as arising from the body although from sometimes indeterminate locations. This is what allows him to say that, in the case of bodily sensations, 'their *esse is sentiri*' (ibid.:50).[4] In other words, to *have* such a sensation is to *feel* it, and there are no externally measurable criteria that are applicable. Such 'felt' bodily sensations include the motion and position of the limbs, the position and posture of the body relative to the earth, the pressure of one body part on another, or the stretching of tissue incurred when exercising strenuously. To ask where such sensations are located is often indeterminate or inappropriate, and even misleading in the case of the phantom limb. It is difficult, as Armstrong says, 'to give any *alternative* account of "first-person reports of present experience" which will do justice to their apparent ineffability, yet avoid the assumption that they are reports on "private items"' (ibid.:80). Locating and clarifying these sensations is a notoriously difficult enterprise, based on potentially erroneous reflective introspection, and subject to learned associations and habitual perceptions that might be misleading. Examining the bodily sensations, and the relationship between somatic sensations and tactual perception, it will be useful to bear this indeterminacy or ineffability in mind as we return to phenomenologies of touch and somatic sensation.

When writing of kinaesthesia and proprioception, and despite differences in approach and method, Merleau-Ponty does acknowledge his debt to Husserl. For example, in the second volume of *Ideas* (1989a) Husserl posits a *kinaesthesen*, the kinaesthetic functioning of different parts of the body, as a background of sensory receptivity against which material objects are perceived. Husserl speaks of the '"I can" of a corporeal, kinaesthetically functioning being' (in Landgrebe 1981:49). Merleau-Ponty adopts this Husserlian expression in contrasting a static, visual notion of perception with a motile or kinaesthetic notion of perception that combines the different senses into a coherent unity. It leads us 'to understand motility as basic intentionality' (1992:137), that kinaesthetic capacity is key to anticipative action, and stands behind our interaction with things. 'Consciousness is in the first place not a matter of "I think that" but "I can"', he declares; and motility links together diverse somatic and sensory experiences, 'not by placing them all under the control of an "I think", but by guiding them towards the intersensory unity of a "world"' (ibid.:137). This is a reasonable initial statement of the meaning and usefulness of the phenomenological project for thinking about the sensory body and movement, and is consistent both with the experiences of blind subjects regaining sight and with those of neonates, where movement forms part of the active correlation of visual and haptic worlds into a coherent unity. The significance of movement and the correlation of vision and touch forms the core of the following chapter.

The late Husserlian approach, being sympathetic to embodiment, places touch and kinaesthesia as a central aspect of the orientation toward the world and of bodily intentionality. Like Merleau-Ponty, his approach accommodates fairly novel perceptual content, in both his 1903 book *Ideas* (1989a) and his 1907 lectures *Thing and Space* (1998), kinaesthesia is addressed as an important enframing set of sensations, especially the 'kinaesthetic manifold' in the latter. A brief sketch of his ideas about kinaesthesia and his related notion of 'holding sway' will lead us to a discussion of Merleau-Ponty's treatment of kinaesthesia and touching. In *Crisis*, kinaesthesia is apportioned the role of uniting the different motilities of the sense organs. Merleau-Ponty's distinction between the 'I think' and 'I can' finds its echo in Husserl's 'I do', where even the static body unites its various motilities (eye movements, arms, etc.): 'All kinestheses, each being an "I move", "I do" [etc.] are bound together in a comprehensive unity – in which kinaesthetic holding-still is [also] a mode of the "I do"' (Husserl 1970a:106). In other words, whether moving or static, the body persists in its anticipative stance, and kinaesthesia has a constitutive role in this intentionality. The kinaesthetically functioning living body (*Leiblichkeit*, ibid.:106) therefore organizes perception such that the particular kinestheses of the various organs cohere through 'holding sway' (*walten*) in *Crisis* (ibid.:107), the wielding of one's lived body (*Leib*) and its organs in order to have some control over its surroundings:

> And this 'holding-sway', here exhibited in all perception of bodies – the familiar, total system of kinestheses available to consciousness – is actualized in the particular kinesthetic situation [and] is perpetually bound to a [general] situation in which bodies appear, i.e. that of the field of perception. (ibid.)

To achieve a form of harmonious perception, then, some perception must be anticipative, must stand in advance, and so Husserl admits there is a hidden intentionality to such quotidian perception:

> The actual kinestheses here lie within the system of kinaesthetic capacity, which is correlated with the system of possible following events harmoniously belonging to it. This is, then, the intentional background of every straightforward ontic certainty of a presented thing. (ibid.:162)

Remaining sceptical of Husserl's dichotomy between internal sensory representations and external actions, and of the possibility of 'ontic certainty', clearly one notes that the various kinaestheses are inextricably woven into the perceptual background, and that kinaesthesia helps constitute the very possibility of perceiving objects in their solidity and three-dimensionality. Whether newly born or newly sighted, for example, the active correlation between various senses is achieved through actual or potential motility, consonant with Husserl's 'holding sway'. Movement or potential movement, a kinaesthetic background, helps cohere the various patterns of sensations in order to actively correlate visual blobs of colour and tactile forms. From a phenomenological viewpoint this involves not only the active correlation of the immediacy of sensation within the visual field (through the eyes) and the tactile field (through the hands, the skin), but also an anticipatory orientation that makes use of the various potential and actual kinaestheses, or motile patternings of sensations. All this coheres – literally 'makes sense' – within the framework of the anticipative stance, the intentional, felt unity of the body.

Husserl's Hands, Merleau-Ponty's Grip

This bodily intentionality is predicated on kinaesthesia, then, but also on what Husserl calls 'the privilege of the localisation of touch sensations' in *Ideas* II (1989a:150). Touch as both active movement and passive receptivity, its dual aspect, remains a constituent of the kinaesthetic background of bodily intentionality, and potentially poses questions concerning the quasi-objectivity of measurable touch and its simultaneously subjectively felt qualities. When 'looking' for lost objects, for example, eyes and hands explore and we realize that vision and touch are equally prehensile and kinaesthetic. This kinaesthetic touching is a significant aspect for the lived, sensible body. It constitutes a necessary part of 'acting corporeally', the 'I can' rather than 'I think', as Husserl shows in *Cartesian Meditations*:

> Among the ... bodies (*Körper*) of this nature I then find uniquely singled out *my body* (*Leib*) ... the only one in which I immediately *have free rein* (*schalte und walte*), and in particular govern in each of its *organs*... I perceive *with* my hands, touching kinesthetically, seeing with my eyes, etc., and can so perceive at any time, while these kinestheses of the organs proceed in the *I am doing* and are subject to my *I can*; furthermore, putting these kinestheses into play, I can push, shove, etc., and thereby directly, and then indirectly, act corporeally (*leiblich*). (1960:97)

Hands and eyes roaming, actively associating sensory stimuli in order to solidify perceptions, is evidently kinaesthetic and anticipative, an 'I can', and therefore orchestrates a felt coherence to perception. Thinking of the relation between vision and touch one notes that a newborn infant is all hands and eyes, performing frantic saccadic movements in order to perform active correlation and, literally, to 'get a grip'.

Focusing on hands and touching reveals both similarities and differences in terms of approach and method between the work of Husserl and that of Merleau-Ponty. A rigorous textual analysis would be inappropriate here, but two aspects of touching that Merleau-Ponty derives from Husserl are notable. First, the notion of the 'double sensation' of touch, of hands touching each other, is significant for both. Secondly, Merleau-Ponty's extension of Husserl's kinaesthetic intentionality into an anticipative stance, through a 'motor intentionality' (1992:110) that resolves figure from ground, allows him to talk of getting a 'grip' on a situation or context. The aptness of this tactile-kinaesthetic metaphor will be pursued.

Hands

Instead of the body being awkwardly inserted between the material world and the
subjective sphere, as Husserl had asserted (1989a:161), the dual aspect of touch
(being transitive–intransitive, active–receptive) could usefully lead to explorations
of subject–object dualisms, the biological facticity of the body and its relation
to the felt coherence of somatic sensation, and the self-affirmation of the lived,
sensible body through the example of reflexive touch, of one hand touching another.
This is indeed what Merleau-Ponty accomplishes later (1992; 2000). Indeed, for
Husserl the reflexive experiencing of one's own body as a body at all is reliant on
touch. It 'becomes a body only through the introduction of sensations in touch, the
introduction of pain sensations, etc., in short, through the localization of sensations
qua sensations' (1989a:151). Experiencing one's own lived body, for example,
can occur through permutations of these localized sensations, one hand touching
another, or eyes perceiving hands. As Carman explains, 'The body as such emerges
in the coincidence of sensing and being sensed, specifically in my sensing my
body sensing itself' (1999:213). Sight alone is insufficient for this. You cannot see
yourself seeing, but by touching oneself this involves the dual aspect of touching
(simultaneously touching and being touched), grounds the localized sensations, and
fragments the felt coherence of the body in the natural attitude.

When touching one hand with the other, in a particularly resonant passage
Merleau-Ponty seemingly follows the gestalt logic of the Necker cube, applying the
oscillation between visual aspects of the cube into the tactile realm of the hands:

> the two hands are never touched and touching at the same time with respect to each other.
> When I press my two hands together, it is not a matter of two sensations felt together
> as one perceives two objects placed side by side, but of an ambiguous arrangement in
> which the two hands can alternate in the role of 'touching' and 'touched'. What was
> meant by talking about 'double sensations' is that, in passing from one role to the other,
> I can recognize the hand touched as the same one that will in a moment be touching.
> (1992:93)

On first reading his observation seems trite or mundane, even. Yet it expresses a
significant phenomenological truth, as the hand actively touching the other loses
its own localized sensations. Its proprioceptively felt qualities recede. Flipping the
orientation of this dynamic, so that the hand passively touched becomes the active
toucher, is an easy mental exercise to perform and reveals an anticipative orientation,
as Merleau-Ponty acknowledges in the last sentence, that the 'touched' will be
'touching'. This is not simply an awareness that the felt localization of sensation,
in this case within the hands, is the foundation of bodily intentionality. For Husserl,
the kinaesthetic capacity of the touching hands, and the localization of sensation, is
still orientated within a quasi-objective thinking of body, a body awkwardly inserted

between objective world and subjective sphere. Katz' pioneering psychophysics of touch in *Der Aufbau von Tastwelt* (partly translated as 'The world of touch' in 1925, see Kreuger 1982), for example, turns such tactile qualities into measurable quantity, entirely consistent with Husserl's interpretation. Instead, thinks Carman, for Merleau-Ponty 'the body is not a kind of quasi-objective thing with which I identify thanks to the localization in it of my subjective sensations, rather the attribution of sensations to myself in the first place presupposes my own prior identification with my body' (1999:223). The perceiving mind is an already incarnated mind, and even when I'm intensely scrutinizing my hands they remain proprioceptively mine, able at any time to be called to action or to instinctively intercept unexpected threats.

Merleau-Ponty's unfinished work of 1968 *The Visible and the Invisible*, published posthumously in 2000, revisits hands and touching again. His examination of our tactile being he famously compares to the two halves of an orange; our *becoming a tangible being* is opened up by simultaneously touching and being touched. As before in his *Phenomenology of Perception* it follows the gestalt-type mental operation of switching hands from toucher to touched. But here he also incorporates a kinaesthetic component, allows other sensations alongside the imaginative visuality of the Necker-type analysis. Acknowledging other somatic sensations, this moment, the opening up of a tangible being into a tangible world, is equally present in the abnormal psychology of post-operative vision, the perception of the body and felt sensation in the phantom-limb phenomenon, or the developmental psychology of an infant's discovery of self-touching. In such significant moments the split between the visual and tactile worlds temporarily applies. For others, it is only through the phenomenological attitude rather than the natural attitude that the felt coherence of the body is cleaved into its visual and tactile components which, with a nod to Husserl, are inherently kinaesthetic:

> This can happen only if my hand, which is felt from within, is also accessible from without, itself tangible, for my other hand, for example, if it takes its place among the things it touches, is in a sense one of them, opens finally upon a tangible being of which it is also a part. Through this crisscrossing within it of the touching and the tangible, its own movements incorporate themselves into the universe they interrogate, are recorded on the same map as it; the two systems are applied upon one another, as the two halves of an orange. (2000:133)

Clearly, becoming a 'tangible being' is a corollary of the Husserlian impulse of kinaesthetic touching, yet admits the possibility of something outside the enclosed circuit of hands touching hands. Other possibilities, such as an openness to the thickness and porosity of sensations between bodies, is revisited in later chapters. The significance of hands touching other hands, in particular, will form a significant motif for an analysis of flesh and 'feeling-with'.

Grip

Whereas Husserl is content to consider kinaesthetic touching as mostly associational, the one arising through the action of the other, Merleau-Ponty employs a gestalt approach that differentiates between figure and ground, as we saw. For example, sitting in a stationary train one is peripherally aware of a neighbouring train starting to move (cf. his example, 1992:47, which follows from Husserl's discussion of perceptual motivation). Sometimes this offers a kinaesthetic illusion, the sensation of movement. Looking up from the newspaper, visual attention fixes the context of foreground and peripheral background, and the kinaesthetic sensation (is it this train or the neighbouring train that is moving?) becomes resolved and recedes. Fixing the context or, in Dreyfus' memorable phrase, maintaining a 'maximal grip' on things (2004:137–9), occurs not just through the association of sensations but with an anticipative stance. As 'a mass of tactile, labyrinthine and kinaesthetic data' (1992:249), or a 'system of possible actions' (ibid.:250), Merleau-Ponty claims a potentiality in our various contexts that awaits confirmation through other means:

> my body is geared to the world when my perception offers me a spectacle as varied and as clearly articulated as possible, and when my motor intentions, as they unfold, receive from the world the responses they anticipate. This maximum distinctness in perception and action defines a perceptual ground, a basis of my life, a general milieu for the coexistence of my body and the world. (ibid.)

The resolution of this gestalt-type kinaesthetic illusion is certainly an example of attaining 'maximum distinctness', although Dreyfus' phrase is more memorable. In our ongoing everyday operations with an anticipative stance, indubitably at times our senses mislead us. While the somatic sensations that lie outside Aristotle's five-sense classification are often indistinct or vague, what is remarkable is that perceptual illusions through unresolved somatic sensations occur, and frequently enough to be recognized as such. Again, what in everyday experience seems to be non-thematic, the under-explored series of somatic sensations and their interactions become suddenly prominent as a result of these uncanny kinaesthetic and proprioceptive illusions.

Conclusion: Toward a 'Felt' Phenomenology?

While the sensible body allows seemingly continuous and multisensory experience of the world, to Rita Lauria the loss of touch, more than any other sense, leads to feeling like an orphan in that world (2000:149). Correspondingly, loss of sight embeds the subject in a far more tactile world, a world that retains a felt unity, a coherence. Like several recorded cases, the eponymous blind character in Brian

Friel's play *Molly Sweeney* undergoes an operation to restore her vision, revealing a huge amount about the relationship between vision and touch, to be detailed in the following chapter. But reflecting on a time before her vision was restored by the operation, Molly nostalgically expresses the merging of self and tactility, of sensuous envelopment, remembering fondly her previously tactile and kinaesthetic world without visual distractions. Perhaps reminding us of the active undergoing of sensation that Aristotle conceives as *aesthesis*, which started this chapter, Molly's feelings are clear and resonant:

> And how could I have told those other doctors how much pleasure my world offered me? From my work, from the radio, from walking, from music, from cycling. But especially from swimming. Oh I can't tell you the joy I got from swimming. I used to think – and I know this sounds silly – but I really did believe I got more pleasure, more delight, than sighted people can ever get. Just offering yourself to the experience – every pore open and eager for that world of pure sensation, of sensation alone – that could not have been enhanced by sight – experience that existed only by touch and feel; and moving swiftly and rhythmically through that enfolding world; and the sense of such assurance, such liberation, such concordance with it. (Friel 1994:24)

What better illustration of the role of the somatic sensations of kinaesthesia, of the diverse pleasures of touching (warmth, movement, pressure), than Molly's swimming experience? Not simply the pleasure of cutaneous sensation, Molly articulates something of the manifold of tactile sensations, delight in those somatic sensations of kinaesthesia and proprioception without separation, without classification: simply a world of pure sensation. Our reflexive attempts to write and represent such complexes of sensations may easily fall into the realm of deeply introspective subjectivity.

Instead, to treat subjective sensation not simply as reflective introspection, but as situated within ongoing affective and intercorporeal relations of *proximity* and *distance*, is one approach. Feeling in other words is more usually a feeling-with, a *mit-gefühl*. This is the central topic of this volume's final chapter, subtitled 'flesh and feeling-with'. Meanwhile our question becomes: How can we use the rich descriptive insights of phenomenology, including what presents itself to our embodied consciousness as a sensuously receptive and kinaesthetic body, to interpersonal tactile experience? Departing from individual introspection something of the processual, intersubjective nature of bodily sensations is considered, for example, in the anthropological study of the Anlo-Ewe people of West Africa by Kathryn Linn Geurts (2002; 2005). Briefly, her cross-cultural psychology suggests ethnographic approaches to the sometimes indeterminate yet interrelated nature of somatic sensations discussed above. Her fieldwork revealed an Anlo conceptualization of the senses as simultaneously interoceptive (inward-looking, somatic) and exteroceptive (outward-looking) senses, failing to map neatly onto the Aristotelian construction of five senses:

Anlo individuals and I found that their sensory order did not map well onto a five-senses model... Instead, they pointed to *seselelame* as a more generalized feeling in the body that includes both internal senses (such as balance and proprioception) and external senses, as well as other perceptual, emotional, and intuitive dimensions of experience (2005:166).

Geurts' cross-cultural perspective concerning somatic sensations augments what has here been framed phenomenologically. Most notably the notion of *seselelame* ('feeling in the body', or literally 'feel-feel-at-flesh-inside', 2005:175) inextricably combines what are conventionally held to be somatic sensations, such as kinaesthesia, proprioception and the vestibular senses, with bodily postures, language, and even a person's character (2005:171–4), and effortlessly conflates various forms of embodied perception with emotion (2005:165). Geurts' ethnographic approach is cursorily mentioned here as an alternative investigative pathway that can follow our previous theoretical discussions. Her ethnographic insights will be revisited in the context of a qualitative approach to a 'felt' phenomenology that accommodates and tries to articulate the manifold experiences of touching and feeling others. Furthermore, she also reveals that the study of hitherto under-examined somatic sensations is only novel in a culture that has systematically undervalued or forgotten them. Before discussing the forgetting of touch from a Western historical perspective, we now look at the philosophy and history of blindness, documenting and discerning the process of 'learning to see', to better articulate the complex relationship between vision and touch, eyes and hands.

–3–

Seeing with the Hands, Touching with the Eyes

The Blind Man of Puiseaux

In his famous *Letter on the Blind* of 1749, the French essayist and philosopher Denis Diderot writes of the experiences of a blind man in the French town of Puiseaux. Asked whether he would be overjoyed if he ever regained the use of his eyes, the blind man of Puiseaux supposedly replied:

> I would just as soon have long arms: it seems to me that my hands would tell me more about what happens on the moon than you can find out with your eyes and your telescopes; and besides, eyes cease to see sooner than hands to touch. I would be as well off if I perfected the organ I possess, as if I obtained the organ which I am deprived of. (Diderot 1916:77)

Knowing that the moon was far away and that the eye could gain no direct knowledge, this congenitally blind man asserts the necessity of touch as a more reliable path to knowledge, and analogizes the process of seeing with the eyes with that of touching with the hands. The blind man's testimony was used as empirical evidence in a long-running philosophical debate initiated by the so-called 'Molyneux question', the answer revealing much about historical and contemporary attitudes to blindness, touch and space. What this hypothetical debate reveals, and why it captured the public imagination of the time, is a popular conception of the non-visual spatial experience of the blind, in other words a spatial imaginary. The urgency to validate this spatial imaginary through appeals to empirical evidence in the late seventeenth and early eighteenth centuries reveals the beginnings of a naive phenomenological psychology. Yet this spatial imaginary of the blind by the sighted, of 'what the blind see' (the subtitle of Sacks' 2003 essay), remains of interest, as recent literature suggests (e.g. Gregory and Wallace 1963; Hull 1991; Magee and Milligan 1998; Kleege 1999; Sacks 2003; Gregory 2004). This chapter therefore investigates the historical and philosophical basis of this interest.

We can identify three related strands of inquiry that characterize Enlightenment conceptions of blindness which analogize hands and eyes, touch and vision, addressed in sections of this chapter. First, in the section 'Hands and Eyes', the Molyneux question. William Molyneux's 1692 monograph *Dioptrica Nova* initially pitted his question concerning blindness, touch and vision couched in terms of hands and eyes, cubes and spheres: 'If a man, blind from birth, suddenly gained vision, could he tell a sphere from a cube by sight alone on the basis of a lifetime of solely tactile experience?' (in Riskin 2002:23).[1] This question was posed in a letter to British empiricist philosopher John Locke, and initiated an ongoing dialogue between figures such as Berkeley, Condillac, Diderot and Voltaire. In fact the Molyneux problem was regarded by Ernst Cassirer in 1951 as *the* central question of eighteenth-century epistemology and psychology (in Gallagher 2005:153). Secondly, in the section 'Eyes and Hands', the related question of 'what the blind see' is addressed as an area of philosophical enquiry. In order to conceptualize the tactile imagery and spatial experience of the blind, Descartes and Diderot again consider the analogy between hands and eyes, touch and vision to be appropriate. This analogy was forged in 1637 in Descartes' philosophical treatise on optics, *Dioptrique*, where he hypothesized that the blind 'see with their hands' (in Gregory 1967:171). Further, how the congenitally blind (without any visual experience whatsoever) conceive of vision and the function of the eye, as revealed by the blind man of Puiseaux, deepens this analogy between eyes and hands. The third section, 'Condillac's statue' examines the outcome of these debates in terms of a more general philosophy of sensation, as Etienne Bonnot de Condillac's thought-experiment in his *Traité des Sensations* of 1754 concerns a hypothetical statue that progressively comes to life, like Pygmalion's statue in Ovid's *Metamorphoses* (also discussed in chapter 5), but through the successive addition of each sense. But a crucial stage in the organization of sensation, the development of spatial relations and perspective is when the statue commences touching. Recounting this thought-experiment highlights the parallels with infant development, the relationship between space, body and world that arises due to sensory orientation and successive sensation.

Here we start from Descartes' original analogy and follow through Molyneux's hypothetical question, both concerns which predated reliable cataract operations and therefore any available empirical data, and sample subsequent discussions once the first cataract operations were performed. An assessment of the post-operative evidence is discussed in the section 'Touching with the eyes'. My concern is not simply to recapitulate previous discussions in philosophy (e.g. Morgan 1977; Eilan 1993) or experimental psychology (e.g. Von Senden 1960; Jones 1975). Instead, I wish to investigate the role of touch within the long historical reach of a spatial imaginary that stretches from Descartes' *Dioptrique* (1637) to current concerns in psychology (e.g. Sacks 2003, Gallagher 2005, Streri 2005), and my slant on this is threefold. First, the assumption of an equivalence of the senses, substituting hands for eyes, touch for sight, is fundamentally to ask whether sensory perception is straightforwardly *cross-modal* (or *inter-modal*, sensory information being transferable from touch to vision) or actually *amodal* (sensory information being prior to its processing as specifically audile, visual, tactile, etc.). Secondly, it shows how the Molyneux question remains unresolved to this day, despite the availability of post-operative evidence, and even recent literature (e.g. Jacomuzzi et al. 2003; Gallagher 2005) explicitly addresses this problem, albeit with modified terms of reference. And thirdly, it brings questions of relevance to modern technologies of sensory substitution systems in thinking about the equivalence, or otherwise, of vision and touch, of 'seeing with the hands' through electronic means. The fact is, as Josipovici observes, in thinking about blindness after Molyneux 'we are all heirs of the seventeenth century' (1996:69).

Hands and Eyes: Molyneux's Question

Although Descartes had written of the analogy of eyes and hands in his *Dioptrique* of 1637, the problem of space and touch in the congenitally blind as an issue in the philosophy of perception was raised by Irish philosopher and scientist William Molyneux in a letter to John Locke, after the publication of the first edition of Locke's *Essay Concerning Human Understanding* in 1690. Berkeley, Diderot, Condillac and Voltaire subsequently became involved in a discussion of the philosophy of blindness. The letter was reprinted in later editions of Locke's work, and became known in empiricist scholarship as 'Molyneux's question'. It concerned the hypothetical case of a man born blind who could now see, at a time before cataract operations could answer this definitively. Locke posed the problem thus:

> Suppose a man born blind, and now adult, and taught by his touch to distinguish between a cube and a sphere of the same metal, and nighly of the same bigness, so as to tell, when he felt one and the other, which is the cube, which the sphere. Suppose then the cube and sphere placed on a table, and the blind man be made to see: *quaere*, whether *by his sight before he touched them*, he could now distinguish and tell which is the globe, which the cube? (1991:67)

Remembering that the question was formulated before cataract operations had been performed successfully, the theoretical content of the question gauges whether the empirical content of the touch experience has a specificity of its own, or whether it can be equated *a priori* with the sensory experience of sight. Answering 'yes' to the question therefore presumes 'that our perceptions are amodal in their spatial content' according to Eilan (1993:237), a position for which she claims there is much empirical evidence especially from child-development studies, for example Piaget and Inhelder (1956; 1969). Conversely, answering 'no' to Molyneux's question, as did Molyneux, Locke and Berkeley, is tantamount to arguing for the specificity of the senses, and what Eilan (1993:240) describes as the 'radical incommensurability' of the different sensory systems. Inter-modal (or cross-modal) perception, the translation from one sensory system to another, must be learned through repeated experience, a systematic perceptual correlation that commences at birth for the sighted, or after the cataract operation for the congenitally blind. Inter-modality seemingly requires that it be organized through an apprehending, unifying subject who transcends immediate sensory experience. Being an empiricist, Locke could allow no transcendence of the immediacy of experience, and therefore sided with the incommensurability of the sensory systems. Molyneux's question and the issue of the specificity of the senses, especially touch and vision, is important for later theories of the psychology of blindness, and in particular the issue of spatial cognition in the blind. For the empirical psychologist Von Senden in his book *Space and Sight* (1960 [1932]) for example, what was felt by touch would produce a separate and differentiated series of sensory impressions from what was seen. The specificity of the sense modalities does not allow a higher-order integration of sensory information, such that an abstract concept can be built up from different sense impressions. But this viewpoint has found support from Révész (1937; 1950) who claims that the distinct and independent modalities of visual, tactile and kinaesthetic functions lead to separate and incommensurable spatialities for each. For Jones (1975:467–70), echoing Berkeley's argument for the empirical association of the senses over time, vision is only one element in a mutually supportive system of the senses which becomes actively correlated through movement. Indeed, Berkeley's aim in his *Essay Towards a New Theory of Vision* was 'to show the manner wherein we perceive the distance magnitude and situation of objects', but as a significant correlate to this aim also 'to consider the difference there is betwixt the ideas of sight and touch, whether there be any idea common to both senses' (1983:13). We will revisit these positions through the lens of psychology and developmental psychology later. The problem is perhaps compounded by the fact that first-person historical accounts of visually impaired and blind subjects rarely speak of the specifically tactile experience of space, and those physicians involved have neither investigated nor problematized it rigorously. Early accounts of cataract operations also failed to make the crucial distinction between congenital and adventitious blindness, relative sensitivities to light, or even differing capacities for learning (e.g. Von Senden 1960 [1932]:220; Monbeck 1973:91; Gallagher 2005:168).[2] Molyneux's question therefore stands as a challenge to the scientific and physiological knowledge of the time, eliciting selective empirical testimony to a philosophical problem, and – through discussions of space, touch and sight – interprets it as a key issue in the debate between innate ideas and sensory experience.

In 1709 Bishop Berkeley provided a new twist to the debate, arguing for the specificity of the modalities of touch and sight and denoting a stark separation between the senses. In asserting that there are no 'general ideas' that stand outside immediate experience he agrees with Locke, but goes so far as to deny that space is visual at all. For Berkeley's *Essay Towards a New Theory of Vision*, spatial experience was predominantly a tactile phenomenon:

A man born blind, being made to see, would, at first, have no idea of distance by sight... The objects intromitted by sights would seem to him (as in truth they are) no other than a new set of thoughts or sensations, each whereof is as near to him as the perceptions of pain or pleasure, or the inward passions of the soul. (1983:19)

In such a view there is no conflict between visual and tactile space, since for Berkeley there simply is no visual space. Additionally it means there is no space common to all the senses, no 'general idea' or innate concept of space, as Morgan explains (1977:179). One of the fundamental premises of Berkeley's empiricism, space is therefore not visual but haptic. Yet he concedes the possibility of amodal perception of sorts, speaking of 'the extension and figure of a body, being let into the mind two ways, and that indifferently, either by sight or touch' (1983:lxviii). It is from this form of empiricism that Hume later argues in *A Treatise of Human Nature* of 1739 (1978) that the notion of the spatial extension of objects is derived from the association of experiences of touch and sight. The array of light on the retina for example, in and of itself, has no inherent meaning. Echoing Berkeley's sentiment, psychologists Warren and Rossano have more recently stated: 'The observer learns to attribute meaning through the visual array through the establishment of associations between patterns of visual stimulation and patterns of tactile and motor experience' (1991:128). In other words, instead of the empirical view of Berkeley that 'touch teaches vision,' Warren and Rossano update this in terms of developmental psychology to say that 'tactile/motor experience "calibrates" visual experience' (ibid.). This is supported by some psychological studies of touch in early infant development (e.g. Piaget and Inhelder 1956 and 1969; Jones 1975; Warren 1982; Millar 1994; Rose 1994; and neonates in Gallagher 2005).

So far we have acknowledged the spatial character of tactile perceptions in philosophical debate. In inter-modal perception there are no actual equivalences between sensory data, say between hand and eye. Through associations of sensations and perceptual experience, however, a single, coherent perceptual content can occur so that familiarity with the *look* and *feel* of an object will make its subsequent recognition, through whichever sense modality, easier. The empiricist legacy continues from Molyneux through to recent developmental psychology, where spatial cognition is constituted by both tactile-kinaesthetic and visual experience. So far this discussion has been predominantly couched in philosophical terms. But what difference does the empirical evidence actually make?

Touching with the Eyes: Cheselden's Patient

At the time Molyneux's question was posed in 1690 little empirical evidence existed, mainly due to the fact that cataract operations were not routine. Although Von Senden makes brief reference to an operation in the eleventh century, more detailed reports start to appear with a celebrated set of experiments on youths with cataracts by the surgeon William Cheselden in 1728. It was Cheselden's report to the Royal Society in London that was subsequently discussed in France by Diderot (1916 [1749]), Buffon (1749, in Morgan 1977:16), Condillac (1930 [1754]) and Voltaire (1992 [1738]). Voltaire introduced a French readership initially to Cheselden's case study in his *Elements of Newton's Philosophy*, published in 1738.

These ongoing discussions initiated by Molyneux's question were part of a larger Enlightenment fascination with the link between the senses and cognition, thinks Barasch (2001:149), in a climate where musing on experiences of blindness and visual impairment were the topic of conversation in fashionable salons. Neither Diderot nor anyone else 'went beyond the boundaries of abstract psychological speculation', says Anagnos (in Farrell 1956:18), and these questions would have remained hypothetical for both philosophers and public alike were it not for the historic surgical operations performed by Cheselden in 1728. When Cheselden's patient saw for the first time he is also quoted as performing an equivalence between hands and eyes. Supposedly misconceiving space and distance, he initially collapses the distance between the object and its retinal impression, saying that visual objects 'touch' the eye (in Von Senden 1960 [1932]:219). In his account, Cheselden comments on the difficulties that his patient had with the new-found visual world: 'For a long time he distinguished neither magnitude, distance, situation, nor even figure… Everything he saw seemed at first to be upon his eyes, and to touch them, as the objects of the sense of feeling touch the skin' (in Morgan 1977:23–4). More crucially as regards Molyneux's question, Cheselden's patient was unable to distinguish with his sight what, with the help of his hands, he had been able to distinguish through touch. Whether cube or sphere, whether above or below him, his sight allowed him to recognize neither these objects nor their relative position in space. Perspective and distance were similarly problematic. Reportedly, when examining a painting he had to reach out and touch the surface to confirm there was only a two-dimensional representation, rather than three-dimensional solid bodies. Voltaire reports, surprised, that the blind man asked 'which of the senses deceived him, that of feeling, or that of seeing' (1967 [1738]:65; also Diderot in Morgan 1977:52).

Writing explicitly about the Molyneux problem, and similarly with the benefit of Cheselden's report, in his *Letter on the Blind* of 1749 Diderot theorizes a relation between touch and space such that touch aids and informs the eye. Diderot conjectures:

> It has to be agreed that we must perceive in objects an infinite number of things that the infant or the blind-born [given sight] do not perceive at all, even though such objects be painted upon the back of their eyes the same as ours; that it is not enough for objects to strike us, that we still must be attentive to their impressions; that as a consequence *we see nothing* the first time we use our eyes … that experience alone teaches us to *compare* sensations with what occasions them; that since sensations have nothing that resembles

objects essentially, experience has to construct about us analogies that seem to be purely conventional: in a word, it cannot be doubted that *touch serves a great deal to give the eye precise knowledge of the conformity between an object and the representation of it that the eye receives*. (in Creech 1986:119, emphasis added)

In this Diderot finds agreement with Berkeley's speculation. In his questioning of the blind man of Puiseaux, Diderot assumes there is a spatial component to tactile experience, and that such tactile experience informs the eye. However neat a solution, the publication of Diderot's *Letter* is questioned by later findings. Platner in 1785 casts doubt on the veracity of Diderot's empirical information. Against Diderot's deduction that tactile experience is inherently spatial, Platner concluded after investigation that the congenitally blind literally have no awareness of space, and in the words of Von Senden, that the sighted are simply 'deceived by the verbal habits of the blind' when speaking of space, since they cannot share spatial understandings with the sighted (1960:28).

After several hundred years of experimental evidence and surgical operations, should the question not be resolved? As Heller summarizes, 'the many studies of the restoration of sight do not provide unequivocal answers to Molyneux's question' (1991:241). The answer is negative, therefore, for the following reasons. First, it is a classic example of an attempt to gain privileged access to the contents of another person's mental state and cognitive processes, in this case of the blind by the sighted. However sophisticated the questioning, qualitative inquiry is hampered by the attempt to gauge empirically the sensory contents of another person's consciousness, and this problem persists in current examinations of experiences of blindness. There remain only fragments and imaginations. Secondly, there are complexities in the interpretation of the evidence over what counts as 'blindness' and 'sight', and in historical accounts these have not been systematized or standardized. Whether congenital or adventitious, and irrespective of the differing sensitivities to light that is a continuum from sighted to non-sighted, the historical evidence remains difficult to unpick as this information was not identified in the accounts. And thirdly, the post-operative experience varies greatly between patients, so that 'learning how to see' (Gregory 1967, 2004; Sacks 1993, 1995) is different according to the plasticity and adaptability of each individual patient, and the level of previous retinal damage.

For example, Von Senden in 1932 agrees with Platner's findings, arguing that tactile experience of the blind is entirely non-spatial, the blind person having no proper spatial representation of the objects touched. 'What are features of shape to us are for him [sic] wholly unspatial, purely tactile distinctions of sensation or dynamic movement,' he argues, 'they are distinctions in the constancy of sequence and ordering of impressions' (1960 [1932]:49). Consequently he concludes there are no 'absolute spatial concepts' for the blind, and that for the blind person there are only 'relational concepts, ordered sequences and schemata' (ibid.:61). This he infers from a selective reading of post-operative accounts. Their descriptions of phenomena while sightless are related primarily to the peripersonal touch-space around the body, making it difficult to conceptualize a shape or figure lying beyond reach of hand or cane. Interviews conducted and published in a weekly newspaper with the congenitally blind subject Joan Getaz, questioned in 1928, fuelled further the public imaginations of blind spatial experience. Without prior visual experience she conceptualized a tree serially and schematically as a temporal, textural sequence of trunk, branch and leaves. Due to confusion over relative sizes compared with the body, Ms Getaz apparently assumed the tree was not much larger than a man. It was from his reading of newspaper reports, rather than rigorous psychological studies, that Von Senden concludes there is a difference between the visual and the tactile fields. The schema or ordered sequence is therefore not a 'real consciousness of space', he maintains (1960 [1932]:69).

This view is not widely held. Recalling Berkeley's dogmatic assertion that our spatial knowledge comes primarily through touch, and that touch informs and appends vision, Warnock (in Von Senden 1960 [1932]:322) and Jones (1975:461) regard Von Senden's view, that the congenitally blind have no spatial concepts, as equally dogmatic and unsupported by evidence. A more recent report examining tactile mapping suggests that the congenitally blind 'may encode space in a serial, egocentric manner', say Kitchin et al. (1997b:233), a self-referential, route-type representation of space. This perhaps encapsulates the contemporary spatial imagination by the sighted of the congenitally blind: the assumption of tactile-spatial 'images' or inner mental representations, especially of the static kind. More recent psychology endeavours to escape such straightforwardly representational models, and from Gibson (e.g. 1950; 1968) and Piaget (e.g. 1955; with Inhelder 1956) onward have stressed how spatial perceptions can occur without spatial 'pictures' or inner mental representations, a spatiality resulting from active movement informed by kinaesthesia (Gibson 1950:224; Karlsson and Magnusson 1994:10 footnote 1). The specificity of haptic space and tactile 'images' is revisited below. Meanwhile, Jones (1975:466) argues specifically against what he calls the 'visual map' theory, and asserts instead the importance of motor organization, citing empirical evidence for this.

Returning to an insight by Diderot it can be noted that when first opening our eyes we learn to compare sensations by experience, thereby admitting a *temporal* component to spatial perception. For cross-modal perception to occur, for the Molyneux patient or for Diderot, there is a temporal aspect to sensory experience that forges associations between the sense modalities, thereby involving kinaesthesia, the memory of touch-patterns and other sensory-motor interventions. These observations would entail a modified answer to the Molyneux question, where what is commonly known as 'visuo-spatial working memory' (Baddely 1992) relies on 'mental images' in the blind that are neither specifically visual nor spatial, as Graven observes (2003:102), and so memory allows the transfer of information between modalities. But at some level there is convergence between the sensory modalities, Graven argues, so that 'a cognitive vision-touch link [is] derived from converging subsystems' (ibid.:108). In terms of the absolute pragmatic experience of working memory his evidence suggests that memory alone is not the intermediary of cross-modal transfer. Instead, there are underlying encoding processes at a 'lower cognitive level' than memory (ibid.), encoding experiences from different sensory subsystems. In other words, while memory might allow cross-modal transfer between modalities such as vision and touch, perception is more amodal than cross-modal. Where does this leave the experiences of eyes and hands, of blindness and spatial imagination?

Eyes and Hands: Diderot and Descartes

Let us return to historical accounts. From the discussion of Molyneux and Locke in the section 'Hands and Eyes', we now consider Diderot's response to the post-operative evidence, which is more aligned with that of Descartes. Before Diderot nobody had actually elicited the testimony of blind subjects to contribute toward the Molyneux discussion, and so Diderot stressed that his subject was a real, not hypothetical person (in Morgan 1977:32; Kennedy et al. 1992:176). He was convinced of the spatial character of tactile impressions in his subject, and questioned his subject about the spatiality of tactile impressions and the successive presence of the hand in different places. We are now familiar with the clear hierarchy of the senses, sedimented since Aristotle's *De Anima*, in which vision was primary (also Crary 1990; Jay 1994), but also how the absence of vision necessitated a substitute for sight. In discussing the way the blind negotiate the world through the use of a stick, it is unsurprising that Descartes invoked a simplistic version of a hypothetical blind man in his *Dioptrique* of 1637:

> Without long practice this kind of sensation is rather confused and dim; but if you take men born blind, who have made use of such sensations all their life, you will find they feel things with such perfect exactness that one might say that *they see with their hands*. (in Gregory 1967:191, emphasis added)

The Cartesian concept of vision is therefore modelled after the sense of touch; the ability to 'see with the hands' implicitly regards tactility as a lesser substitute for sight, even if it is the primary mode of spatial awareness and navigation to the blind. Such equivalence of sight and touch extends even to the idea of the fovea, the rodless part of the eye that affords the most acute vision. It is recognized that the most accurate part of our touch perception comes from the hands and especially the fingertips (e.g. Angell 1906:147), due to the concentration of nerve endings. It is only natural to expect an analogy between the high-definition optical discrepancy of the fovea, and the highly discriminatory tactile sensing of the hands and fingertips.

The accidental discovery in 1786 by Valentin Haüy that embossed script could be read by the fingers, for example, implied in the words of Farrell that 'sensitive fingers ... could take the place of insensitive eyes' (1956:93). The substitution of the sense of touch for the sense of sight, of hands for eyes, was therefore crucial in terms of the development of education for the blind.

Clearly Descartes' analogue between touch and vision, eyes and hands, is one of sensory poverty. Yet unusually for the time the exact same sensory analogue for Diderot instead proves the richness of the sensory world for the blind, and this fascinates him. This sensory analogue between hands and eyes, the haptic and the optic, persists in the education and psychology of the blind and in 1930 Pierre Villey echoes the words of the blind man of Puiseaux, and similarly analogizes the neurophysiology of hands and eyes, or haptic foveation without colour, implying the amodality of perception. While Diderot augmented Descartes' analogy by considering proximity and distance ('seeing' the moon with long arms), Villey furthers this distance aspect in his comparison of the senses: 'Sight is long-distance touch, with the sensation of colour added. Touch is near sight minus the sensation of colour, and with the sense of rugosity [texture] added. The two senses give us knowledge of the same order' (in Farrell 1956:93). Even more recently, psychologists concerned with blindness make the distinction between the near-space of haptic exploration and the far-space of locomotor exploration. Ungar (2000) for example observes: 'In a sense, haptic exploration is like foveation without peripheral vision, in that the positions of objects not currently being attended to must be maintained in memory[,] and no cues are available to draw attention in any particular direction.' Noting the use of 'foveation' as a term of equivalence between sight and touch, we find that in addition our attention is drawn to the distinction between the haptic (or prehensile) and locomotor explorations of space, of great importance for the congenitally blind. The reach-space of the hand and fingers is said to be 'prehensile space', hence the foveation analogy, while 'locomotor space' implies the movement of the entire body. Whether in immediate prehensile space or in the locomotor space afforded by movement, the notion of externality and the cognition of space for the blind is often performed and mediated through the hand and its prostheses, such as a cane or stick.

The same analogy concerning hands and eyes is extended to the hand's prostheses, and finds expression once again in Diderot. Instead of the hypothetical unnamed blind man of Descartes' *Dioptrique*, the blind man of Puiseaux is asked directly how he conceives of the function and purpose of eyes. The answer confirms Descartes' interpretation of touch in terms of vision, as if there is an equivalence. "'Madame,'" entreats Diderot, "open the *Dioptrique* of Descartes, and you will find there the phenomena of vision related to those of touch, and illustrations full of men occupied in seeing with sticks. Neither Descartes nor those who have followed him have been able to get a clearer conception of vision'" (quoted in Morgan 1977:34). Making the same analogy between the touch-space of the stick around the body and the visual field, he replies:

> When I place my hand between your eyes and an object, my hand is present to you but the object is absent. The same thing happens when I reach for one thing with my stick and come across another. (in Von Senden 1960:64)

Seeing with hands and seeing with the hands' prostheses afford different fidelities of touch, however. If foveation occurs within the fingertips, the hand and its prostheses are more peripheral and insensitive. In the same work, Diderot extends this foveation analogy:

> Should ever a philosopher, blind and deaf from birth, construct a man in the image of Descartes', I make bold to assure you, Madame, that he will place the soul in the fingertips, for it is from there that he receives all his sensations, all his knowledge. (1977:40; also De Fontenay 1982:157–8)

Diderot acknowledges Descartes' view of the prosthesis and cane as an extension of perception, and in so doing accepts the observation that the sensorium is thereby extended. It is perhaps not the soul that is situated in the fingertips, as Diderot muses, but an acknowledgement that cognition is extended, literally reaching from brain to the peripersonal, prehensile space around the body. This reminds us of Kant's assertion that the hand is the 'outer brain of man', heavily involved in spatial cognition (in Merleau-Ponty 1992:316). Diderot therefore takes Descartes' encephalous model of the senses, the sensorium being situated in the head or a set of internalized spatial representations, and makes it more acephalous or distributed. As Diderot argues, try telling the congenitally blind and deaf man that 'the head is the seat of our thoughts,' and he will report otherwise: 'the sensations he will have derived from touch will be, so to speak, the mold of all his ideas; and I would not be surprised if, after protracted meditation, he were to find his fingers as tired as we do our head' (in de Fontenay 1982:165). Although this is a naive imaginative projection, it nonetheless remains indicative of an embodied spatial imaginary.

Seeing with the hands, considering touch and sight as analogous (if not equivalent) in this way, is to conceive perception as amodal, disregarding the specificity of each of the senses in order to postulate some underlying correspondence. Hence the analogy between the hand, the stick and the eye in Descartes' *Dioptrique* and Diderot's *Letter on the Blind*. So far we have considered the way that 'seeing with the hands' assumes the non-specificity of the senses. While the congenitally blind are able to make compensations and adjustments in terms of object recognition and spatial navigation, this does not mean that spatial perception is necessarily amodal or cross-modal *per se*. But by observing the blind man's ability to recognize objects tactually, Descartes' *Dioptrique* assumes that the capacity to form a whole representational framework was an innate property of the mind, not derived from the experiences or associations of the different senses. Now let us consider for a moment the exact opposite viewpoint, that there is no representational framework without the successive correlations of sensory impressions that are derived from experience.

Condillac's Statue: Touch, Movement and Space

In his *Treatise on the Sensations* of 1754, Condillac begins by observing that 'We do not know how to recall the ignorance in which we were born; it is a state which leaves no traces after it' (I,i). This sets the scene for a thought-experiment in empiricism, an imaginative reconstruction of the way that, from a blank, impressionless state of no prior experience or knowledge, immediate sensory impressions build into complex cognitive activities, and more complex concepts such as space and perspective arise directly as a result. This piece of cognitive retro-engineering is akin to Merleau-Ponty's project in *The Primacy of Perception* (1964a) of conducting an archaeological investigation into the mechanisms of perception to reveal the hidden mechanisms behind the immediacy of sensory experience, discussed in chapter 2. Condillac's unfolding narrative endeavours to find plausible explanations for the current organization of the adult sensorium, and simultaneously insinuates an explication of neonatal development. In Gallagher's words, it works as 'a heuristic place-holder for both the newborn infant and the congenitally blind subject of Molyneux's question' (2005:154). While an empirically informed piece of plausible speculation, resulting from a synthesis of second-hand post-operative evidence and philosophical musings on the development of the body and the senses, the limitations of this model will become evident shortly.

In order to understand the processes by which the senses leave impressions on the subject, then, Condillac imagines an immobile, statue-like figure with the potential to receive sensations, beginning with smell and successively adding the other senses. Although clearly alluding to infant development this imaginative figure also echoes the myth of Pygmalion in Ovid's *Metamorphoses*, the beautiful marble statue coming to life. The touch of the artist Pygmalion in making this statue become flesh will be revisited in chapter 5. Condillac asks us to imagine an originally inanimate and insentient human being, to consider what it could come to know were it to acquire each of the senses, either in isolation from the others or in various combinations. This question is in fact a more radical version of the question Molyneux had posed to Locke, but now opens up the question to speculations concerning combinations of the other senses. For example, Condillac asks what a person endowed solely with the sense of smell would think upon acquiring hearing; or what a person endowed with vision would know if incapable of motion, and unaware of any tactile sensation. While seemingly a series of random or listless speculations, the background of this questioning is an attempt to solidify a radical form of empiricism. All that is required is a rich array of sensations that correlate over time in order to build up more complex ideas and cognitive abilities. His speculative psychology based on a range of Molyneux-type questions sought to explain how a statuesque being might acquire ideas of space and of external objects, based solely through the acquisition and subsequent association of sensations, coordinated by movement over time.

According to Condillac's narrative, first comes smell. After opening its eyes the statue moves, and by discovering movement realizes touch. The other senses follow, and Condillac's thought-experiment affords us an opportunity presently to think through the coherence and unity of the senses through movement, a kind of speculative psychology or, like Herder's aesthetic approach to Pygmalion's statue in *Sculpture* (2002), an imaginative proto-phenomenology. Indeed, one of the remnants of the Enlightenment philosophical conception of blindness is that tactile or haptic space is derivative of bodily movement. As in the discussion earlier on Cheselden's patient, the whole notion of the extension of objects in space (*extensio*) can only be revealed through motility. In fact it was from discussing Molyneux's question that Locke's famous simile arose comparing the mind to a 'white paper', a *tabula rasa* (1991:II.i.2), a blank sheet that awaited experience.[3] From this Berkeley inferred that it was through the awareness of the body's own movement that the notion of spatial extension occurred, 'which then provides structure for tactile and visual sensations' (Kennedy et al. 1992:175). It is with a more biological basis that Condillac took Locke's empiricism and the notion of movement to be the basis for all sensory knowledge. Considering the relationship between memory and sensation allowed Condillac to do away with Locke's separation of the senses from the faculty of reflection. Locke had to distinguish between immediate 'sensation', which he described as the way 'our senses, conversant about particular sensible objects, do convey into the mind several distinct perceptions of things, according to those various ways wherein those objects do affect them' (1991:II.i.3), and 'reflection,' being 'the perception of the operations of our own mind within us, as it is employed about the ideas it has got' (ibid.:II.i.4).

To escape this separation between abstracted reflection and the immediacy of sensation, both Berkeley and Condillac stressed the importance of motility, the subject experiencing physiological sensation and performing active perception. As outlined above, Berkeley (1983 [1709]) had argued that the knowledge of spatial structure originates in perceptual learning and experience. He observed that knowledge of distances cannot occur by vision alone, and that tactual cues are necessary for such distance perception. Thus haptics for Berkeley was 'the vital substrate to vision' (Kitchin et al. 1997:2). Berkeley also argued that the structure that united these tactile and visual sensations was an awareness of the body's own movement. In short, for Berkeley, body motility and the correlation between tactile and visual sensations is how spatial apprehension takes place. Both Berkeley and Condillac agree on this point, and their views in turn influenced later psychology such as Lotze's prominent work of 1856, *Mikrokosmus*.

Condillac's statuesque thought-experiment exemplifies the crucial role of the integration of sensory experience through movement, and therefore of the production of the concept of space and perspective through the body. After beginning to smell, with that modality's ambiguous spatiality, the statue opens its eyes. However, sight by itself is similarly unsuccessful in revealing distinctions between boundaries or shapes, and by opening its eyes the statue is unable to recognize one location or spatial boundary relative to any other (*Treatise* I.xi.8–9). Condillac maintained that it is only through the sense of touch that we first acquire an awareness of space as an external continuum that extends outward beyond the bounds of our body, and an awareness of other objects in this space. After beginning to smell and having opened our eyes, touch allows us to attribute smells, sounds, tastes, and colours to external objects. The tactile (cutaneous, kinaesthetic) sensation of solidity is crucial for the development of an awareness of space, and the ability to recognize and manipulate external objects. Much like Merleau-Ponty's discussion of sensory unity, the section 'The Spatiality of One's Own Body and Motility' in *Phenomenology of Perception*, we transpose these reflections into the body of the statue.

The Touching-touched Relation: the Spatiality of the Statue's Body

Once again, touch grounds the experience of solidity and spatial extension and the organization of further sensation. This is no different for Condillac, and a key moment in the developing consciousness of the hypothetical statue is in touching and being touched. Condillac explains in the *Treatise* (II,v) that tactile experience of the sensations of solidity allow us to infer that our bodies are spatially extended, and that something else exists outside of them. In the comparison between touching ourselves and touching something outside of ourselves, a crucial differential emerges. This is the relation of toucher-touched, a fundamental moment in the emergent sensory consciousness of the statue. The profoundly significant realization of self and non-self such a moment affords, of the cognition of external objects that occurs in relation to oneself, is discussed variously by Maldiney (see chapter 5), Merleau-Ponty (see chapters 2 and 8) and Derrida (on Nancy and 'self-touching', 2005:270). For Condillac the self-touching and touching of another by the statue is considered not only as underlining the significance of the boundary of self and non-self, but also forms the basis of sensory evidence for solidity and spatial extension. We now walk through Condillac's unfolding sensory narrative to understand that crucial relation between touch, the sensorium and spatial cognition.

Consider first the touching of one's own hand. The feeling of solidity in one hand has a corresponding sensation of solidity and being touched in the other. Touching here imparts two instances of solidity, the one passively felt and the other actively touching. For a primitive statue-like consciousness coming into sensory awareness for the first time, duration also comes into play. Manual explorations such as tracing a path with one hand around the other, and subsequently building up a continuous sequence of sensations around the entire body, would indicate how different parts of the body are spatially related to others. Thus the statue initially acquires an awareness of its own spatially extended body.

Consider next the case of touching something other than one's own body. Touching another object, the sensation of solidity is not met with a corresponding feeling of being touched. An absence of sensation infers the solidity of other objects, and awareness of the shape and location of such objects in surrounding space is acquired. Based on this distinction derived from touching, other sensory properties such as smells and sounds are now attributable to other objects in a space relative to the statue. From the statue's point of view, moving objects within circumambient space makes sensations appear or disappear (*Treatise* III, i-ii). So, whereas Locke had assumed the distinction between an inner and an outer world, Condillac endeavours to generate this division by considering the statue self-touching and touching another, thereby postulating two sources of ideas. Furthermore, touch now becomes the tutor of the other senses, training sight to provide depth to the visual field for example. There is increasing awareness of distance through the correlation between visual sensation and touch; to the statue, when moving its hands in front of its eyes, colour sensations appear then disappear, thought at first to exist on the surface of the eyes (like Cheselden's post-operative patient), then as being beyond the arm's reach, and eventually correctly attributed to particular tangible objects beyond arm's length by discovering correlations between visual distance cues and the distance that must be crossed to actually manipulate that object. Having originally no concept of space, then, perspective and relationships of distance are learnt through continually sedimenting tactile-visual and kinaesthetic associations, starting from the egocentric spatial framework of the statue's body.

Condillac's statue starts as detached and immobile but – in accreting sensory modalities, sensations and movement – it begins to be progressively active and involved in developing a sense of space, solidity and perspective. Like Pygmalion's Galatea, the statue becomes *flesh*. If we were to imaginatively invest the statue with an increasing agency that follows from its sensory and cognitive development, like Ovid and Herder, we could speculate on the phenomenology of this sensory unfolding, this process of becoming fleshly. The spatial organization of sensation and the imbrication of body and world is amenable to Merleau-Ponty's analysis of embodied consciousness, especially in *Phenomenology of Perception* (1992). In becoming flesh the statue becomes progressively involved in what Merleau-Ponty calls the 'thickness of the world' (1992:204). This is not the individuated body of the immobile 'subject of physiological vision', in Crary's words (1990), an observer detached from the world he inhabits, where the analogous *camera obscura* worked as a similarly static and detached model of human optics and the retina. Instead, through Condillac's *Treatise on the Sensations* and Thomas Reid's notion of 'combinant sensations' (in Yolton 1984:215), the statuesque being is multisensory and mobile, thereby becoming engaged in the active production of its world. Thinking back to chapter 2, in Merleau-Ponty's terms this is the 'natural perception' of the 'body-subject' (1992:225). From active exploration, movement, the statue learns how to perceive, and by so moving opens up a space of sensation that integrates the various senses into a higher-order cognitive spatial framework.

Like a child wriggling on the floor and encountering objects, tactile sensation is the aggregate of motion and touch; a visual field becomes three-dimensional and the learning of depth perception occurs thereby. As Politz writes, 'Self-motion and touch are our first spatial experiences' (1979:279), and this neatly mirrors Condillac's statue. Therefore the collocation of the senses of sight and touch bound through motility is held to be productive of spatiality in the subject, in the hypothetical statue of Condillac and developmental psychology alike. From the beginning of the *Treatise* onward, the hypothetical statue has a clear parallel with the unfolding development of human neonates. Touch is crucial for Condillac's thought-experiment, and some current developmental psychology attempts to gain empirical support for comparable speculations on the relationships and correlations of senses such as vision and touch, eyes and hands in early infancy, such as Arlette Streri's and Yvette Hatwell's work (e.g. Streri 1993 and Hatwell 2003). An empirical response in terms of developmental psychology has self-conscious roots within the Molyneux problem, in terms of the relation between hands and eyes, and Condillac's statue in terms of the formation of the sensorium, as Streri herself notes. Elsewhere, Streri offers a way to reconcile the specificity of information gathered from separate sensory modalities (vision, touch, smell) to form a structural unity in the experience of an object:

> Indeed, when a baby explores an object with its eyes, its hands and its mouth, the different pieces of information gathered are neither added together nor multiplied. A synthesis or a perceptive organization is necessary to give the object some coherence. Furthermore, the bimodal exploration of objects has an important consequence: the infant has to judge as equivalent certain information gathered simultaneously by the haptic and visual systems, in spite of their structural and functional specificity. (Streri 2005:340)

Here are clues in considering the debate between amodal or cross-modal perception, and Streri is clearly in the latter camp, although she also finds evidence for haptic recognition of objects by the hands at birth (2005:329–30). However, although there are clear parallels between Condillac's thought experiment and concepts of neonatal development, it would be misleading to burden what is essentially a speculative model based on Condillac's second-hand digestion of post-operative evidence as a complete explanation for the unfolding sensorium. Likewise, Diderot's assertion that 'vision must be very imperfect in an infant that opens its eyes for the first time, or in a blind person just after his operation' (1916:52) assumes a naive parallel between blind subject and neonate that does not admit complexities of varying stages and levels of blindness, nor does it admit fully developed processes of cognition within an adult subject without sight.

Condillac's experiment in speculative proto-phenomenology is also potentially useful to us in light of twentieth-century psychology. For example, active exploration through movement and touch through this personification of the statue illustrates Gibson's (1979) notion of active perception, although earlier Révész (1950:100) had differentiated between a 'receptive' and 'purposive' attitude. After all, *percipere* in Latin means 'to take hold of, to feel, to comprehend.' As Rodaway has observed, it is a reaching out (1994:10). Apart from Weber's research on the psychophysics of active touch in 1834 (1978) it was Gibson's work on the senses (1968 and *passim*) that fully embraced the active nature of perception, imagined by Condillac through the statue. After Von Senden, Révész (1937) had posed the separation and specificity of sensory spaces, noting their differentiation but also their necessary collocation in order for space to exist. He noted they are 'different, independent, and qualitatively unrelated sensory space-structures' (1937:434), but that they were interwoven and unavailable for separate analysis in terms of the sensory production of space. Even the *visual* perception of the world, he argues, has a tactile and kinaesthetic component, and therefore there is no separate visuo-spatial image that is distinct and identifiable without the 'tactual-kinaesthetic functions' (ibid.). This works both ways, as Révész suggests:

> It would be far more probable to realize *haptic space* and haptic space-images because it is quite possible, at least for people who were born blind, to exclude visual images; but those who see can receive only a partial idea of pure tactual space and space-images perceived through touch, because an act of touch automatically initiates also visual impressions or sensations. Even when this transformation or this visualization of tactual sensations does not take place, we cannot obtain a pure tactual configuration. (ibid.:434–5, his emphasis)

The predominantly visual-haptic and kinaesthetic nature of space should be familiar to us through the later Husserl's discussion of the specific kinaesthesias of different sense-organs and bodyparts (in chapter 2). It is echoed by James Rowland Angell (1906), a contemporary of George Herbert Mead and William James. In addition to noting the relation of the haptic and optic, the eyes and hands in the production of space, Angell also acknowledged the separate movement of the eyes, adding optic motility and body motility to build up elaborate space perceptions. Like Husserl's discussion of the separate kinaestheses of the different organs (examined in chapter 2), Angell argued that movement was the all-important factor for the 'building up and correlating with one another of our various spatial sensations'

(1906:146). Following neatly from Condillac's statue then, the collocation of the senses of sight, touch and kinaesthesia is for Angell a prerequisite for the production of sensory space, making such sensory space a *multimodal, motile space*: 'Our space, as we know it in adult consciousness, is, then, a distinctly synthetic affair, developed from two or three sensory sources, through the intermediation of localizing and exploring movements' (ibid.:153–4).

Returning to the subject of blindness and visual impairment, those post-Molyneux insights from Condillac concerning the synthesis of visual and haptic information and the beginnings of spatial awareness find unequivocal support even today, for example by psychologist Gunnar Karlsson, who is similarly able to claim:

> [T]he condition for the possibility of the experience of space is sight and/or tactile experiences, that is to say, if a person has *never* had sight or tactile experiences (and, one might have to add, neither kinaesthetic experience), that person could never experience spatiality. (Karlsson and Magnusson 1994:10)

In the absence of one of these crucially spatial senses it is nevertheless possible that another sense can become associated, one that offers the necessary spatial component such as audition. For Révész and Karlsson this allows blindness to produce a non-visual, tactile and kinaesthetic space independently from visual space, thereby reasserting the existence of true spatiality for the blind after Von Senden's denial of it. Bringing back vision and touch into the production of spatiality through the body, after Condillac's thought-experiment we are usefully reminded of Oliver Sacks' newly sighted patient Virgil who, having had his sight restored through surgery, walks through the city. He visualizes those familiar objects he had previously known so well through touch, and thereby learns to see (1993; 1995). The narrative of the awakening sensory consciousness of the statue, starting with smell, eyes then opening, followed by touching and movement, therefore finds a parallel in Virgil. He actively correlates familiar haptic sensations with newly visual sensations through repetition and continuous exploration after the operation. Bodily movement unites these divergent sensory realms, and it is through walking around that Virgil obtained a sense of 'space, solidity and perspective', says Sacks (1995:120). The ready fusion of vision and touch in sighted experience, in which the one modality informs and modifies the other (intermodality), means there is a re-ordering of the remaining sensory modalities in the absence of vision. Warren notes in addition that 'the nature of intermodality organisation in the congenitally and later blind may be qualitatively different' (1978:78–9). In other words, Warren acknowledges the difference that prior visual experience may have in the constitution of the sensorium, the sensory ordering of spatial experience. Thinking through Condillac's unfolding narrative, this does not preclude the possibility of a purely tactile-kinaesthetic or *haptic* space that informs – and is informed by – any available visual data, whether congenitally blind, visually impaired or sighted. The question then becomes: what is the relation between haptic and visual spaces, of hands and eyes? Condillac's statue is another imaginative thought experiment in considering the interrelations of the senses and the production of space, of thinking through embodied perception, a proto-phenomenology that takes touch seriously, and which questions whether our experiences are amodal or cross-modal.

Seeing with the Hands, Touching with the Eyes

Now, to return to where we started, with Descartes' analogy of 'seeing with the hands' in *Dioptrique*. Rather than being rooted in any particular sense modality, then, Descartes thought of the process of constructing a spatial representational framework as amodal, independent of any specific sense modality (Jacobson and Kitchin 1997). The argument for amodal spatial perception necessarily elides the specific perceptual content of the different sense modalities and makes them contribute to an underlying, unifying faculty that makes sensations cohere at some cognitive level. As we saw, Aristotle terms this unifying faculty *sensus communis* or 'common sensibility' in *De Anima* (424b–425a). As a result, for both Descartes and Diderot, 'the senses are conceived more as adjuncts of a rational mind and less as physiological organs', as Crary puts it (1990:60). As rational adjunct rather than distinct sensory modality, context and memory inflect the suitability of vision as an analogy to touch, or eyes with hands, and *vice versa*. If conceived as adjuncts in this way, the sometimes diverging and sometimes converging sensory subsystems dynamically inform and shape our perceptual experience of the world. Amodal spatial apprehension occurs as the result of just such a 'unity of the senses' (Marks 1978), while the case of Cheselden's patient and Condillac's statue underlines the distinctness yet interdependence of newly acquired sensory experience. The fundamental unity of the senses still holds currency in some circles, such as Carreiras and Cordina (1992). But, sagely enough, Diderot was actually arguing in the eighteenth century for something close to Graven's (2003) recent articulation of converging-diverging sensory subsystems and Gallagher's (2005) discussion of intermodal neonate vision. He was to hold a *correspondence* rather than an *equivalence* between the senses, while conceding the possibility that the senses have a specificity of their own: 'It is easy to conceive that the use of one of the senses can be perfected and accelerated by the observations of another; but it is not easy to conceive that between their functions there is an essential dependence' says Diderot (1916:62). Presciently, this can be translated into the psychological idiom of amodal and cross-modal perception, where cross-modal perception equates with correspondence.

This debate, and speculation concerning intermodal and amodal perception, as we have seen, has been updated in recent neuropsychological writings. Space does not allow a complete survey or development of these ideas, but it is sufficient to note that the same debate concerning visualization and cognition between vision and touch persists. Indeed, the question of 'visualization' in the blind, of what the blind 'see', is addressed specifically as an indication of the brain's organization of sensory information as amodal and adaptable, for Sacks (2003) and Motluk (2005). Such recent popular science articles about what the blind 'see', with Sacks in *The New Yorker* interviewing a number of blind respondents, and Motluk in *New Scientist* profiling a blind artist, can be seen as a continuation of Diderot's attitude of inquiry. Sacks for example writes of mounting neuropsychological findings that reinforce Crary's view (1990: 60) that the senses are no longer distinct modalities, that the 'sensory modalities can never be considered in isolation':

> There is increasing evidence from neuroscience for the extraordinarily rich inter-connectedness and interactions of the sensory areas of the brain, and the difficulty, therefore, of saying that anything is purely visual or purely auditory, or purely anything. (Sacks 2003:55)

Relating this back to his case studies, and more usefully in the context of this chapter's discussion of vision and touch, eyes and hands, and the possibility of cross-modal perception, Sacks then states: 'The world of the blind, of the blinded, it seems, can be especially rich in such in-between states – the intersensory, the metamodal – states for which we have no common language' (ibid.). Imaginations of the experience of blindness, from Descartes onward, have furthered the substitutions of sensory experiences, of hands and eyes, as we have seen. These and other incidences of cross-modality, such as Condillac's hypothetical statue, have implications for the synaesthetic richness of experience in blind and sighted alike, an important area of inquiry in phenomenology ('synaesthetic perception is the rule' Merleau-Ponty argued famously in 1945 (1992:229)) and more recent psychology and cognitive science. And cross-modal transfer from vision to either audition or touch is the basis for technologies of sensory substitution systems for the blind and visually impaired, as investigated in the work of Karlsson and Magnusson (1994) and Kitchin et al. (1997), and exemplified by Bach-Y-Rita (in e.g. Morgan 1977).

Returning to the theme of eyes, hands and the spatial imaginary, it is fitting to state the full title of Diderot's essay, 'Lettre sur les aveugles, à l'usage de ceux qui voient'. The subtitle, translated as 'for the benefit of those who see', is obviously intended as part of the Enlightenment fascination with the sensory world of the blind by those who can see, arguably reducing a phenomenology of blindness into a speculative parlour game for the sighted, notwithstanding the assumption of an absolute distinction between 'blind' and 'sighted' experience which has been complexified in the course of this chapter. Yet, reminding ourselves of Gregory's blind subject who underwent an operation to see in 1963, one phrase resounds, both in the psychological case study by Gregory and Wallace (1963) and in Sacks' report (1995). Being able finally to touch a mysterious object, correlating the newly visual blobs of colour he sees with what was familiar in his previously tactile world, with great relief he announces: 'Now that I've felt it, I can see!' (in Sacks 1995:126). We started with the words of the blind man of Puiseaux, who similarly analogizes touching with seeing, and underlines the continuity of the theme of eyes and hands. Now, from the intermodality of touch and vision, the next chapter historically investigates the place of hands and eyes in measurement and geometry.

–4–

The Forgetting of Touch: Geometry with Eyes and Hands

> We like Euclidean geometry because we are men [*sic*], and have eyes and hands, and need to operate a concept of space that will be independent of orientation, distance and size.
>
> Lucas, Treatise on Time and Space

Losing Touch

> **Forget,** *v*: from Old Teutonic *getan* ... in the sense 'to hold, grasp'... The etymological sense is thus 'to miss or lose one's hold'. (OED, 2nd edn, 1989)

To 'forget' means to lose remembrance of something, to let go. But in a stronger sense it is more deliberate, even a wilful neglect. It could be argued that the non-visual senses have not been casually forgotten but actively forgotten, deliberately written out of the cultural history of the West, with its emphasis on the eye as the dominant sense organ. As we know, this visualistic bias is well documented by a number of scholars such as Crary (1990; 1999), Classen (1993) and Jay (1994). Perhaps the most representative single encapsulation of this assumption occurs in an essay tellingly entitled 'The nobility of sight' by Hans Jonas (1954). To forget touch in particular is to disregard the whole array of the bodily senses, to emphasize the eye (and an abstracted visualism or, as Jay terms it, 'ocularcentrism') rather than the hands and feet (haptic experience). In this chapter I want to achieve two things. First, to advance another critique of the discourse of visualism, analysing certain practices historically assumed to be visual and abstracted; and, secondly, thereby reveal the underlying haptic (tactile, proprioceptive, kinaesthetic) aspects of spatial experience and reinscribe them into that cultural history. If to 'forget' touch means it has lost its hold, then it would be worthwhile to grasp its history and meaning back.

Arguing this assumes that our spatial experience is more than visual. We have already seen the importance of the somatic senses of movement (kinaesthesia), the body's felt position (proprioception), and balance (the vestibular sense). These somatosensory experiences of space have usually been disregarded due to the philosophical correlation of abstract thinking with visual experience, especially since the Greeks.[1] The *forgetting* of touch and the bodily senses, one could say, *forges* a set of idealized, abstracted visual representations, perpetuating the discourse of visualism. In other words, it fashions or constructs something, a rational process and a set of inscriptive practices. One example that shows particularly well the entrenchment of visualism in spatial terms is geometry, as it originally involves an embodied performance of measurement, yet in the necessity to make it communicable, forgets this. It ends up becoming the epitome of abstracted visual representation, and even, as we shall see, a model for universal reason, the *mathesis universalis*. If previous chapters introduced and validated the Aristotelian *aesthesis* and the rediscovery of the somatic senses, this chapter charts how this sensory experience becomes abstracted and made universal: from *aesthesis* to *mathesis*. Now we literally remember the body in abstracted visualistic practices such as geometry by adding 'hands' (the haptic, the somatic) as well as eyes (the optic).

Geometry: The Empirical Art of Mensuration

Before it becomes an abstracted, visual set of symbols on a surface, at one stage geometry involved the actual bodily process of measuring space. In the measuring process the hands, feet, eyes and body are all involved in spatial apprehension and perception. Spatial relations mediated through the body become represented in abstract form through a set of visual symbols. As we know, such visual symbols become part of a whole system of representation, geometry, which is subtracted from the original, embodied measuring process. Literally the measuring (*metros*) of the earth (*geos*), geometry involves formally fixing objects in spatial relations of order and measure. But how does the embodied process of measuring actual multidimensional spaces become abstracted into two-dimensional symbols and relations? What happens to the original, embodied encounter with space, the walking, pacing, the use of the hands and of measuring tools? Husserl briefly considered this in his essay 'Origin of geometry' originally published in 1939. In previous chapters we became acquainted with Husserl's later interests in the lived body (*Leib*) and kinaesthesia (especially 1970a). But his essay on geometry is notable for being an investigation into geometry not as a practice in itself but as a pursuit of abstracted visualism. The body is barely present, but its traces are evident.

This chapter's structure is threefold. In the first section, 'Geometry and the eye,' the power of the metaphor of geometry as a template for other areas of thought is examined, and how this transpires in terms of mathematical and cultural history. In other words, geometry becomes itself an 'optic' through which empirical observations are made, becomes the standard for other areas of knowledge and – as a template outside of the purely mathematical realm it bridges with other areas – becomes married to empirical observation through the use of instruments and measuring objects. The world of empirical observation receives validation from such a geometric template, involving the forgetting of body, of touch and of somatosensory experience in general. Secondly, in 'Geometry and measure', various explanations for this pattern are traced back historically in the records of agronomy and field-surveying, writings that helped to disseminate the study of geometry throughout the Middle Ages. Measurement and the notion of metrological space through hands and bodily movement are traced historically through medieval sources. Historically, practical discourses of measurement accompanied the dissemination of Euclid's and Proclus' theoretical geometry. Attempting to negotiate through various phenomenological problems concerning the origin of geometry through the body and the body's boundaries, the third section of the chapter is therefore an exposition of a 'Geometry with eyes and hands', *contra* Lucas, to see how measurement is performed through haptic as well as visual perception, and yet communicated intersubjectively as an abstracted, universalizable model through the use of objects that augment the senses, within a distributed network of tools and operations. But more generally the chapter is, throughout, an extended critique of this tendency toward visualism, the origin and deployment of geometry as metaphor, noting its historical importance and expressive power.

Geometry and the Eye

> Thus the geometer ... will not think of exploring, besides geometrical shapes, geometrical thinking.
>
> Husserl, 'Origin of Geometry'

Once the result of measure mediated through the hand and body in Greece and Egypt, geometry tied together objects and spatial relations by means of the body. By the time of the Renaissance supposedly, the conventional history of geometry tells a story based on distanced, disembodied, abstracted vision, substituting the abstracted and visual for the previously more intimate and tactile. But this is historically unqualified and will be challenged in due course. Prefiguring the initial measuring process is bodily investigation and experience of space, entailing somatic movement and the use of the senses. Such bodily investigation of space is what Cassirer terms the 'empirical art of mensuration' (1950:47) and cannot be accomplished without using both eyes and hands. Kant's (1990:A29) synthesis of rational order (the eyes) and empirical investigation (the hands and feet) neatly binds the body's experience of space with the geometry of abstracted visualism in spatial measurement. Yet the philosophical history of geometry, written and rewritten many times, ignores the body and the role of the hands and feet, concentrating predictably on the eyes, perpetuating this discourse of abstracted visualism.[2]

So, what of the model of geometry, why is it predominantly visual, and why so pervasive? There exists something that Pascal termed the 'geometric spirit' of mathematics which he contrasted with the 'subtle spirit' of philosophy, where certainty was exemplified in the former, and informed speculation in the latter, observes Knight (1968:18). As a model the geometric was the standard, exemplified by contemporary Enlightenment advances in the sciences. It is this universal model, a standardized ideal of all inquiry, that pervades from this time onward. But the seeds were sown much earlier in the sixteenth century, where the substitution of quantification for qualification was occurring. The transformation of the sensible realm into quanta, this tendency toward universal measurement was termed 'panto-metry'.[3] For Galileo, geometry was the only standard of intelligibility in explaining nature, and it was necessary to apply the principles of geometry to the natural world, claims Maull, thereby uniting geometry and physics (1978:256).

This is the tendency to reduce other observable facts into abstracted, visual terms and to impose a geometric template onto other areas. It is an ethos that Bachelard terms 'geometrism' (1994:215). Seemingly universal and translatable, geometry has existed as a generalized, generalizing model for all the sciences and for metaphysics.[4] In his essay 'The Origin of Geometry', Husserl shows geometry to be a co-construction, something mutually manufactured, and in his words a product of 'coconsciousness' (1989b:173) that seems to stand for a set of communicable, inter-subjective truths. Geometrism undeniably has an expressive power, then, resulting from the urge to abstract and visualize within whatever domain of knowledge that is examined, be it physics or organizational flow charts, making relations between observable facts or truths communicable and therefore inter-subjective. Geometry becomes 'geometrism' when the template of abstract visualization, the ordering of relations, becomes applied to very different domains. It becomes an 'optic,' appropriately enough, through which standardized measure and spatial relations are mapped and observed.

This theme continues with the so-called father of analytic geometry, René Descartes. In the *Dioptrique* (1637) he wrote that truth could only be revealed in the form of 'rational conceivability', the ideal of knowledge being an abstract geometry, a *mathesis universalis* or 'universal learning'. 'The word mathematics [derived from *mathesis*] in ancient Greek means: that which is taught or learned', explains Michel Serres (1995:114), and this opens up one of the central concerns here: how metric relations become abstracted into universal learning, become inscribed as an artificial form of memory, and are then intersubjectively communicable. The metric relations between bodies or objects were important to determine for Descartes, and part of his theory of perception was to ask how a specifically three-dimensional, Euclidean geometry was applicable to the natural world. He rather aptly confides in a letter shortly before publication of the *Meditations*: 'The whole of my physics is nothing other than geometry' (in Lachterman 1989:187). This optic, then, of the geometrical characteristics of bodies, and the geometrical relation between bodies that Descartes seeks to understand is what Maull calls the 'geometrization problem'; this I understand in the same way as Pascal's 'geometric spirit' (in Knight 1968:18), Bachelard's 'geometrism' (1994:215), or Husserl's 'geometric thinking' (1989b:158).

It is not simply that the practice of geometry denudes and diminishes the richness of multisensory experience, then, but that geometric thinking tends toward an abstracted, generalized model. The variability of sensory experience becomes converted into a stable, invariant model; as Serres puts it, the 'coarse senses' become converted into 'pure understanding' (1995:115), the *mathesis* of universal learning. As we will see, the need for stable invariance in our sensory experience and understanding is echoed by the need for stable invariance in our measuring tools. By insisting on the purity of the *mathesis*, this is simultaneously to doubt the veracity of sensory information, occurring clearly in Descartes' *Meditations* (1968 [1641]). The progress from sensory information to abstraction, in effect the Platonic move from the sensible to the intelligible, and its culmination in Descartes' mathematical philosophy, is summarized by Welton:

> The essences of things become reduced to their mathematizable features, their measurable spatio-temporal extension, their geometric configurations; this means they are reducible to quantity, for, as Descartes was the first to show, geometry can be reconstructed as algebra. (1999:40)

Famously in his 'First Meditation' he suggests as a starting point the thought experiment of having no senses to doubt. For, having no senses, there should remain only the basis of rational thought, without fear of doubt or uncertainty. Descartes proceeds: 'I will consider myself as having no hands, no eyes, no flesh, no blood, as having not a single sense' (1968:100). A more wilful form of forgetting all the senses could hardly be imagined. Against the possible illusions and uncertainties of his senses, then, Descartes looks to the hard inner core of certainty, the *mathesis* as pure reason, as being a generalizable model applicable in all cases to the phenomena of the outside world. In making the *mathesis* model applicable to other situations he relegates the senses to a far more contingent, minor position. The *mathesis universalis* unites what are seemingly very different objects into manifestations of an underlying geometric structure. The *mathesis* 'does not relate to number, to spatial form, to motion as such,' writes Cassirer, 'but extends to everything that is determined according to order and measure' (1985:351).

When writing on the 'tradition' of geometry Husserl realized the importance of the *ethos*, the way geometry has been co-constructed – that is, establishes a demonstrable field of delimited knowledges and practices that are intersubjectively communicable. Thus in 'The Origin of Geometry' he states succinctly: 'the geometer ... will not think of exploring, besides geometrical shapes, geometrical thinking' (1989b:158). While he explicitly raises this problem, he himself fails to adequately investigate such thought processes. For geometrical thinking is applicable to any form wherein the visual imposes a consistency on a measured space, the subtraction of multisensory experience in order to impose a monolithic visual order. Ivins, in *On the Rationalisation of Sight* (1973), has termed this 'optical consistency': the ability for objects and shapes to be transported through the medium of an universally translatable, homogeneous space. It is an optic that captures, that binds together. The optic ideal is therefore a standardized form of measure, with the promise of universal translatability between three-dimensional objects in space and the two-dimensional representations of these on paper, and could not have occurred without the geometrized model of the *mathesis universalis*.

The packaging into quanta of measure is made possible by vision and an assumed isotropic uniformity of space, hence producing a whole realm of 'quantitative representation' that was later accelerated by the two-dimensional printing process (Crosby 1997:228). The forgetting of touch and the bodily senses, and the subsequent emphasis on the visual therefore expedites the production of a whole set of visual representations. Summarizing the shift into the new geometric, quantifiable model, and exemplifying a universalizing, visualistic geometrism, Galileo famously compared geometry to a language through which, once learnt, the entirety of the natural world could be interpreted and understood.[5] The desire to translate the world of experience into a realm of pure representation makes this possible, and Galileo's language is an obviously visual one. So it is entirely in keeping with Galileo's project that Descartes wanted to form an indissoluble whole through the *mathesis universalis*, a synoptic model applicable to all areas of thought, irrespective of the 'specialist tendencies' of knowledge (Cassirer 1950:18). As a model it becomes increasingly concentrated in order to expand into other realms of knowledge and become universal. Geometrism not only forges a relationship with epistemology; in fact, says Cassirer, it *becomes* an epistemology, perhaps through the visualistic bias of the philosophical imagination, which is clearly the case for Plato:

> In antiquity there had been indissoluble partnership between geometrical and philosophical ideas of truth; they developed with and within one another, and the Platonic concept of the theory of ideas was possible only because Plato had continually in mind the static shapes discovered by Greek mathematics. (1950:22)

Geometrism therefore becomes an epistemology in its own right in order to impose and continually maintain the order of the *mathesis* against disorder or disunity, and in this imposition of unity displays a 'subtle violence', argues Cassirer (1950:18), to the heterogeneous, the different. Even now there is a continuity between this historical formation of geometrism and current developments in disciplines such as AI, cognitive science, and philosophical theories of mind. Writing relatively recently, Gärdenfors for example outlines his theory of 'conceptual spaces' in terms remarkably akin to the *mathesis universalis*, and not dissimilar in spirit to those of Galileo:

The primary application of the theory of conceptual spaces is to function as a framework for *representations*. When the framework is complemented with assumptions concerning the geometrical structure of particular domains and how they are connected, one arrives at empirically testable theories. (2000:48, original emphasis)

So, undeniably, abstracted visualism and geometrism remain evident and are still pervasive. But how did this transpire historically?

From Sense to Abstraction

Sometime in the sixth century BCE, Thales, regarded as the first Greek philosopher, measured the shadow from the pyramid of Cheops by the Nile, noticing the shadow's invariability in form despite changes of scale. Serres suggests that whatever Thales was actually observing, say the height of a stick, a body or a pyramid, was insignificant. 'This is science without a subject, science which dispenses with the senses or does not operate through them' (1995:86), he says. Yet the knowledge derived through this process of measurement remains unchanged. In order to remain communicable and universally translatable, the development of geometric thinking relies on the subtraction, or indeed active forgetting, of the senses, to go from the variability of the senses and sensory experience to the static invariability of a desensualized, abstract space. Serres describes this in a now familiar way: 'the geometric model of the world emerges here without the intervention of organs, functions or faculties' (ibid.).

Like Serres' observations, Latour's phrase 'optical consistency' (1986:7; see also Ivins 1973:9) implies the construction of an abstracted, smooth, isotropic space within which translation from one realm to another may occur. This space is the result of that 'geometrical thinking', or 'geometrism' discussed earlier. It implies universalizable, isometric translation. Optical consistency maintains its universalizability by de-emphasizing the particularity of sensory epistemologies, for example through the detachment and abstraction into disembodied 'sight' as opposed to the whole perceptual system of 'vision' that includes other sensory information and somatic sensation. The crystallization of optical consistency occurs especially alongside the rise in scientific methods, as Latour argues: 'The rationalization that took place during the so-called 'scientific revolution' is not of the mind, of the eye, of philosophy, but of the *sight*' (1986:7). In this observation Latour identifies rational thought with the desensualized, disembodied language of abstract visual representations.

To summarize, putting the senses through the machinery of abstraction means a collapse of the vast array of bodily sensations and perceptions that we are now familiar with, from Aristotle's *aesthesis* to Husserl's and Merleau-Ponty's kinaesthetic body, into a detached, optical geometrism.[6] But how did the abstracted perception that is 'sight' supposedly become detached from 'vision' and bodily perception in the first place? If geometrism is an idealized model of epistemology, as Kant also assumed in linking geometry with synthetic a priori knowledge, then sensory epistemologies are by comparison increasingly disregarded and unreliable. If certainty exists, it is a certainty of the *understanding* and not of the senses themselves, and this is what makes it a *mathesis universalis*. To pursue a series of metaphors, the 'grip' on certainty is tenuous; by mediating space through instrumentation, such as surveying equipment or an architect's square, reliance on actual bodily senses seems less certain or absolute, and the measurer becomes unsatisfied with anything other than an exact measurement of truth.

To come up with a set of two-dimensional representations designed to reveal spatial relations in their entirety is obviously to push away the empirical content of those earlier multisensory investigations. In the words of Husserl, we put a 'garb of ideas' over the things encountered in the sensible world, and thereby go from 'sense' to 'abstraction' (1989b:118). This conceptual attire is a mechanism for manufacturing abstraction from sensation, the self-same geometrism of before. While something like an immanent, embodied phenomenology of spatial measure could be postulated, it is disregarded by Husserl in favour of a pure, idealized, transcendent geometry. A less transcendental phenomenology of geometry could take account of the empirically derived 'practical reason' that underlies what later becomes 'scientific reason'. Taking such a phenomenological view, the senses could be reinscribed into the abstract language of visual representation, and we could start to remember the sensory content of empirical measure, as Beck describes in terms we can immediately recognize:

> But mathematics and especially its prototype, the geometry of Euclid, were originally only an empirical way of measuring... This means that geometry, too, does not find mathematical objects in the real world but constructs them only by means of the imagination in order to govern nature practically and to fix it on a generally valid base by measuring it. (1941:480)

What lay at the base of geometry, so-called empirical mensuration, involved the hand and thereafter an instrument, the active touch of the hand in its use of the measuring instrument. Among psychologists and philosophers such as Berkeley, Révész and J.J. Gibson, there is a greater conviction and certainty about the material world through the mediation of touch than there is with the visual alone. The link between epistemology and touch, indicated in chapter 1 through the expression 'seeing's believing, but *feeling's the truth*', is also exemplified when asking a shop assistant 'Can I *see* that, please?' when what demonstrably occurs is the need to hold the object, manipulate it. Apart from an epistemological argument, the promise or possibility of touching and grasping is implicit in this notion of 'seeing', and their quotidian nature is underlined by the fact that most interactions with material culture are not thematic, are unreflecting, without theoretical correlates, immediately graspable or touchable. Husserl describes these interactions, and notes their intersubjective constitution: '[they are] things we see, grasp, and touch, just as we, and other people, see them, grasp them, etc.' (in B. Smith 2000:319). In other words, as in our previous discussions of habituated perception, the intuitive palpability of everyday objects is unproblematic, and indicates the intuitive practice of grasping and of tactile contact; to reach out and touch in order to 'see' an object, for example. In those originary acts of measurement prior to geometrical abstraction perhaps there is a similar intermodal impulse, as much 'grasping' as 'seeing'.

A paradigmatic example of this lies within pictorial representations, which show the relation of touch to knowledge, through the hand and also the use of instruments. For example José de Ribera's painting *The Sense of Touch* (1613, reproduced on the cover of this book) depicts a blind man touching a skull. Doubting Thomas, who similarly needed to touch in order to understand, is sometimes portrayed on canvas as having an architect's square in his hand, and his need of an instrument of measurement suggests to Elaine Spolsky the convention of 'the insufficiency of unmediated sense perception as a guide to knowledge' (1994:114). Truth is measured no longer by hand but by instruments, sets of apparatus that are constant, invariable; objects such as the set square, the plumb line, but especially in Serres' example of the *gnomon*, to which we shall return, a tool that measured shadows and 'constructed a geometric model of the universe' (1995:81). In pictorial representations of Thomas the implication is that his doubt as an epistemological problem is due to the uncertain grip by which he can *say* he has knowledge. It is a fragile, tenuous grip because if the instrument malfunctions or is misread, that certainty becomes instantly misplaced and erroneous. Reliance on such instruments entails a fundamental distrust of everyday sense-perception. It also circumscribes the limit of what is knowable, what can be known, imposing a boundary-limit on knowledge as such. The instrument through which we gain knowledge of objects becomes the mediator between sense-perception and the world, another method or channel therefore for that notion of optical consistency. But the instrument must remain stable, constant throughout. Thus all our geometrical measurement, writes Helmholtz, 'depends on our instruments being really, as we consider them, invariable in form' (1971:240). He confirms then that the abstracted language of visual representation is reliant on absolute invariability, consistency and rigidity, in both the tools of measurement and also in the geometric model of understanding, the *mathesis*, these unyielding qualities being desirable for any scientific model. Yet our embodied spatial experience is never entirely unmediated, as Helmholtz assumes. As has been discussed, our spatial experience is always kinaesthetic, informed by somatic sensations and haptic memory through the body and limbs, whether we go on the 'feel' of space or whether we quantify it with instruments we manipulate with our hands. The next section will explore the implications further.

Geometry and Measure

> The name of 'geometry,' where could it come from? Geometry got its name from the measurement of the earth, by means of which the boundaries of everything upon the earth are commonly established.
>
> Boethius, *Liber de Geometria*

Moving from the philosophy of spatial measurement and geometry, I now wish to ground the discussion by looking at the historical record. Examining historical sources can be an active form of remembrance, to recover lost memory by bringing forth information, in this case concerning the somatosensory content of spatial measurement alongside the development of geometric practices. We discover that the dissemination of geometrical ideas in the Middle Ages occurred alongside extremely practical information, including field-surveying manuals and the study of gromatics (surveying techniques). So far we have considered what is lost in the move from the richness of embodied sensory experience to theoretical abstraction, without imagining that the reverse could also historically be the case. Before that, I wish to examine the way that optical consistency collapses three-dimensional, lived and embodied knowledges into two-dimensional representations or inscriptions on paper, for example, in order that they may join that same form of consistent, universally translatable organization as geometry, the *mathesis universalis*. This influences the practical concerns of record keeping and bureaucracy, incorporating objects and files into what Latour calls 'metrological chains' or inscriptive practices (in 1986:22).

Latour gives the examples of the reduction of experimental data, of rat injections, of petri-dish growths and scientific paraphernalia from three dimensions to the two-dimensional form of inscription – piles of paper printouts and charts and diagrams that go to bolster a scientific status quo or else to attempt to transform it (1986; pursued further in his *Science in Action*, 1987). In so doing, the reduction of multi-sensory and multidimensional experience into two-dimensional inscription is the major characteristic, and hints at the haunting of earlier sensorimotor investigations within these abstracted forms. The forgetting of such multisensory experience fosters a different form of mnemotechnics, however, achieved through inscriptive practices. The paper-based inscriptions that result are therefore a form of externalized memory, one that is visual, clearly demonstrable and communicable between people (hence Husserl's description of 'co-construction', and Serres' characterization of geometry as 'transcendental' yet as 'intersubjectivity', 1995:117). A two-dimensional set of abstract, logical relations rapidly becomes the standard by which these specialized knowledges are communicated, especially after Robert Boyle.[7] Similarly, Don Ihde gives the example of the beginnings of anatomy in the Renaissance, where olfactory and tactile experience no longer find representation within anatomy texts after Leonardo, who peels away successive layers of skin and flesh (literally 'cutaways') purely through anatomically correct illustrations (1995:18). Tactile references to hands-on dissection within textbooks disappear in favour of visual representations, which Ihde finds consistent with the Renaissance 'enhancement of the visual' which itself rides on the converse, the 'reduction of the other senses' (ibid.). The promotion of visual distance in the age of perspective, in this case Leonardo's corpse or his engineering drawings, promotes a particular kind of visualism. Through the invention of various drafting techniques that reduce three dimensions to two, such as the exploded diagram, the projective geometry of Desargues, and the rules of geometrical perspective (discovered probably between 1410 and 1420 by Brunelleschi, prior to Leonardo), an 'objective' viewpoint was being established, to be interpreted 'geometrically' as Ihde himself identifies (ibid.:19).

Such techniques therefore involved the reduction of multisensory, multidimensional data into two-dimensional paper-space, usually following a Euclidean metric. Latour remarks on this reduction to this effect: 'The two-dimensional character of inscriptions allow them to merge *with geometry*' (1986:13, original emphasis). In fact,

> *Anything* that will accelerate the mobility of the traces that a location may obtain about another place, or *anything* that will allow these traces to move without transformation from one place to another, will be favoured: geometry, projection, perspective, bookkeeping [sic], paper making, aqua forte, coinage, new ships … (ibid.)

Latour proceeds to make the observation that the conversion from one domain to another is an agonistic movement, in terms of it being both abstractive and practical. It entails the ability to abstract, but also 'the practical work of mobilizing resources without transforming them' according to Latour (ibid.:25). This involves assembling what he calls long 'metrological chains' (ibid.), establishing linkages with some sort of authority over stable measurement and standards over different domains: the birth of the bureau, of records, of file-keeping as well as the construction of the edifice of scientific authority and verifiability. And in this – the drawings of an engineer in the mastery of a machine, or the bureaucrat's assembling of paper-based personal records – is a similar movement from three to two dimensions, to inscription based on the idea of universal exchangeability and absolute consistency. This exchange now occurs in a refined optical space, exerting a mastery through these means on the environment around it.

Nevertheless, processes of empirical measurement would always involve, as Ivins succinctly and memorably puts it, 'the counted motions of men's bodies' (1964:103). But in the translation from one realm into another, establishing optical consistency, the metrical legacy of these bodies becomes distant. As we have seen, the geometric becomes a model in and of itself, extending geometrical imagery even into the style of philosophical reasoning in the early Middle Ages, and furthering the association between geometry and epistemological certainty in Descartes. But this all could be read and interpreted otherwise. Let us turn this around. For example, Zaitsev argues that there is evidence for a congruence between mathematical geometry (coming through fragmented and incomplete translations of Euclid's *Elements* before the twelfth century), passages from Roman land-surveyors, and metaphysical or 'pseudo-philosophical' digressions (1999:523). This curious amalgam came to be known as 'geometry', at least until full translations of Euclid were made from the Arabic, and this disseminatory model finds a parallel in Biblical scholarship. Serres argues that in the same way that commentaries on the Bible became successively incorporated into the published book, interpretations and commentaries on Euclid's *Elements* became an increasingly established system of geometry (1995:114). In the Medieval mind, however, where *geometria* came to be translated literally in Latin as *mensuratio terrae*, again, the measuring of the earth, land-surveying or agronomy was as valid as the more abstracted pursuit. It was still geometry, but a geometry informed and disseminated by praxis. Some fragments of the translation of Euclid were compiled by Boethius and his contemporary Cassiodorus, while yet others appeared in various forms. In his *Commentary on Euclid*, Proclus shows an antagonism toward the incredibly practical nature of measurement, talking of the movement from the imperfection of sense-perception to the perfection of calculation and reason. In this work he ties in the Egyptian birth of geometry with extremely practical considerations of measure that were made necessary by the contingent climatic conditions of the area. Proclus declares:

> [G]eometry was first discovered among the Egyptians and originated in the remeasuring of their lands. This was necessary for them because the Nile overflows and obliterates the boundary lines between their properties. It is not surprising that the discovery of this and the other sciences had its origin in necessity, since everything in the world of generation proceeds from imperfection to perfection. Thus *they would naturally pass from sense-perception to calculation and from calculation to reason*. (in Suppes et al., 1989:v, emphasis added)

Proclus provides further evidence, therefore, of the process of abstraction being a move toward perfection, and of the purposeful forgetting of its historical origins – from the remeasuring of lands to an abstracted, visual model of pure rational thought. The practical context is overwritten, like a palimpsest, leaving only the barest traces of a memory. For example, a text identified as by 'Pseudo-Boethius' included the word 'demonstration' (*demonstratio*), which did not then mean the usual deductive procedure but, in Zaitsev's words, 'was associated with a practical operation of reconstructing the boundaries of fields' (1999:525). Parts of surveying manuals appeared among fragments of translated Euclid in manuscripts; it is clear that only those fragments pertaining to field-boundary calculations, and therefore having a utility value, were included in these manuscripts. In addition, surveying manuals without any Euclidean content were still referred to as 'geometric'.

The consistently visual basis of many of the measuring terms in the manuals underlines our observation that any inscriptive practice must have the ability to reduce raw three-dimensional, multisensory perception into sets of two-dimensional, abstracted representations. This, more than anything else, is the *ethos* of geometrism. Yet almost contemporaneously with Descartes, at the height of analytic geometry and the fascination with optics, another conceptual reversal is possible. Desargues forged what came to be called 'projective geometry' from a composite of the geometrical knowledge of artists, engineers, stonecutters and architects. Desargues, himself an engineer and architect, attempted to write his postulates in a form that craftsmen and artisans could understand, notes Ivins (1964:87). Thus the motions of men's bodies, of hands and feet, whether in architectural drawing or the steady chipping of stone, informed geometry in much the same way that agronomy and Roman land surveying had informed and disseminated Euclid's geometrical postulates in the Middle Ages.

Geometry once again cannot be divorced from the influences of the empirical art of mensuration or of practical work with the hands shaping forms. In the transition of the material forms recognized by the hands of medieval architects, surveyors, stonecutters, masons, sculptors and other artisans (so-called 'haptomorphs'), being translated into visual imagery ('optomorphs') and vice versa, we rediscover the importance of the sensory and empirical in the formation of the supposedly transcendent and universal. The divorce of pure mathematics and measurement has not always been the case historically. As Crosby has argued, surveyors must have known the Pythagorean theorem and operationalized it through everyday practice before the philosophical and mystical implications were realized (1997:14ff). Similarly, the Master Masons of the Gothic cathedrals, probably ignorant of Euclid, had an entirely practical geometry, practising it through manipulations of basic geometric figures, with the knowledge mostly being disseminated orally rather than through two-dimensional representations. Apprenticeship presumably involved mimetic skill, a set of tactile-muscular orientations and hand-eye co-ordinations, and an ability to work haptically with the material, before the finer points of divine order and ratio became significant. Away from paper-based representations, then, this transmission of haptic practice occurs through such mimetic skill, which has a sensorimotor, indeed haptic, basis. Echoing geometry's claim to be communicable and intuitively understood without recourse to a whole set of knowledges, the psychologist Donald discusses further the manual (motor) and visual aspects of mimetic skill:

> Mimetic skill results in the sharing of knowledge without every member of that group having to reinvent that knowledge... The primary form of mimetic expression was, and continues to be, visuomotor. The mimetic skills basic to child-rearing, toolmaking, cooperative gathering and hunting, the sharing of food and other resources, finding, constructing, and sharing shelter, and expressing social hierarchies and custom would have involved visuomotor behavior. (in Wilson 1999:48)

Such visuomotor behaviours or mimetic skill in this context are shown to be demonstrable, shared within the community, communicable and therefore intersubjective or co-constructed in the Husserlian sense. Yet unlike the *mathesis*, the understanding that can be learned or taught is more than visual. Utilizing muscular memory, the transposition of movements and the transmissions of embodied skills, there are clear implications for taking so-called tacit knowledges seriously in this respect.

Geometry with Eyes, Hands and Feet

To try to escape the primarily visual connotation with geometry and measure, it has been important to reassert the importance of the other sense modalities, including the haptic. In this section I want to explore further the phenomenological aspects of spatial measure. A brief historical overview will help contextualize this. Historically, measuring space has often been done with the body, hence the Graeco-Egyptian notion of cubits (a forearm's length), digits (a finger's breadth, ¾ inch) and so on. Using body parts as an investigative aid to the perception and measurement of external space also involves moving them in relation to a core orientation of the torso, for example. Body parts therefore become components of the mechanisms of measure; the body itself becomes instrument. Measurement occurs through an assemblage of mechanical constructions and prostheses – augmentations of the body and its senses – such as compasses, yardsticks, dividers and so on. In order to produce isotropic, measured space, material tools and instruments are brought into the ordering and measuring process, even the limbs or body parts of the one who measures. For example, Helmholtz in 1878 traced the genesis of measurement through the body in this way to a set of geometrical axioms:

> In measuring, we are simply employing the best and surest means we know to determine what we otherwise are in the habit of making out by sight and touch or by pacing. Here our own body with its organs is the instrument we carry about in space. Now it is the hand, now the leg that serves for a compass, while the eye turning in all directions is our theodolite for measuring arcs and angles in the visual field. (1971:259)

As we have seen, the transplantation of geometry as *praxis* in Egypt to geometry as the object of theoretical inquiry, the primarily visual *theoria* in Greece involved the idea of 'measure' at the heart of the Greek enterprise. The empirical art of mensuration in Egypt becomes instead the model or template of a true, philosophically recognizable form of knowledge, especially through Cartesian analytic geometry. Underlying such abstracted geometry, re-emerging in projective geometry and elsewhere, is the relation between body movement and measure: the set of tactile-muscular experiences that go to make up the measuring process, 'the counted motions of men's bodies' (Ivins 1964:103). Greek geometry began with these motions, so geometry as we recognize it already entails haptic forms of perception. Measure has therefore always involved muscular sensations of movement (kinaesthesia) and position (proprioception) interacting with vestibular balance. We can see current echoes of these practices in the teaching of geometry in the classroom to children, getting an initial 'sense' of geometry perhaps in the playground through pace and measure (legs, feet), marking out shapes in space with chalk (hands) – that is, being haptic, being kinaesthetic, being visuomotor. The counted motions of men's bodies, the somatosensory informing the visual determination of mark and measure, must therefore be a whole-body geometry, with hands and feet as well as eyes.

The previous chapter invoked the long-running debate concerning the relative merits of vision versus touch, of eyes versus hands, in spatial perception stemming from Descartes' *Dioptrique*. Related to this debate, Berkeley in his 1734 essay 'A New Theory of Vision' (1983) contended that touch is indispensable in the perception of the visuo-spatial field, and therefore of the ordering and measuring of objects within that field. Early in the twentieth century, psychologist Geza Révész harked back to Berkeley's philosophical take on the topic, arguing that the haptic sense is inherently a 'geometric' sense. Révész attempted to repatriate the importance of touch within spatial measure. As opposed to the two-dimensionality of visual space, with its distance estimates based on learned perspective, he saw haptic or tactile space as originally three-dimensional, and therefore inherently more geometrical than vision alone. While vision shows spatial relationships, he admitted, touch is necessary to measure and compare:

> In contrast to touch, vision has the advantage of being able to recognize spatial relationships in a direct act of intuition, whilst the organ of touch is forced to employ a method which is not habitual in visual experience, namely, a procedure which both measures and compares. This comprehensive measuring activity justifies us in designating the haptic sense, with certain reservations, as the 'geometric' sense. (1958:31)

In this active touching of measurement, movement is also necessary. But it is because of the relatively invariable width of hand and length of foot, he argued, that haptic space is therefore *measured* rather than estimated, and so haptic space may be characterized as 'geometric-space-measure' (1937:439). Révész's privileging of the hand's and body's exploration of space, and the hand's more intimate relation with measure, was unusual and untimely. In a move inspired perhaps by the centrality of touch for Berkeley, and sedimenting the second half of the dictum 'seeing is believing, but feeling's the truth', Révész makes much of the invariability of tactile, as opposed to visual, sensations. He therefore ascribes a pivotal role to the constancy of hands rather than the variability of eyes in the measuring process. 'Through our tactual sense we comprehend *the constant, the approximate, the invariable, the general,* or in other words, *the sensory and perceptible content of geometry* [original emphasis]', he argued (1937:440).[8] Further, for Révész the idea of the continuity of objects and of their spatial relationships is constituted by their tangibility, their ability to be apprehended and manipulated through touch.

We may now bring together the earlier discussion about mimetic skill with the geometric-space-measure of Révész. Assuming that the youngster who wants to become a surgeon, sculptor or needleworker has some sort of predisposition to use the hands and their sense-returns, Wilson likewise argues that the movement of the hands of these budding handworkers occurred, among other things,

> to obtain information that could only be obtained by acting upon the object being held. The information returned to the brain was written in the tactile and kinesthetic language of manipulation and was compared with information coming from the visual system, as part of a process through which the brain creates visuospatial images. (1999:276)

The coming-together of a set of sense-returns based on visual, tactile and motor feedback occurs especially through the hand, as the hand has a 'calibrating' or measuring function in relation to the brain. It extends the brain, it helps the brain reach out in space to extend beyond the confines of its spatial fixity, and creates a new orientation of the organism to its environment, what Wilson calls a 'new class of situational knowledge' (ibid.:59). The creation of contexts or situational knowledges through the manipulation and active investigation of the space immediately surrounding the body unsurprisingly returns us to Husserl and Merleau-Ponty's 'natural attitude' (e.g. the latter's 1992:281). It is in this way that everyday weighing, counting and measuring as praxis, which involves visual-tactile-kinesic modalities, creates somatic spatial contexts. But the creation of contexts that Merleau-Ponty discusses is a way beyond the distinction between transcendent, geometric, or abstracted space on the one hand, and immanent, situational or phenomenal space on the other. Contra Révész and the invariability of haptic experience, the creation of contexts is a dynamic, kinaesthetic framework that includes the motile body but also what can be incorporated into that body, for example instruments, tools, or spatial measuring equipment (e.g. Merleau-Ponty 1992:143), even if the equipment fosters two-dimensional inscriptions, as Latour outlined. In the extension of our hand into the world, for example, an act seemingly of pure exteroception through which we gain the perception of an 'outer' sensory world, Merleau-Ponty argues that movement is the basis of the unity of the senses such as touch and sight, and that perception is always a 'reaching-out' in encountering objects. Thus the background against which perception occurs, the 'bodily attitude', is always a 'kinaesthetic situation' (ibid.:234, 325, 303), as was discussed in chapter 2. Merleau-Ponty's kinaesthetic situation, or Wilson's situational knowledge based on visuo-motor sense returns, reaffirms for me the assumed, hidden, somatosensory basis of quotidian spatial perception and spatial measure, and this extension of phenomenology to haptic spatial contexts places hands and eyes within a larger philosophical narrative, opening the discussion out into rich conceptual and, later, empirical territory.

Drawing Conclusions about Measurement

The hand is at the forefront of calibration; it is the extension of the mind, according to Kant, and therefore a machine of measure. And likewise we can extend beyond the hand toward the visuo-motor in general, incorporating the feet, the limbs, the somatic senses. This is to link haptics with spatial experience, particularly in this case with processes of spatial measurement and geometry. Some concluding remarks are now in order. In tying up some of the themes of somatosensory phenomenology and visualistic geometry, I would like to allude further to the larger networks and practices in which measurements find passage, find translation from realm to realm through the distributed, somatic measuring process on the one hand, and the fluid teaching and interpretation of these as quanta on the other. In the process of measurement, which is the basis for a visual fixing of order and measure of objects in space, the body and therefore multimodal perception become forgotten so that something of a visual order, an abstract set of visual representations, can be forged instead. Spatial measurement is not just the importation of a set of plans or mental schemas into the world, but results from a performative act in which we are in practical engagement with our surroundings. So argues Ingold, at least, in 'Building, Dwelling, Thinking' (1995, especially p.76). The use of tools of measurement are practical extensions of the hand's reach, the bodily measure of space, and these tools are further extensions to Kant's description of the hand as the 'the outer brain of man' (in Merleau-Ponty 1992:316), heavily involved in spatial cognition. Furthermore, the involvement of the hand-eye, visuo-motor or simply 'haptic system' (Gibson 1968) is crucial in the performance of measurement, drawing, and subsequent construction of an abstractive geometry. As we have touched upon, historically there are numerous techniques of measure involved within land surveying, agronomy, architecture and so on. Such techniques have existed for millennia across many cultures, so solidly historically sedimented that they appear, in Husserl's words, 'always already there' (1989b:178). Conversely, Helmholtz sees the building up of Euclidean geometrical axioms gradually through 'a succession of everyday experiences', going to make a practical framework in which the axioms make sense, operate, and become practical for surveyors or stonemasons (1971:246). The culture of systematic measurement is born from this, those practices of mimetic skill in the workplace (see e.g. Kyburg 1984:257). Serres elsewhere echoes this relation between mimetic skill in the workplace and the abstracted space of geometry and measure when he contends that 'Euclidean space was chosen in our work-orientated cultures because it is the space of work – of the mason, of the surveyor, or the architect' (1982:44). If the framework was always already there, then for Husserl a meditation on the objects and their geometry surrounding him could bring forth ideal shapes, pure thinking, transcendent geometry. Husserl thinks that the philosopher can supposedly see the significance of such techniques, and it is interesting to see how the realm of engaged, sensory, spatial experience becomes *theoria*, a set of objects of mental contemplation assumed to be visual in nature. For Husserl's philosopher, excusing in this instance his exclusive use of the masculine pronoun:

> As a philosopher proceeding from the practical, finite surrounding world (of the room, the city, the landscape etc. ...) to the theoretical world-view and world-knowledge, he has the finitely known and unknown spaces and times as finite elements within the horizon of an open infinity. But with this he does not yet have geometrical space, mathematical time ... and with his manifold finite shapes in their space-time he does not yet have geometrical shapes, the phoronomic shapes; (his shapes, as) formations developed out of praxis and thought of in terms of (gradual) perfection, clearly serve only as bases for a new sort of praxis out of which similarly named new constructions grow. (1989b:178–9)[9]

Again there is the idea of increasing perfection, like Proclus, from sense to abstraction. And the 'new sort of praxis' Husserl mentions, which brings forth new constructions and understandings, is that *forging* of visualistic, abstracted geometric knowledge which itself is derived from the *forgetting* of sensory experience. The geometrical measuring techniques that are inexplicably 'already there' are mediated through hands, forearms, feet, body lengths and instruments, building up abstraction through a series of praxes. Becoming transformed into paper-based inscriptions allows another set of praxes to emerge – the paper acts as an externalized form of memory that allows the intersubjective communication of geometrical thinking. But of course this externalized memory comes at the price of the forgetting of the original 'bodily attitude' or 'kinaesthetic situation' of which Merleau-Ponty speaks.

Cartesian optics, as we saw, leads to a sense of detachment from the world, one might say from the 'thingness' of things, and this is famously exemplified in the case of the *camera obscura* and perspective machines in use in the Renaissance, as Crary has argued (1990). This detachment is of the eye, we might say, whereas the hands and feet draw us into the world. As we draw to a close, a suitable ending falls to Henri Focillon. Focillon rather poetically extends this idea, incorporating the feet as well as the hands into his measuring of space, and providing something like a phenomenological-experiential account for haptic perception. And it provides some indications of where we might take Merleau-Ponty's idea of situational knowledges in contextual space:

> Sight slips over the surface of the universe. The hand knows that an object has physical bulk, that it is smooth or rough, that it is not soldered to heaven or earth from which it appears to be inseparable. The hand's action defines the cavity of space and the fullness of the objects which occupy it. Surface, volume, density and weight are not optical phenomena. Man first learned about them between his finger and the hollow of his palm. He does not measure space with his eyes but with his hands and feet. The sense of touch fills nature with mysterious forces. Without it, nature is like the pleasant landscapes of the magic lantern, slight, flat and chimerical (1992:162–3).

Experiencing and measuring space with eyes, hands and feet therefore integrates the visual elements of spatial perception into a kinaesthetic, bodily orientation to the world. To mark and to measure involves the eyes, hands and feet, and here we have discussed the re-inscription and re-membering of the bodily, especially the haptic, within a realm historically and conceptually associated with detachment and optical abstraction. Along with this, geometrism or the tendency toward geometric thinking has been examined, and contrasted with the actual performance of the taking of measure and our quotidian, engaged spatial experience. After forgetting touch, re-membering measure through the hands and feet, perhaps, is a way of grasping some of its history and meaning back.

–5–

'How the World Touches Us': Haptic Aesthetics

A Touching Experience

Art can and should be a touching experience. Standing in front of a painting, appreciating a sculpture, or walking through a building, even if we are not permitted to physically touch the work we should at least be touched *by* it. In a famous essay of 1935, Walter Benjamin wrote of the metaphorically tactile quality of some artwork and film:

> From an alluring appearance or persuasive structure of sound the work of art of the Dadaists became an instrument of ballistics. It hit the spectator like a bullet, it happened to him, thus acquiring a tactile quality. It promoted a demand for the film, the distracting element of which is also primarily tactile, being based on changes of place and focus which periodically assail the spectator. (Benjamin 1999:231)

Along with his comments of the tactile quality of artwork consistent with a German art history tradition, Benjamin also wrote about what he called 'tactile appropriation' (1999:233) and the influence of habit in this form of perception. From the position of thinking with eyes and hands in terms of geometry, we now proceed toward a more explicitly haptic manner of speaking, the consideration of a 'haptic aesthetics'. From the active touching, reaching out and measuring of space, we consider how we become touched and affected by things through artworks. This will be one of two chapters explicitly addressing a haptic aesthetics, the second one being 'Tangible Play, Prosthetic Performance', examining contemporary examples of digital art and performance. By contrast, this chapter is rooted mainly between the nineteenth-century art history of Johann Gottfried Herder, the early twentieth-century thought of Alois Riegl and Walter Benjamin, the twentieth-century aesthetic writings of Maurice Merleau-Ponty and the philosophy of Gilles Deleuze. Both chapters share a common structural organization, however, each containing three sections roughly corresponding to the physiology of touch: first, the 'skin', with its cutaneous tactility; secondly the 'flesh', with its deeper, more muscular feelings of movement; and thirdly, the 'body' as a somatic set of sensations. An obviously artificial separation, this loose classification helps us clarify the various senses of touch employed in particular artistic examples.

Walter Benjamin never offers us a complete theory of perception per se. Instead he offers fragments, and likewise we too will assemble fragments considering aesthetic relations between touch and affect. Benjamin's visceral, affective metaphor of being 'assailed' or being hit 'like a bullet' when looking at a film is indicative of the way that we can be affected in a palpable way, or in Merleau-Ponty's words, of 'how the world touches us' (1969:245). Starting from Benjamin's evocation of the tactile quality of an aesthetic encounter, I wish to pursue and extend his ideas of 'tactile appropriation' further. Quotidian embodied experience involves a self-evidently tactile component, as in the perception of weight, mass, texture, density and so forth, and this is nowhere clearer than in the aesthetic encounter with an art form, whether two-dimensional canvas, three-dimensional sculpture, or a building with its surrounding environment. Benjamin argues that, in the case of architecture especially, this tactile component of perception is fundamentally based on habitual bodily perception. And we have seen how our tactile-spatial perception occurs through what Husserl terms the 'aesthetic body' (e.g. 1999:11), that is, the way the body unifies the various senses in space.

From a philosophy of fragments that characterizes Benjamin's work, equally it would be appropriate to look at fragments or snapshots of affective experience. For the sake of narrative as well as conceptual development, we can think of each of these successive sensory experiences in isolation. A conceit offers itself, a way to bind the haptic fragments through a variety of artistic forms: that of an ivory statue progressively coming to life. In the first section, 'Pygmalion and Galatea: Feeling and Becoming Flesh', the story of the Cypriot sculptor Pygmalion and his crafting of a beautiful female form which he prays will come to life, from Book X of Ovid's *Metamorphoses*, works as a narrative device. Using this device allows us to reimagine the commencement of sensory experience of the statue, and literally embodies the experience of the different artistic genres, their sensuality and their spatiality. Furthermore, a large number of philosophical works and treatises were inspired by the myth, including Herder's seminal aesthetic work *Sculpture* of 1778, subtitled *Some Observations on Shape and Form from Pygmalion's Creative Dream* (2002). Condillac's *Treatise on the Sensations* of 1754 was similarly inspired, using the myth as a thought-experiment 'for the single purpose of a hypothetical exposition of empiricism', mostly Locke's, thinks Carr (1960:254).

So this is how the chapter will be organized, with Pygmalion's statue becoming more fleshly and feeling, proceeding through increasingly multisensory and spatially multidimensional artistic examples. A narrative pathway into thinking of the interrelatedness of feeling and sensation, of the tactile and the visual. To understand the 'tactile properties' of objects and materials, as Bernhard Berenson most famously characterizes (1909:4ff), is also to attempt to understand their capacity to affect – or 'touch' – us. Perhaps this position further widens the definition of 'haptic' in the way that Young (1990:182) sees it, as 'an orientation to sensuality as such' that includes all the senses, an orientation that reduces the abstracted distance of the gaze, and which implicitly includes affective response. The second section, 'Aesthetics', starts from the position that 'aesthetic' is etymologically ambiguous. While traditionally aesthetics is concerned with the philosophy of art, we are reminded of Aristotle's conception of *aesthesis* as the sensory faculty that undergoes alteration. Aesthetics and sensory perception being related in the premodern sense, it is entirely fitting that art works are employed as illustrative of our embodied capacity for feeling (affects) as well as sensing (percepts). The ambiguity of touching as feeling, of touch as reaching out or as being affected, will effectively bind together touch and affect throughout. Touch and the promise of tactility in aesthetics will be developed through the haptic/optic distinction in art history, that 'shift in perception' that Benjamin (1999:216) borrows from Riegl (1995 [1901]) and which is later used in Deleuze and Guattari (1988) and Deleuze (2003). The haptic/optic distinction is applied to a series of artistic examples in the third section, 'the aesthetic body'. The aesthetic body is comprised of physiologically apt figures, the two-dimensional pictorial surface of painting (skin), the three-dimensional volumes of sculpture (flesh), and the opening out into space of installations and architecture (body), and we follow Pygmalion's statue as she proceeds through these increasingly spatial art forms in order to better articulate a haptic aesthetics.

Pygmalion and Galatea

As told in Ovid's *Metamorphoses* Book X, the story of Pygmalion is an imaginative exercise ascribing a living, breathing, embodied sensory consciousness to an inanimate object, a statue crafted by a man in the startlingly realistic form of a woman. Shunning the company of real women, the sculptor Pygmalion's energies were redirected toward fashioning an ivory statue, the perfect semblance of a living maiden. Stepping back from this incredibly naturalistic creation to admire his own handiwork, he began to fall in love. So startlingly lifelike, he needed to lay his hand upon its ivory surface to confirm that it remained ivory, to reassure himself it was not actually living. In Dryden's translation of 1717 this is rendered: 'The Flesh, or what so seems, he touches oft,/ Which feels so smooth, that he believes it soft' (Ovid 1976:340). He caressed this ivory maiden, gave it presents, dressed it in clothes and jewellery, as any lover would. Although beautiful when clothed, she was equally dazzling when naked. Pygmalion called her his wife, and placed her head on a pillow of the softest feathers, as if she could enjoy their softness.

Presently the festival of Aphrodite arrived, celebrated with great enthusiasm in Cyprus. Victims were offered and odours of incense suffused the streets. Having performed his part in the ceremonies, Pygmalion stood before the altar and yearned to be married to the statue, imploring: 'Almighty Gods, if all we Mortals want,/ If all we can require, be yours to grant;/ Make this fair Statue mine' but felt ashamed, and instead prayed: 'Give me the *Likeness* of my Iv'ry Maid' (1976:341, emphasis added). Aphrodite, who was present nearby, overheard him and divined his secret wishes. Returning home, he went straight to his statue and, leaning over, gave a kiss to its mouth. It seemed to be warm. Again he kissed, laying his hand upon its stony flesh, but this time the ivory started to yield to his fingers:

> But next his Hand on her hard Bosom lays:
> Hard as it was, beginning to relent,
> It seem'd, the Breast beneath his Fingers bent;
> He felt again, his Fingers made a Print,
> 'Twas Flesh, but Flesh so firm, it rose against the Dint:
> The pleasing Task he fails not to renew;
> Soft, and more soft at ev'ry Touch it grew;
> Like pliant Wax, when chasing Hands reduce
> The former Mass to Form, and frame for Use.
> He would believe, but yet is still in Pain,
> And tries his Argument of Sense again,
> Presses the Pulse, and feels the leaping Vein. (Ovid 1976:341)

Astonished, doubtful and fearing he was mistaken, with a lover's ardour he repeatedly touched, seeking verification. Startlingly, it was indeed alive! When he pressed the veins on her warming limbs, the springy flesh indented then resumed its shape, as only real flesh can do. Thanking the goddess Aphrodite, he pressed his lips upon lips as real as his own. The maiden felt the kisses and blushed, and opening her eyes to the light, fixed them at the same moment on her lover. This union between Pygmalion and Galatea was blessed by Aphrodite, and later the child named Paphos was born. The city of Paphos remains sacred to Aphrodite even today.

The story of Pygmalion's statue, its living, breathing fleshiness could obviously be interpreted as erotic wish fulfilment with misogynistic overtones. An anthropomorphosis, the mineral statue becoming human flesh, becoming animated. Nevertheless, the story involves familiar tropes of touching: the erotic touch of flesh with stone; the touching of doubt, of disbelief and verification; and finally the touching of carnal union, of lips and flesh – the vascularity of flesh, the living, pulsing, sensing first moments of a sensory being (such as occurs in a newborn infant). An anthropomorphic figure carved from the minerals of the earth, the correlate of Vitruvius' and Le Corbusier's generic figure in architecture that projects human proportion, scale and measure into architectural spaces. But this is to come. Pygmalion's statue will be a suitable companion to accompany us through the variety of fragmented sensory and spatial experiences of various art forms, a hypothetical entry point for our own embodied perceptions in the apprehension of the surfaces and volumes that invoke tactility or prompt affective response. In other words, a companion with which to think through a haptic aesthetics.

Aesthetics

Can the aesthetic body within an aesthetic encounter reveal insights into the mechanisms and memory of sensory perception in general? Is there some relation between Aristotle's *aesthesis*, the aesthetic body, and encounters with art? I am reliant on the fact that, by his own admission, Merleau-Ponty's aesthetics has much to teach us about the functions of everyday perception. But I take comfort in the fact that Gombrich (1991), Shaviro (1993), Taussig (1993), Lant (1995), Marks (2000), Ione (2000) and Colebrook (2002) for example take a similar approach. In two key essays on aesthetics, 'Eye and Mind' (1964a) and 'Cézanne's Doubt' (1969), Merleau-Ponty concentrated on the painting of Cézanne to reveal the multisensory nature of aesthetic experience, and in particular the tactile within the visible. Quite simply, for Merleau-Ponty, Cézanne exemplifies 'the phenomenological work with paint done by this artist' (Johnson 1993:5). Painting therefore works as a non-philosophical example of thinking through perception, and especially the relation between eye and hand. In Cézanne's own words, the painter 'thinks in painting' (Merleau-Ponty 1964a:178). Moreover, aesthetics – our capacity for feeling, sensing and being affected – involves a sense of touch, texture and mass, those qualities which inform our worldly encounters with things.

Traditionally, aesthetics is regarded as the branch of philosophy that deals with the arts, especially fine art, and whether in the philosophy or the history of art, accounts are usually ocularcentric, rarely considering 'other modes of experience and forms of attention' such as tactility, as Johnson (2002:61) observes. Yet the etymological and historical derivation of aesthetics reveals a different story, able to be defined as dealing with physical, material things perceptible by the senses. Tellingly, 'aesthetics' derives etymologically from stem *aesthe*, 'feel, apprehend by the senses' (*Oxford English Dictionary*, 1989). Plato's extreme scepticism concerning the value of sensory information and art is evidenced for example in Book X of *The Republic* (1986), art being reduced to pure imitation or representation (*mimesis*), capable of revealing no truth, and being a potentially corrupting influence. Conversely, Aristotle defended the importance of both sensory experience and cathartic value of the arts in *Poetics* and *Politics*. As we now recognize, for Aristotle *aesthesis* was the 'sensory faculty', standing in for an undeveloped philosophy of perception by articulating sensation as an alteration of this faculty. In 1750 Baumgarten revisited this derivation, in the words of Shusterman, coining the term 'aesthetics' and defining this as 'his project of a science of sensory perception' (2006:237). 'The end of aesthetics', wrote Baumgarten, 'is the perfection of sensory cognition as such, this implying beauty' (*Theoretische Ästhetik* §14, in Shusterman 2006:239). Although beauty was an important consideration in terms of the arts for Baumgarten, true to its etymological root as *aesthesis*, Baumgarten's emphasis on the aesthetic encompassed not only the arts but also sensory perception, including natural beauty and everyday perceptual practices. Kant formalized this further, solidifying the link with sensory perception whereby aesthetics was 'the science which treats of the conditions of sensuous perception' (1990:66n), or 'the science of the rules of sensibility in general' (1990:93). It was only in the nineteenth century that aesthetics became reduced in its application to the philosophy of art, especially concerning judgement, taste and beauty, as a result of the English translation of another of Kant's works, *Critique of Judgment*.[1] Hegel also limited his application of the term aesthetics to the fine arts, and while Baumgarten and Kant had included nature as worthy of aesthetic judgement, Hegel did not.

In 1994 Seremetakis, herself a Greek, re-examined the Greek origins of the word while writing about the sensory content of memory. In her etymological reflections she notes that *aésthema*, which is 'emotion-feeling', and *aesthetikí*, which comes to be 'aesthetics', are both derived from *aesthénome* which she translates as 'I feel or sense, I understand, grasp, learn...' (1994:5). Following Seremetakis we revert to the Aristotelian definition of aesthetics, via Baumgarten. Its meaning 'of or pertaining to sensuous perception, received by the senses' is marked as 'obsolete' in the *Oxford English Dictionary* (1989), but this derivation is useful in combining the sensory apprehension of material artefacts with affect, illustrating how the world touches us. For Jennifer Fisher's project of a haptic aesthetics, 'recuperating the premodern meaning' of aesthetics not only returns us through etymology to sense perception, but ushers forth other questions including the political when she asks: 'what are the implications of mobilizing aesthetic analysis to understand the play of agency in configurations of living, feeling, experiencing, producing and perceiving, all of which manifest dimensions of the political?' (1997:4). The sensory and corporeal aspects which foreground this approach to aesthetics is certainly compatible with feminist frameworks, she notes. This question is revisited in chapter 6 of the present volume. The corporeal aspect involves a 'sensorially nuanced aesthetics' for Fisher that effectively links the sensory with the affective, considering the combination of the somatic senses and the affective dimension together a 'haptic' or 'relational' aesthetics, 'an aesthetics which refers to experience as well as objects' (ibid.:6). While the haptic is traditionally associated with closeness and proximity, denoting contiguity and contact, the optic is supposedly associated with distance and transcendence. Yet for Fisher the haptic encompasses distal as well as proximal perception:

> In this sense haptic perception can elucidate the energies and volitions involved in sensing space: its temperature, presences, pressure and resonances ... it is the affective touch, a plane of feeling distinct from actual physical contact. (ibid.)

Thus affective touch is separate from actual proximity or distance. A felt proximity separate and distinct from actual physical contact, for Fisher the haptic includes affective touch. Later, Fisher makes an analogy between haptic and optic 'lines of sight', as it were. 'While the visual gives trajectories – sightlines – between the viewer and the surfaces of art, the haptic defines the affective charge – the felt dimensionality – of a spatial context' (ibid.). Fisher's call for a haptic aesthetics effectively brings together touching and feeling, tangibility and affective forces. Nevertheless, it rests on a distinction between the haptic and the optic that figures in art history, as the next section explores.

The Haptic and the Optic

Armed with our initial discussion of Benjamin, to which we shall return, and from Seremetakis' *aesthénome* as feeling, sensing, and grasping, we are in a better position to understand Deleuze and Guattari's return to Riegl's distinction between the 'haptic' and the 'optic' in *A Thousand Plateaus* (1988:492–9). In his 1901 book *Late Roman Art Industry*, Alois Riegl had made the distinction between haptic and optic forms of perception within Greek and late Roman art. Opposing long-distance, disembodied vision (the optic) with close-range tactile perception (the haptic), Riegl's argument connected these aesthetic habits of perception with distinct historical epochs, and how the associated art forms utilized space and perspective. Ancient art worked in a shallow space, the space of relief, and emphasized the tactile connection of the parts. Much earlier, Herder in 1778 similarly generalized that the Greeks 'perceived as do blind people, and through feeling, saw' (2002 [1778]:78). The development of Greek art from Egyptian art lies in this tactile-optical realm, thought Riegl, part way between close vision (*Nahsicht*) and distant vision (*Fernsicht*) – the realm of normal vision (*Normalsicht*). Thus late Roman art became more purely optical and distant (*Fernsichtig*, e.g. Riegl 1995 [1901]:124). The plane of reference is no longer haptic. Such space is not strictly 'tactile' space, because the tactile is a particular sense modality, usually associated with skin contact. Instead, 'haptic' refers to the whole hand-eye-movement system, and is investigated in psychology by J.J. Gibson (e.g. 1968). Deleuze and Guattari go on to relate this close-vision (haptic) and distance-vision (optic) to 'smooth' and 'striated' space, taking the concepts elsewhere.

But in returning to the art history of Riegl, Wilhelm Worringer, and to an extent Henri Focillon, the distinction between haptic and optic occurs as part of a long-standing debate within a venerable tradition. Bernhard Berenson, in his influential *The Florentine Painters of the Renaissance* of 1896, indeed elevates tactility to a crucial position in painting and the reception of a work. His scholarship concentrated on representations of human figures, and Giotto is exemplary, but his conclusions are universal. 'The essential in the art of painting', he proclaims, '... is somehow to stimulate our consciousness of tactile values, so that the picture shall have at least as much power as the object represented, to appeal to our tactile imagination' (1906:5). Painters may appeal to our tactile imagination, as Berenson explains, because even a primitive psychology of perception admits that the sense of depth and perspective arises within infancy through touch and the muscular senses of movement. Those cases of post-operative vision after blindness, in chapter 3, are testament to this. Berenson even argues that this connection between tactile experience and the sense of depth and perspective is subsequently forgotten when we reach adulthood. However, when our eyes fall upon a shape or an image, we are in fact 'giving tactile values to retinal impressions', he argues (ibid.:4). Exploiting this psychological feature, the implications for the painter are clear:

> Now, painting is an art which aims at giving an abiding impression of artistic reality with only two dimensions. The painter must, therefore, do consciously what we all do unconsciously,– construct his third dimension. And he can accomplish his task only as we accomplish ours, by giving tactile values to retinal impressions. His first business, therefore, is to rouse the tactile sense, for I must have the illusion of being able to touch a figure, I must have the illusion of varying muscular sensations inside my palm and fingers corresponding to the various projections of this figure, before I shall take it for granted as real, and let it affect me lastingly. (ibid.:4–5)

Quite apart from Berenson's argument that the painter must rouse the tactile sense, the fundamental observation of tactile values within retinal impressions admits a form of intermodality, the translation from vision to touch, which is exploitable by the painter. It admits non-optical elements (tactility) to seeing and rendering visible. This is different from Riegl's position concerning distance and the haptic. We return to Deleuze and Guattari who – after Riegl and consistent with Berenson – show the importance of the 'nonoptical function' within vision:

> 'Haptic' is a better word than 'tactile' since it does not establish an opposition between two sense organs but rather invites the assumption that the eye itself may fulfill this nonoptical function (1988:492).

Thus haptic space 'may be as much visual or auditory as tactile', they argue (ibid.:493). Thus the haptic is not in opposition to the optic. It does not oppose the eyes with the hands, but acknowledges the sensory interdependence of the whole haptic (hand-eye-motion) system. But neither is it merely shorthand for 'multi-sensory', or for the mysterious neurophysiological workings of the somatic senses. As Fisher argues, the haptic and the visual are implicated in one another: 'The issue is not to replace the visual by the tactile, but to explore the complexity of the senses in aesthetic experience' (Fisher 1997:11). Deleuze echoes this, asserting it wrong to 'simply oppose manual and optical space' since they enter into 'new correlations and combinations' in painting, at least (2003:131). And this mutuality of tactile and visual, eye and hand is revisited and developed by Deleuze in his *Francis Bacon: The Logic of Sensation* (2003). From Riegl's art history through Deleuze and Guattari, the haptic is consistently formulated in terms of closeness, of proximity. As Fisher had argued, the haptic as affective touch cannot be reduced to mere physical distance. It is what Carol Armstrong calls the 'nearly manual' field as opposed to the 'optical' field in an essay on photography (2002:32). Within photography and film, a haptic orientation brings into proximity, portrays texture, and invites intimacy (see Lant 1995; Marks 2000; 2004). The haptic therefore recasts the aesthetic relation between a work and its embodied reception.

Whereas in the next chapter we explore a haptic aesthetics of digital performance and multimedia installations, here we concentrate on more 'traditional' art forms to explore historically the role of touching and feeling in aesthetics. The first stage is to identify how, in the aesthetic encounter, our awareness of the relation between touch and space comes into play. This occurs in the visual arts as well as the plastic arts, and it is clear from Merleau-Ponty's celebration of Cézanne (1964a; 1969) and the structure of the visible and the invisible (2000) that the visual arts have been considered as an underpinning for his phenomenology, as Bate documents (1974:349). How the aesthetic encounter invokes tactility in its manifold forms will be examined in three stages, and we can imaginatively enter into the world of Pygmalion's statue as we do so, perhaps, seeing through her eyes and feeling with her flesh the successive sensations and surfaces on offer, and increasingly spatial forms that require oculo-motor and kinaesthetic movement. First, in painting on a pictorial surface that is predominantly visual but, through texture and technique, appeals to a tactile sensibility. Secondly, considering the volumes occupied and played with by the so-called plastic arts, starting with sculpture, the paradigmatically tactile art form.[2] Lastly, the larger-scale concrete spaces of architecture, an unfolding of space and sensation. This sequence indicates different degrees of physicality in the aesthetic encounter, progressively engaging more complex senses such as kinaesthesia as well as tactility, involving the multisensory body to increasing degrees as the spatiality of the works unfold. The discussion of painting and surface, for example, starts with the synthesis of touch and sight located in the eye (the tactile within the visible), but as we progress through examples of sculpture and architecture more of the motile, multisensory body becomes involved. Although only fragments of experiences and case studies are offered, we correspondingly explore fragments of the aesthetic body, fragments of skin, of flesh, of body. By an imaginative projection into a figure such as Pygmalion's statue, an empty receptacle for novel sensory experience, perhaps a coherence can be imposed by the reader, and a progressive sensory-spatial unfolding may be experienced through her.

The Aesthetic Body

Surface, Painting, Skin

[The artist] touches, he feels, he reckons weight, he measures space, he molds the fluidity of atmosphere to prefigure form in it, he caresses the skin of all things. With the language of Touch he composes the language of Sight – a 'warm' tone, a 'cool' tone, a 'heavy' tone, a 'hollow' tone, a 'hard' line, a 'soft' line. But the language of speech is not so rich as the impressions conveyed by the hands. (Focillon 1989:167)

Cézanne himself rather boldly declares that 'Talking about art is almost useless', since 'the man of letters expresses himself in abstractions whereas a painter, by means of drawing and colour, gives concrete form to his sensations and perceptions' (in Cézanne 1995:303–4). In his essay 'Eye and Mind' (1964a) Merleau-Ponty recognizes that the intimate relation between sight and touch allows a sense of immersion in the world. 'Sight-space' and 'touch-space' are in the same world, a world that, by being embodied and having the requisite senses, we all share. Ostensibly, the paradigmatic artistic example would be sculptural. But in 'Eye and Mind' he looks at Cézanne's paintings. Cézanne was attempting to portray 'ideated sensations', another term borrowed from Bernhard Berenson, as Martin (1981) notes, preceding the scientific splitting of the sensations of touch and sight. Indeed, one of Merleau-Ponty's chief concerns was the entirely theoretical separation of the data of the senses, which does not occur in the flow of conscious experience (Bate 1974; Merleau-Ponty 1969, 1992). Repeatedly, Merleau-Ponty employs aesthetic arguments concerning specific art works in order to support his larger claims about perception. While some might see this as problematic, a kind of aesthetic fallacy, the phenomenological approach to art can remain consistent with his psychology of perception. Painting becomes a valid phenomenological exercise, reconstructing what is 'seen' through experimenting with shifting and fragmented forms. Not learning how to see, like Virgil, but learning how to make visible those invisible structures of perception. 'Eye and Mind' (1964a) follows this argument concerning the eye and rendering visible, how a depth is given to the canvas, which bespeaks the relationship between vision and touch and is exemplified beautifully in the painting of Cézanne. Shiff adds that Renoir talked of the brush stroke (*'touche'*) on the canvas (1991:134). There are three ways that touch is significant in terms of the pictorial surface, and these are interrelated. First, in painting on canvas the brush stroke is a mark, evidence of the manual touch of the painter; secondly it is also the touch of the paint mark as a visible form – something that eventually looks like Cézanne's *Pommes et Oranges* (1899) or *Mont Sainte-Victoire* (1906) for example. Thirdly, both the painter's and the viewer's experience of the painting is touching, affective. In between the viewer and the painter, the touchmarks or brushstrokes on the canvas are a physical point of translation of sensation, of affect. 'Each mark could be regarded as the representation of a moment of sensation and experience, of a continuing encounter with the world,' writes Shiff (1991:136). The brushstroke or *touche* is the mark or sign of the hand, and the activity of the hand in the shaping of material is familiar in discussions of sculpture, too, as we shall see. Like Riegl, Henri Focillon regarded the importance of the artist's touch. Whereas Riegl considered handcrafts as comparable to fine art in this respect, Focillon concentrates on painting. Even so, writing in 1934, he remarks on the imprint of the manual process of painting, using richly expressive terminology that betrays a haptic orientation: 'Even the most moderated and uniform execution betrays the artist's touch – that decisive contact between man and object, that *grasping of the world* that we can see emerging gently or impetuously under our very eyes' (1989:172–3, emphasis added). The artist's touch is present whether the material is clay, stone, wood or the fluid texture of paint on canvas, Focillon continues. Likewise, Deleuze speaks of the significance of 'manual traits' in painting, especially that of Francis Bacon, where the movement and rhythm of the hand assumes independence from the eye, through marks by rag, stick, brush or sponge (2003:100); it is a 'liberation of the hand' (ibid.:106), proceeding from optical chaos to manual rhythm on the canvas. Just like Merleau-Ponty and Fisher, then, Deleuze also acknowledges the haptic function of the eye (ibid.:133), a closeness of vision that occurs in essence through use of colour on the planar surface, evoking texture and volume.

The attempt to render 'how the world touches us' can occur through any art form; it is not simply a matter of the visualization of tactility, nor a simple evocation of the tactile in the visible through the artwork. In depicting something visually the painter's view is not from the 'outside', that is, not merely a 'physical-optical' relation with the world, where 'the world stands before him through representation', argues Merleau-Ponty (1964a:181). Paul Klee's famous characterization of modern art, 'not to render the visible, but to render visible' (e.g. in Deleuze 2003:56), placed the painter in the role of heightening our perception of the underlying structure of things. Deleuze and Guattari say this is to make perceptible 'the imperceptible forces that populate the world, affect us, and make us become' (1994:182). Merleau-Ponty also carries Klee's idea forward. The painter must make 'visible' a whole realm of experience, achieved 'by breaking the 'skin of things' to show how the things become things, how the world becomes world' (1964a:181). From this language it is clear he uses the aesthetic encounter as an exemplary strand in his archaeology of perception, a pathway that returns to the primacy of perception (discussed in chapter 2). This is reinforced in a later essay, 'Cézanne's Doubt':

> Cézanne does not try to use color to *suggest* the tactile sensations which would give shape and depth. These distinctions between touch and sight are unknown in primordial perception. It is only as a result of a science of the human body that we finally learn to distinguish between our senses. (Merleau-Ponty 1969:240)

The body for both Merleau-Ponty and Husserl is, unsurprisingly, the locus of aesthetic experience and imposes a structural unity on sensations, the 'primordial perception' of which Merleau-Ponty speaks. Similarly, the body for Husserl is always 'the aesthetic body' (1989a:60; 1999:11), which is subject to 'aestheta' (sense or sensation). The painting process is never entirely separate from the artist, for Merleau-Ponty. As Roberts summarizes, 'painting virtually emerges out of perception and its presence to the world through the body' (1998:133), the body of both artist and beholder. While Husserl has much to say about the implication of the aesthetic body, the materiality of the art object, and the significance of flesh in the phenomenological apprehension of an artwork which could be of interest (e.g. 1999:24ff), Merleau-Ponty's analysis of Cézanne in particular lies on a path which extends beyond a phenomenology limited to the body or the subject; it strains toward the affective power of the work which stands in between the artist and the beholder.

Therefore in our quotidian perceptual experience, just as in the aesthetic encounter, there is an 'invisible' background against which we perceive, for example, a red dress. Redness is never perceived in isolation, argues Merleau-Ponty, as 'this red is what it is only by connecting it up from its place with other reds about it, with which it forms a constellation... In short, it is a certain node in the woof of the simultaneous and successive. It is a concretion of visibility' (2000:132). His argument is revealing, for in that parallel between perceptual reflections and the phenomenological work performed by the painter the concretion of visibility is not thematic, treated as an examinable conscious event, and its sensory content is not limited to colour alone. The texture of the dress' material, as a play of light and a memory of touch, also forms this concretion of visibility. As Vasseleu summarizes, 'Our experience of a thing's colour cannot be even confined to visual experience, but has a texture that includes other perceptions of the thing, for example dimensions of tactility, sonority and smell' (1998:44). Seen in a different light, the same red dress will show differences in colouring and texture, yet we know it is the same dress. In this case we invoke a sensory memory, by 'substituting the actuality of colour for the memory of colour' (ibid.:47; also Merleau-Ponty 1992:304). Even the surface of the canvas may invoke a sensory assemblage through the body, not just tactility through the *touche* of the brush-stroke.

Painting's phenomenological significance for Merleau-Ponty therefore consists in its 'disclosing the mode of our insertion into the world' (Crowther 1993:107). This makes visible the 'invisible' aspects of bodily orientations and perceptual capacities through form and texture, aspects which we are not immediately aware of. Cézanne's painting shows for Merleau-Ponty the *way* that we actually see. And for Deleuze, too, the imperative for Cézanne is to 'paint the sensation' (2003:35). The way objects are depicted on canvas, made to obtrude or shine forth in our perception, overcodes more traditional techniques and laws that govern 'correct' optical perspective, for example, to bring forth haptic qualities. This is the 'invisible' which for Cézanne constructs or produces the 'visible'. That 'grasping of the world' as Focillon put it, our mode of insertion into the world, is fundamentally pre-reflective but inescapably embodied, and this is reflected in the aesthetic encounter. The world is given a pre-reflective structural unity not as an intellectual operation but, as Crowther remarks, as 'a function of all our sensory, motor, and affective capacities operating as a unified field' (1993:103).

Therefore, after Klee's talk of rendering visible through painting, Cézanne additionally exemplifies how the materiality of the object – or at least, a sense of the materiality of the object – is also made visible. In Merleau-Ponty's words:

> The object is no longer covered by reflections and lost in its relations to the atmosphere and to other objects: it seems subtly illuminated from within, light emanates from it, and the result is an impression of solidity and material substance. (1969:237)

And, later: 'We *see* the depth, the smoothness, the softness, the hardness of objects; Cézanne even claimed that we see their odor' (ibid.:240, original emphasis). Thinking about the body in the apprehension of Cézanne's painting in 'Eye and Mind' therefore enables him to consider the thingness of the body, its materiality and its kinaesthetic properties. Deftly and continuously shifting between the examination of a painting, the intention and technique of the artist, and the embodied aesthetic experience, Merleau-Ponty, like Cézanne, is able to think *through* painting, for in the phenomenology of embodied perception and the phenomenology of the aesthetic encounter alike, the body is indeed a thing:

> Visible and mobile, my body is a thing among things; it is caught in the fabric of the world, and its cohesion is that of a thing. But because it moves itself and sees, it holds things in a circle around itself. Things are an annex or prolongation of itself; they are encrusted into its flesh, they are part of its full definition; the world is made of the same stuff as the body. (1964:163)

While talking of painting in this instance, the sense of the materiality of the object in the aesthetic encounter, along with the motility of the perceiving body, is perhaps more evident in sculpture and architecture than in painting. Martin (1981) certainly applies this physical, fleshy analysis to sculpture and the feeling of 'withness' with things. So the following sections will therefore try to extend the discussion into the plastic and spatial arts, progressively unfurling bodily sensations and senses of touch, and considering the haptic and affective elements of an increasingly spatialized aesthetic experience.

Volume, Sculpture, Flesh

> But we woodcutters, modellers, masons, painters of the shape of man and the face of the Earth, we still retain a wholesome respect for the *noble weightiness* of matter.
>
> Focillon, *Life of Forms in Art*

Whereas the two-dimensionality of painting seemingly separates the viewer from the viewed, implying a necessarily scopic distance, sculpture entails more of an involvement with, and sharing of, the three-dimensionality of that sculptural space.

Michèle Roberts writes about the aesthetic encounter in terms applicable to painting at the surface, sculpture in terms of volume, and architecture alike:

> Volumes, colors, lines of force, etc. are not rediscovered or constructed by the sensory apparatus, but, as 'lived objects'; they present themselves to us as the center from which sensations radiate. The sensations are thus discovered in the world, since our bodily perceptions are equally in the world and in us. (1998:131–2)

This dynamic between the material and the sensation reminds us of that space Deleuze and Guattari described as 'where material ends and sensation begins' (1994:166), where 'affects' are wrested from 'percepts'. But something of the intersensoriality of embodied perceptual experience, and of the conception of flesh as the intermediary between body and world, is reminiscent of Merleau-Ponty and the various sensations and associations present in the concretion of visibility. Along similar lines to Berenson's characterization of 'tactile values' in Renaissance painting, Margaret Boden, writing about the lush Pre-Raphaelite textures of Lord Leighton's paintings, claims that 'one can – and often does – imagine reaching out to touch them, to feel their sensuous folds with one's fingertips or to lay them gently against one's face'. But, she continues, 'painting only rarely produces this sort of response' (2000:293). Instead, sculpture more directly invites to touch the surface, especially when representing or recalling bodily contours, since 'it engages one on a bodily level' (ibid.). Something about the material presence and three-dimensional form of a sculpture often evokes a more embodied, multisensory response, appealing to the somatic senses. But there are historical precedents in aesthetic theory concerned exactly with this. One such figure in the aesthetics of sculpture is now examined.

In words that reveal an almost proto-phenomenological awareness of aesthetics as embodied perception, Johann Gottfried Herder in his seminal 1778 treatise *Sculpture* (2002) recognizes the centrality of touch, or at least the promise of tactility, in appreciating sculpture. 'While sculpture is created for the hand,' he says (ibid.:50), 'painting is made for the eye' (ibid.:56). His observations are prescient, remarkably prefiguring more recent aesthetic writing like Read (1961), Merleau-Ponty or indeed Focillon (1989), yet Herder limits himself to an analysis of that most conservatively representative of sculptural forms, that of classical Greece. Were we to have a hundred eyes like the giant Argus, states Herder, 'without a hand to touch', we would only have a distanced or abstracted 'bird's-eye view' (2002:40). Instead, and redolent of what we have identified as the 'premodern' meaning of aesthetics as *aesthesis*, Herder shows the possibility of tactility, the significance of the hand, and solidifies that association of tangibility and epistemology:

> The living, embodied truth of the three-dimensional space of angles, of form and volume, is not something we can learn through *sight*. This is all the more true of the essence of

sculpture, *beautiful* form and *beautiful* shape, for this is not a matter of color, or of the play of proportion and symmetry, or of light and shadow, but of *physically present, tangible truth*. (ibid., original emphasis)

Later, Herder explicitly considers the appeal to tactility that the sculptor makes in his craft. Unlike two-dimensional art forms, which cannot portray the multiformity of the human figure, Greek sculpture allows every muscle or vein to stand out. Thus one skill of the sculptor is in manipulating this form, inviting the eye and hand of the beholder to touch: 'Almost without wishing it, our *sense of touch* is *drawn toward* every pliant curve and every delicate form' (ibid.:91, original emphasis). By so doing, this promise of tactility for Herder he explicitly links to feeling, since sculptural forms and the evocation of tactility appeal to 'inner sympathy', an affective component to the aesthetic experience that occurs through touch. For example, incidentally reaffirming the primacy of touch,

> Everyone knows that as regards contemplation and the awakening of ideas the sense of *touch* is the obscurest, tardiest, and most sluggish of the senses, but that it has *primacy* and stands as the *judge* when it comes to feeling beautiful form. Forgetful of imitation and ideas, it simply feels what it *feels*, awakening a response of inner sympathy that is all the more profound for being obscure. (ibid.:57, original emphasis)

Like Herder, Herbert Read in his 1961 work on sculpture elevates it as the haptic art form *par excellence*, discussing its three-dimensionality and weighty materiality in startlingly similar terms:

> For the sculptor, tactile values are not illusions to be created on a two-dimensional plane: they constitute a reality to be conveyed directly, as existent mass. Sculpture is an art of *palpation* – an art that gives satisfaction in the touching and handling of objects. That, indeed, is the only way in which we can have direct sensation of the three-dimensional shape of an object. (1961:228, original emphasis)

What is made present in our awareness in 'touch-space', according to Read's aesthetics of sculpture, is the weightiness, mass, or what Khatchadourian terms 'ponderability' (1974:336) of the sculpture piece.[3] Apart from the evocation of tactility or the wish to convey the synaesthetic or 'primordial' nature of perception, sculpture makes a space available to play: it draws us in and, like touch, our haptic-visual 'gaze' is closer, more intimate and shared. It lies within the reach-space of the body, or 'prehensile space'.

'Sculpture reveals our physical "withness" with things, our "being-with", much more vividly than painting', argues Martin (1981:28). A sculpture, being a framed object in the sense that it is placed outside the realm of everyday perceptual experience, epitomizes 'withness' with things due to its enactive, crafted materiality, manifested through surfaces and textures without the need to physically reach out and touch the object itself. While sculpture may be the 'art of palpation' for Read (1961:228), our aesthetic appreciation is not necessarily lessened if a piece remains unreachable, behind glass. Rather, it is the *potential* for tactility, the sensory appeal of texture and form, an underlying synaesthesia which is the mechanism for the continual crossover between sensory modalities. Speaking of the apprehension of texture in a comparable way, Merleau-Ponty assumes a synaesthetic correspondence between the senses in embodied experience: 'The senses intercommunicate by opening onto the structure of the thing. One sees the hardness and brittleness of glass... One sees the springiness of steel' (1992:229). These sensory associations are confirmed when, in the case of the glass, the brittleness makes the glass shatter, and the sound of the breaking glass accompanies the visual experience. Following Khatchadourian, these 'tactile associations' (1974:336) occur in the apprehension of the stone of the sculpture. It is not simply about the evocation of tactility by other means, a simple translation from one sense to another. While sculpture exemplifies tactile qualities and associations almost paradigmatically, such haptic experiences are not limited to the framed or rarefied aesthetic encounter. That texture, colour and light are interwoven into the fabric of perception, a continual synthesis of sensory modalities, is an unremarkable everyday occurrence for the aesthetic (touching, feeling) body. Martin gives the example of approaching a stone wall. Moving closer we see various colours, shapes and textures that recall certain haptic information from prior encounters, patterns of light on the stone that indicate texture, relief, massiness. 'We do not know about the surface, volume, and mass of these stones by sight alone but by sight synthesized with memories of tactual and kinaesthetic perceptions,' he articulates (1981:59). A quotidian relation of touch, kinasthesia and memory through the body, called upon in the aesthetic encounter with painting, sculpture, or architecture alike.

As an art of palpation, the haptic experience of sculpture is therefore bi-directional, its reciprocality stemming from the possibility of our touching an object and its touching us. This reminds us of Merleau-Ponty on the reciprocity of the toucher and the touched (2000:133), or as Maldiney puts it, 'Indeed by touching things we touch ourselves upon them, we are simultaneously touchers and touched' (in Chrétien 2004:84). The perceived physicality of the sculpture piece is simultaneously an affirmation of the material fleshiness of the body, and of the beholder's viscerality. Of Henry Moore's sculpture *Family Group*, for instance, Arnheim describes that space between material and sensation invoked earlier, in this case the near-representational but abstract figures of a man, woman and child: 'space appears tangible, stagnant, warmed by body heat' (1966:250). This, despite being apprehended visually, and despite the coldness of the stone from which it is formed. Both Husserl and Merleau-Ponty wished to show how fleshy being was the 'natural attitude' or ground of experience, and Rajchman relates this to perceived spatial orientation. Speaking of Husserlian flesh, then, and returning to Riegl's *haptisch/optisch* distinction, the aesthetic body is ordered and oriented, maintains the order between the optic and the haptic, and grounds us:

> It centers us ... it links oculo- and motor into a single unified field with receding horizons, which permits us to place things in a coordinate space, reidentify objects, and say what's up and what's down; and it makes all the textures of our *haptisch* space come to conform to this *optisch* organization. (Rajchman 1998:46)

In terms reminiscent of the kinaesthetic background of everyday anticipative embodiment discussed previously, this is organization of sensorimotor space around the body, the optic and the haptic, the eyes and hands. Translation of sensory information between modalities, an appreciation of light and texture, is not the ordering of sensation per se, but the ordering of sensorimotor coherence and spatial orientation within the ocular-motor (haptic, optic, kinaesthetic) body – a haptic, visual-tactile-kinesic involvement in the physical withness of things. We are drawn by this into the surrounding enlivened space, thinks Martin, to appreciate especially the sculptural aesthetic encounter, the physicality of withness with things:

> Sculpture revives the withering of the tactual and kinaesthetic senses by bringing us back into direct contact with the raw power of reality: the bumping, banging, pushing, pulling, soothing, palpitating tangibility of our withness with things. (Martin 1981:78–9)

The sympathetically somatic response to a work, the imaginatively kinaesthetic response to a kinetic expression through the material, is charming. (See e.g. Sallis 1994 for a similarly phenomenological tack.) But to bring together the physicality of a work with a physiological and affective response, a return to *aesthesis* and the notion of an aesthetics that involves the entire body, we now unfold another spatial dimension.

Space, Architecture, Body   We have seen the smooth spatial continuum that operates between the canvas of the picture and the material volume of sculpture. Furthering this continuum, there is a place between sculpture and architecture that engages with the kinaesthetic body more fully, that explores three-dimensional material form and its surrounding sensory space. Deleuze and Guattari (1994:186) identify Jean Dubuffet as inhabiting that space between architecture, sculpture and painting. In addition to the multidimensionality of forms in space, what characterizes the work of Dubuffet and others (e.g. Calder, Caro, Paolozzi) is the structuring of an environment that responds to the motility of eyes, hands and body. Sculpture is therefore perhaps the paradigmatic example of an art form involving affect, touch and space, but these properties are shared elsewhere, an aesthetic-spatial continuum that includes installations and architecture. 'We paint, sculpt, compose and write with sensations', argue Deleuze and Guattari (1994:166), noting that when an artist attempts a resemblance to something – a form, a smile, a landscape – the sensation is achieved through working with the material, in each case:

> If resemblance haunts the work of art, it is because sensation refers only to its material: it is the percept or the affect of the material itself, the smile of oil, the gesture of fired clay, the thrust of metal, the crouch of Romanesque stone, and the ascent of Gothic stone. The material is so varied in each case ... that it is difficult to say where in fact the material ends and sensation begins. (ibid.)

The percept and affect of the material itself, its being crafted and shaped to embody other forces or dynamics, has visceral effects. In that space where material ends and sensation begins, tangibility arises. By virtue of the tangible presence of the material or through the textural evocation of tactile qualities, this applies equally to the two-dimensional pictorial canvas and to the three-dimensional volumes of sculpture, architecture and the larger built environment. But it is most evident in sculpture, where for commentators such as Herder (2002 [1778]:35ff) and Read (1961:228), sculpture is the paradigmatic tactile art form. Furthermore, whether representational or non-representational in form, the very physicality of sculpture is met with a physiologically rich, multisensory series of responses that correspondingly reveals the physicality and presence of the beholder's body. 'Sculpture reveals our physical "withness" with things, our "being-with", much more vividly than painting', affirms Martin (1981:28). So it is a condition of our awareness of sculpture's physicality that our own fleshiness and embodied physicality is called to mind.

Relations of tangibility, space and affect are significant in the experience of other art forms, too. For example, the conventional distinction between sculpture and architecture is that the former is concerned with mass, with 'solid volumes that displace or inhabit space', and the latter with 'the voids or spatial relations between material elements', thinks Rogers (1962:297). But the designing of masses in space, and the designing of the spatial relations in which the material forms inhabit, has always been historically blurred, and this is clear in the work of Caro, Whiteread, Long, Goldsworthy and others (e.g. see Causey 1998). The quasi-space where material ends and sensation begins is exemplified in these works, and many of Henry Moore's sculptural figures 'capture portions of space and make them part of themselves,' according to Arnheim, who continues: 'Much less solid than the wood, stone, or metal on which they border, these air-bodies nevertheless condense into a transparent substance, which mediates between the *tangible material* of the statue and the surrounding *empty space*' (1966:250, my emphasis). A related aspect of this felt presence and physicality, of tangibility and 'withness' with things, is a sense of proximity in the aesthetic encounter. The difference between haptic and optic is usually associated with the hands and eyes, where haptic entails manual closeness while optic implies visual distance. But with the increasing artificiality and mass production of images and objects, Benjamin thought that there was a felt distance from things, and an increased need for objects in their original physical presence to assuage this. 'Every day the urge grows stronger to get hold of an object at very close range by way of its likeness, its reproduction', he says (in Taussig 1993:32). The proximal nature of encountering sculpture, its tangible qualities and the promise of tactility, has something of the auratic in it perhaps, something that negates the felt distance between perceiver and perceived. Faced with a 'Do not touch' sign, we appreciate the mass and texture of a sculpture even in our visual apprehension of it.

Therefore, consistent with the discussions of the haptic and the optic in painting and sculpture, it is now entirely appropriate to attend to the notion of haptic architecture. Sensory engagement collapses the distance between the beholder and the work and is comparable to what Benjamin termed 'tactile appropriation' (1999:223). Revealing his own conceptualization of the difference between haptic and optic, as a more subversive hierarchy that pits the haptic as more democratic and everyday, here Benjamin outlines what he means by tactile appropriation:

> Buildings are appropriated in a twofold manner: by use and by perception – or rather, by touch and sight... Tactile appropriation is accomplished not so much by attention as by habit. As regards architecture, habit determines to a large extent even optical reception. The latter, too, occurs much less through rapt attention than by noticing the object in incidental fashion. This mode of appropriation, developed with reference to architecture, in certain circumstances acquires canonical value. For the tasks which face the human apparatus of perception at the turning points of history cannot be solved by optical means, that is, by contemplation, alone. They are mastered gradually by habit, under the guidance of tactile appropriation. (Benjamin 1999:233)

However, Benjamin assumes that most habitual perception is performed in a state of distraction rather than one of attention. Rather than focusing on specific features of a building interior, for example, the notion of tactile appropriation fosters a less distanced, abstract, or contemplative stance. He refrains from flippantly celebrating haptic over optic experience but acknowledges there is a relation between the two, since habitual perception (tactile appropriation) to some extent also determines the optical reception of a building. But there remains the implication that optical distance is collapsed by the more proximal engagement of the tactile. We do not experience architecture geometrically as a pair of disembodied eyes, agrees architect Karsten Harries, who says that '[o]ur experience of buildings is inseparably tied to the experience we have of ourselves, of our bodies, just as our experience of our bodies is affected by the spaces we inhabit' (1997:215). Consequently, the almost ineffable 'feel' of a building, the concretion of habitual, distracted responses over time, is something that characterizes tactile appropriation: how buildings, through their use, apprehension and appropriation, touch us.

Haptic and Optic Architecture   Bloomer and Moore's classic analysis *Body, Memory and Architecture* (1978) is directly concerned with space and measurement, mediated through the hands of architects, masons and dwellers of those spaces. Bloomer and Moore re-examine the importance of the body and the somatic senses in the perception of the building. This is not without precedent, as Norberg-Schulz (1971) and O'Neill (2001) similarly consider the haptic experience of architectural space, the latter in a broad cultural context. But in accommodating new forms of measurement, and seeing the influence of geometry in building design, Bloomer and Moore argue that the birth of modern architecture signified the death of haptic perception, and the distancing of the building from our bodies (1978:21). The promise of an architecture that allows a haptic interaction between *body form* and *built form*, they argued, was lost. For example, changes of texture inside a building affect the movements and the fit of bodies inside the building through the haptic modality; the potential of, say, architecture for the blind is a whole 'choreography of movement' through textural change alone throughout a building, say Bloomer and Moore (ibid.:71). This intriguing possibility is developed in this section, as the haptic/optic architecture distinction has recently been revisited by architect and theorist Juhanni Pallasmaa.

Urban architecture is often in thrall to the visual, straining for the geometric order and measured regularity that is so pleasing to the eye. There is a seeming weightlessness to buildings that strive toward geometric purity, and in the neon-lit metropolis material properties recede in their relevance. To depart from optic architecture and to investigate truly haptic architecture we return to the 'optic' and 'haptic' distinction, this time in the context of design of the built environment and the visitor's embodied perspective. Architect Juhanni Pallasmaa extensively discusses haptic architecture in his larger project of 're-sensualizing' architecture (2000; 2005), offering an initially simplistic and humanistic opposition between geometry and materiality, space and time, strength and fragility, visual and haptic. Expanding *vision* beyond the macular area of intensive focus, a more extensive peripheral *perception* is a more active and engaged mode, not limited solely to the visual. 'Focused vision makes us mere outside observers', Pallasmaa says, whereas 'peripheral perception transforms retinal images into a spatial and bodily involvement and encourages participation' (2000:83). Imaginative use of particular shapes and materials can stimulate the other senses, de-emphasizing the optic, and re-sensualizing architecture (e.g. Pallasmaa 2000; 2005) and design (e.g. Molnar and Vodvarka, 2004) through acknowledging the role of the non-visual and somatic senses in the design process.

The beholder responds to his or her built environment and its manifold sensory qualities of light, texture, colour and acoustics. Architectural techniques that play with perceptions of space in this way, that allow a mobile, multisensory body to explore a spatial narrative through the planned use of these sensory properties, involve this peripheral perception, a haptic (hand-eye) component. No longer dominated by a predominantly visual geometry, haptic architecture at the design stage explores temporal, textural and kinaesthetic experiences of space, and incorporates particular materials for their multisensory properties. As an 'emancipation of the eye', two crucial aspects of architectural experience can be examined. First, familiar now from Merleau-Ponty's discussion of Cézanne's painting, the tactile within the visual, the idea that an unconscious element of touch is already concealed within vision. 'Good architecture offers shapes and surfaces moulded for the pleasurable touch of the eye', as Pallasmaa summarizes (2005:44). And, in a similar manner to that of Merleau-Ponty, 'as we look, the eye touches, and before we even see an object we have already touched it' (Pallasmaa 2000:79). Secondly, emancipation from the distanced or abstracted visual gaze entails a participatory or empathic gaze. Like painting and sculpture, as we have seen, haptic architecture can explore touching and feeling, in both literal and metaphorical senses. From Herder in the eighteenth century, and later aesthetic theorists such as Vischer (1994 [1873) and Lipps (1903), the capacity for empathy (*Einfühlung,* literally 'feeling-into') in their notions of form and space, the somatic, sensory and affective responses to an architectural space is indissociable. After emancipating vision our attention turns to the neglected senses. Numerous architects are therefore attempting, in the words of Pallasmaa, to 're-sensualise architecture through a strengthened sense of materiality and hapticity, texture and weight, density of space and materialised light' (2005:37). As against the architecture of the eye, with its emphasis on control, regularity, geometry and speed, haptic architecture

> promotes slowness and intimacy, appreciated and comprehended gradually as images of the body and the skin. The architecture of the eye detaches and controls, whereas haptic architecture engages and unites. Tactile sensibility replaces *distancing* visual imagery by enhanced materiality, *nearness and intimacy.* (2000:78–9, emphasis added)

Although rather glibly expressed, Pallasmaa clearly identifies with our protracted associations between tactility, proximity and intimacy, associations that recur throughout this book. Furthermore, his unsophisticated opposition between optical detachment and haptic engagement is a historical generalization that bears little scrutiny. But the project of re-sensualizing architecture is a necessary corrective in current architectural theory, following on from Benjamin's subversive formulation of tactile appropriation. And looking to design, one theme that recurs is the transcription of properties of the body into material properties of stone and structure. If buildings can touch us, through the tactile appropriation of a designed environment, then in that process of design the touch of the architect's body is similarly present within the material.

In *The Architecture of Humanism*, George Scott suggests this oscillatory movement. 'We transcribe architecture into terms of ourselves,' he declares, along with its complement: 'We have transcribed ourselves into terms of architecture' (in Harries 1997:215). This latter comment assures the extension of the sensorium, allows spaces of sensation into larger architectural spaces. And I think it characterizes well the relationship of the statue and its surrounding space, the *body form* and the *built form*. The active, embodied, motile, multisensory experience discussed by Condillac and imagined through the statue has obvious connotations for the experiential aspect of architecture and design, the re-sensualization of architecture, to be embraced properly once again. As designers, architects, or potential users of a building, we may imaginatively reconstruct the sensory-spatial experience of Pygmalion's statue Galatea or Condillac's hypothetical statue within architectural spaces, better coordinating the narrative of the spatial progression through a proposed building with textures, sounds, properties of light.

The first written architectural work, Vitruvius' *De Architectura* of 27–23BC, reifies the scale and proportion of the human body, taking a supposedly 'normal' masculine figure which embodies the 'harmonic order of a divinely inspired network of Euclidean geometry' (McAnulty in Imrie 2003:47). Michelangelo's famous illustration *Vitruvian Man* (circa 1492) shows this body as a figural basis from which design could achieve compositional, proportional and harmonic authority; this idealized masculine figure fixes or stabilizes architectural form, leading George Scott to suggest that 'architectural art is the transcription of the body's states into forms of building' (1914:210). Of course, the Vitruvian geometrically mapped body is invariable, healthy, upright, static and male. Such an attitude is revisited in the modernist architecture of Le Corbusier, for example, who regarded the human body as a 'contaminant that countered the ideal of geometrical purity' (in Imrie 2003:47), corrupting the *visual* harmony and *optical* meaning of a building. *Le Modulor* or 'Modular Man' reflected Le Corbusier's understanding in *The Decorative Art of Today* (1925) that the proportions of architecture should be derived from the standard measures of the generic human body. Although the figure of *Le Modulor* is asymmetrical, one arm raised high, an art-deco tweak to a standardized figure, the principle of design from the perspective of a 1.6-metre-high masculine body remains the same. Gaston Bachelard, in *The Poetics of Space*, terms this the 'geometrisation of lived space', the imposition of isometric order and measurable quantities onto space. Indeed, in an empirical study of architects' practices, after interviewing a range of architects, Rob Imrie found that the body is still ignored in (design) practice (2003:52), and found that architects generally imagined the inhabitants of their proposed buildings to be proportioned exactly like themselves, an imaginative projection into similar bodies without imagining anything different, other, incapacitated or even differently gendered. This figurative assumption he terms 'self-imaging' (ibid.:56), an imaginative projection of abstract body into stone comparable to Pygmalion's statue of Galatea, or Condillac's statue which progressively considers the senses and their absence in the perception of space.

Bloomer and Moore had suggested a 'choreography of movement' through textural change alone throughout a building (1978:71). Textural, material change in the space of a building may then produce a set of intensities or affects that shape and modulate the movements of the bodies as they proceed through it. A textural narrative within a built space, much like Zen gardens in Japan, or the alternative materials and sensory cues as you progress through a building designed for the visually impaired.[4] Recent architecture may escape this legacy of geometrical abstraction when spatial construction can be 'loosened up', thinks architect John Rajchman, to become less 'systematic' or 'formless', so that 'its forms or figures become more singular, more original, free to behave in other, less predictable ways or affect us along other, less direct lines' (1998:104–5). Thus the haptic body moulds and can itself be shaped and motivated by the architectural discipline. Architectural space generates sensations just like those of sculpture in this respect, producing a set of affects between the materiality of the building and the haptic/optic body. To view it in this way is to pass from an 'extensive' spatiality of measures and distances to an 'intensive' spatiality of affects, to go from the optic to the haptic, think Deleuze and Guattari (1988:479). Thinking of the intensities, of the affective relationship between built space and individual resonances, we can say that architecture too should strike us as sometimes busy, sometimes tense, sometimes relaxed. Or like choreography, not being only a body but being a body in movement, a kinaesthetic body that experiences lines of force, intensities as well as sensations. It is 'an art of the muscle sense', as Rudolph Arnheim beautifully and succinctly describes dance; 'it may tend toward pure, non-representational movement' (1966:261–2). In other words, the experience of tactility, of kinaesthesia and affect is bi-directional. In touching and affecting the spaces we move within, we are correspondingly touched and affected.

Conclusion

> As a general rule, I am drawn to the visceral: to those points of connection between emotion, theory and life.
>
> Probyn, 'Dis/connect'

Drawing in these disparate strands, I wish to solidify one persistent theme in part-icular, that of proximity and distance. For example, Merleau-Ponty rather poetically declares in 'Eye and Mind' (1964a:283): 'Through sight, the world is in me and away from me.' We might add as a supplement to this: through touch, the world is with us. It is through haptic experience that we feel engaged in the world, and through affect that the world and its objects touch us. We end, as promised, with some words from Walter Benjamin. An aesthetic body, even a metaphorical one such as Pygmalion's Galatea, needs breath to come alive. The word 'aura' derives from both ancient Latin and Greek, meaning breath or breeze. Continuing the development of proximity and distance, Benjamin asks himself: 'What is aura?' The answer: 'A strange web of time and space; the unique appearance of a distance, however close at hand' (1977:49). Imagine someone's breath on a sensitive part of your skin, say the cheek. It is only air, invisible, intangible, yet one feels the caress or touch of the cheek by the breath. I like to think of some of the things discussed earlier in this chapter, those spaces of affect, as feeling like that breath on the cheek. First, it brings touch and vision, distal and proximal together. It forecloses that ordinary relation between the near and the far, between optical space and haptic space, in painting, sculpture and architecture. 'The medical definition of aura brings touch and vision together through the substance of air or breath or vapour... The sensation was of a cold vapour that seemed to rise through the body to the head', observes Shiff (1997:193). The breath on the cheek. Secondly, because of the porosity of the body, the aura as exhalation or as felt breath on the cheek is symptomatic of what was discussed about spatial seepage between material object and perceiving subject. So 'the aura – like breath – could be both inside and outside, both felt and seen' (ibid.). Benjamin's notion of aura can collapse the haptic and the optic, the near and the far, the extensive and the intensive, while thinking perhaps about new art forms and new technologies.

–6–

Tangible Play, Prosthetic Performance

Play may not be literal, but it is very tangible.

Sutton-Smith *Ambiguity of Play*

Tangents

How is the sensory body in general, and touch in particular, being played, displayed and performed? Or, returning to the words of Jennifer Fisher, 'What would it mean to posit aesthetics as both a performative practice and a morphology of feeling?' (1997:4). The investigation of a morphology of feeling, or a *haptic aesthetics*, can be traced through digital artworks that play with the senses, that aim to achieve a re-engineering or remixing of everyday sensory-somatic experience. This somatosensory remixing and tangible play is enhanced and extended by prostheses and technologies, from videogame consoles, the computer desktop and the human-computer interface, the subject of chapter 7, to more complex and immersive multimedia installations and virtual environments, the focus of this chapter. Discussions of immersive technologies have often been accompanied by emancipatory rhetoric (e.g. Rheingold 1991, 2000; Stone 1995; Hayles 1996). We are familiar with the way that, historically, technologies have altered sensory regimes, modified our modes of attention and distraction, especially within modernism (e.g. Benjamin 1999; Danius 2002). The investigation of such a morphology of feeling, a haptic aesthetic, can be extended to more recent digital artworks and performances that play with the senses. Various technologies permit this, a kind of sensory-somatic sandbox: playing with the digital sensorium, altering habituated perception, and exploring the potential for its disruption. The subtitle of Lorraine's book, *Experiments in Visceral Philosophy* (1999), usefully summarizes the focus of this chapter: the engagement with tactility, the body's prosthetic extensions, and the expansion of the sensorium in performance, enhanced by various technologies of skin, flesh and the senses.

Oliver Grau writes of the history of immersive art, from Roman murals and the beginnings of perspective to contemporary interactive media and virtual reality artworks. Virtual reality, he says, 'describes a space of possibility or impossibility formed by illusionary addresses to the senses' and, by fostering immersion, formulates a 'plausible "as if" that can open up utopian or fantasy spaces' (2003:15). This definition is vague enough to be applicable to several technologies of the senses, not just virtual reality. The opening up of spaces of possibility and the illusionary addresses to the senses – in other words, the expansion of the sensorium through technological means – is consonant with a number of digital artworks and performances, involving artist, audience or participant in various combinations of empathic visceral response or absolute sensory immersion. The transforming power of touch and the technological expansion of the sensorium is the focus of this second foray into haptic aesthetics, illustrating this through using a selection of key digital performances and artworks. Rather than using these works to naively celebrate a politics of transgression or emancipation, Grau's 'utopian or fantasy spaces' or as sites for the production of pure difference, say, the examples are grouped so as to apply experiential insights into the folding of the material body, sensation and expression. Through these examples, 'touch' becomes both experience and expression, mediated through various digital technologies, and experienced by audience or participants viscerally as a result. And 'touch' departs from mere cutaneous surface, to progressively unfold the supporting biological strata of the body that help structure sensation. And further, 'touch' encompasses those visceral, affective states that Benjamin spoke of, the tactile quality of an artwork comparable to being 'hit like a bullet' (1999:231), familiar from the previous chapter. Inevitably, insights into such innovative performances and digital artworks loop back into our quotidian 'way of bearing the body (*hexis*)' (Bourdieu 2000:144, using Aristotle's terminology), or our 'natural attitude' (e.g. Merleau-Ponty 1992:281), which forms the background of an everyday embodied stance.

'Tangible play' therefore considers how the senses of touch are mediated, in fact 'remediated', in manifold ways through digital art installations and performances. 'Remediation', explain Bolter and Grusin, is 'the formal logic by which new media technologies refashion prior media forms' (2000:273). The selected performances often explicitly refer back to another artistic medium, such as painting or sculpture, but utilize new technologies to increase the work's immediacy, viscerality and interactivity. Each new medium refashions older media, so that the laws of Renaissance perspective on the canvas are recreated in computer arts and virtual reality, say. Often this intertextuality between media conventions is transparent, and we glide between webpages, books and films for example without being drawn to the specificities of each particular medium. In some cases we become aware of the particularities of a medium, such as the form of interaction and immediacy in videogames, and this Bolter and Grusin term 'hypermediacy', something that 'privileges fragmentation, indeterminacy, and heterogeneity and ... emphasizes process or performance rather than the finished art object' (Mitchell in Bolter and Grusin 2000:31). The mediations of touch in the performances selected certainly exemplify both remediation and hypermediacy, then, as each of the performances is ongoing, processual, performative and fragmented, utilizing various technologies of screens, skins, prostheses and bodysuits to perform tangible play and reconfigure the sensorium. And I would like to highlight another form of remediation, the way that the senses are cast in unusual and heightened ways through the different technologies involved.

Touch and the sensorium is literally mani*fold* in the sense of folding parts of the body into others, re-mapping the topography of the body and its sensory properties, from one mode of mediation to another. Three digital artists/performers who play with different folds of body and sensation and with different media will be introduced in three corresponding, thematically appropriate 'tangents' or cuts of the body.[1] These tangents also correspond roughly to our previous investigation of haptic aesthetics, 'How the world touches us'. In 'cosmetics: folding skin', then 'prosthetics: folding flesh', and then 'aesthetics: folding body', different approaches to sensation corresponding to three 'tangents' are traced, revealing how touching and feeling are enfolded, each section being illustrated through an appropriate artwork. These works explore, first, the cutaneous touch of the *skin* on the screen, being used as a play of presence at a distance; secondly, the mutability of *flesh* and the viscerality of touch in a live performance setting; and thirdly, the exploration of the aesthetic *body* through a multisensory virtual environment, altering the perception of body schema and the spatial apprehension of 'inside' and 'outside'. A morphology of feeling consistently underlies these physiological components of skin, flesh and body as they unfurl and imbricate each other and, through performance, evoke pain, pleasure or pathos. The nexus of sensate, percept and affect, or what Massumi calls the 'degree-zero of sensation' (2002:112), converge in the moments of performance, as we shall see. But first, another necessary tangent.

On the Art of Folding

The model for the sciences of matter is the 'origami', as the Japanese philosopher might say, or the art of folding.

Deleuze, *The Fold*

At first a play of surfaces, the art of origami folds, refolds and folds again, making depth an effect of innumerable foldings of surfaces. As each fold is folded over again, surface metamorphoses into further surface, accruing depth. It is processual. It continually alters shape and depth. 'Folding deforms and disadjusts. There is no avoiding its power of metamorphosis', remarks Doel (1999:162). It is an effect of folding that the skin becomes flesh, and flesh becomes body: that epidermal surface achieves vascular depth. These progressive layers or strata enfold together the cosmetic morphology of the skin, the transmutability of the flesh, and the fluidity of the body. But these folds of skin, flesh and body are not simply for conceptual convenience. Physiologically too, the complex systems of the body are fabricated from layers of skin, and skin appears early in the transition from ovum to foetus, prior to any organs or structures it will subsequently contain (Tobias 2002:44). As Mark Taylor explains, 'the body is, in effect, nothing but strata of skin in which interiority and exteriority are thoroughly convoluted' (1997:12). Separately, the layers of skin, of flesh or of body can be worked and reworked, offering the potential of continual becoming rather than singular, stable identity. This is my purpose in selecting particular digital performances. But together these morphologies and becomings are a form of conceptual and practical experimentation that explore and expand 'senses' and 'sensibilities'.

Importantly, these morphologies are not limited to the usual masculine techno-fetishism that celebrates technology as a form of transcendence. Rather than *transcendence*, the chosen tangents suggest an *immanence* rooted in the immediacy and presence of corporeal inscription, communication and sensation. Folding is immanent, brings the outside inward, collapses distances, and makes presences felt. For example, outlining an ambiguous distinction between the solidity of the phallus and a female, fluid fleshiness that enfolds it, Luce Irigaray ponders about feminine morphology and folding:

> She is not infinite, but nor is she *one* unit: a letter, a figure, a number in a series, a proper name, single object (of a) sensible world, the simple ideality of an intelligible whole, the entity of a foundation, etc. This incompleteness of her form, her morphology, allows her to become something else at any moment ... if she closes up around the unit(y) of [a] conception, enfolds herself around that one, her desire will harden. *Will become phallic because of this relation to the one?* ... Whereas what comes to pass in the *jouissance* of woman is in excess of it. An indefinite overflowing in which many a becoming could be inscribed. (1991:55, original emphasis)

Although her psychoanalytic language intentionally conflates the fluidity of female desire and arousal with a shifting of form, Irigaray underlines the interplay of stability and singular form (the one, the phallus) and dynamicism and continual becoming (morphology, female desire). The figure of the fold appears as that feminine fluidity of desire which responds to, reshapes around, the stable singularity of the phallus. While this conceptualization polarizes them, limiting the role of the masculine and impulsively celebrating the immanent fluidity of the feminine, the morphology is expressed in the rich visceral language of surfaces, movements, sensations, and arousal. And similar insights are suggestive of interoception, the barely-formed perception and raw sensations of the body's interior. Each of the chosen 'tangents' engages with interoception and the somatic sensations to varying degrees, those indeterminate but unmistakably present feelings of folding, of the interior, a sensorium that entwines inside and outside.

A felt morphology of images and surfaces can be cast in phenomenological language, too. The 'lived body' of Husserlian phenomenology quite literally undergoes a morphology in childhood development. In infancy, the acquaintance of body and self-image, the mirror-stage, treats 'image' in predominantly visual terms. But a parallel morphology of the body in infancy also occurs in touching or being touched, argues Welton (1999:184), through an 'image' formed with felt surfaces. Before separation from the maternal breast, the stage of conceptual differentiation between 'self' and 'non-self', is an interplay of surfaces experienceable by touch as well as sight. Before the formation of the 'body-ego', the subjectively experienced autonomous body, 'we can suggest that touch roots the irreducible *presencing* of the body to itself in the *relation* of the body to that of the mother', argues Welton (1999:184, original emphasis). The boundaries of the body form initially from felt surfaces that continue the process of folding into an entirely differentiated body. While this remains psychoanalytic speculation, not only does it highlight the developmental importance of touch and the fluidity of the relationship between interoception and exteroception, but also indicates the role of touching in intercorporeity and intersubjectivity, the focus of chapter 8. A morphology of feeling in these terms charts the unfolding developmental interface between the body and the world experienced through *skin*, through *flesh*, and through *body*.

Tracking such morphologies of touching and feeling, we proceed through a selection of digital performances that progressively unfold the bodily sensorium, performing those 'experiments in visceral philosophy' (Lorraine 1999). These performances allow for an alterity that cannot be experienced so radically or immersively elsewhere, facilitating an experimentation and play not only with the biological facticity of the body but, in Grosz's words, with its 'functions' and 'identities':

> Alterity is the very possibility and process of embodiment: it conditions but is also a product of the pliability or plasticity of bodies which makes them other than themselves, other than their 'nature', their functions and identities. (Grosz, 1994:209)

The pliability and plasticity (moulding, shaping) of skin, of flesh and of bodies, the morphology of biological material, is one theme that unites these tangents. But to what extent is changing their shape actually changing their nature, as Grosz suggests? This will be addressed as we progress through the visceral experiments. We must be mindful of hollow celebrations of pure alterity or difference here. My selection of examples has tried to circumvent simplistic gender stereotypes, whereby the masculine is transcendent and the feminine immanent, for example. All but one involve principally female artists, and each expresses the deeply felt desire to escape externally imposed conditions of masculine constructions of 'beauty' (*The Reincarnation of Saint Orlan*, 1990–present), of the sense of presence, interaction and the virtual body (*Telematic Dreaming*, 1992), of the limitations of the physiology of the body and the folding of inside and outside (*Stomach Sculpture*, 1992–9) and of the usual insertion of the body in the world and its mode of navigation (*Osmose*, 1995 and *Ephémère*). Although technologically dated, these works seem to distil a form of conceptual experimentation and offer a form of reclamation, if not always a viable permanent alternative, from the usual constructions and limitations of the body. Gail Weiss, for example, argues that the body allows 'new morphological fantasies in order to combat self-imposed limitations on our own body images' (1999:86). In digital performance the possibilities for such morphological fantasies increase. Technologies aid this process, from low-level body modification such as piercing, to fully immersive virtual environments. Suggestive as it is of the forces of desire and needs for sexual expression, Weiss sees the technologically extended body as moving toward 'offering new ways of linking bodies up to one another, expanding their interconnections, and, in so doing, increasing their intercorporeal potentialities' (ibid.:115). Intercorporeality, the relations between bodies, is certainly facilitated through technology, although we examine this concept in terms of therapeutic touching in chapter 8. For now, let us explore some of these potentialities through three tangents, three morphologies of feeling, where folding and unfolding are central to sensation, sensibilities, and corporeality.

Rather than an exhaustive survey of performances or installations that deal explicitly with tactility, the 'tangents' are focused on particular fleshy or visceral experiments that distil a particular morphology of feeling. So the 'tangents' of skin, flesh and body have been limited in the interests of clarity. These include the cosmetic performance-surgery of French artist Orlan, the mechanical and electronic prostheses of Australian performer Stelarc, and the immersive virtual environments of Canadian Char Davies. These examples are, respectively, loosely representative of *skin* (Orlan), of *flesh* (Stelarc), and of the *body* and its extensions (Davies). The typology is of course more of a continuum than a discrete classification, but allows a progressive theorization of different sensory and affective aspects of bodily experience: from the play of cutaneous surfaces to the fluid transport mechanisms of the flesh, and finally the actional and relational nexus of the kinaesthetic body. What is conceptually added for each to become the other? Skin is not just surface but also porosity, where principally the cutaneous tactile sensations are engaged. Flesh becomes more complex, involving the cutaneous as well as the vascular in a combination of muscle tissues, nerve endings and fluid transport. And the body is something more complex still, a field of flesh that includes the somatic senses, proprioception, the vestibular (balance) sense and kinaesthesia in an assemblage that spills out beyond mere skin toward action, expression and extended sensation. The progressive folding process that imbricates skin into flesh into body in this chapter is a conceptual-narrative device, taking us through a haptic aesthetics of the digital realm. It assumes the coextensive implication of tactile or sensory surface (skin) into fleshly feeling and embodied action, collapsing any supposed conceptual difference between thinking and feeling, concept and affect, or even the supposed Cartesian separation of mind and body.

Cosmetics: Folding *Skin*

> Becoming-other unfolds across the surface of bodies.
>
> Doel, *Poststructuralist Geographies*

Explaining the surge in popularity since the 1990s of cosmetic surgery, Ellen Lupton declares: 'Skin is the body part most easily altered by human beings, from circumcision and scarification to cosmetics and hair removal' (2002:64). On the surface, literally, the most accessible form of morphology is cosmetic surgery, the nipping, tucking and folding used for purely aesthetic reasons, also known as aesthetic surgery.[2] The phrase 'aesthetic surgery' is befitting. Against the increasing normalization of such practices, argues Kathryn Pauly Morgan, this attempt at self-transcendence escapes the rigid, programmatic 'docile body' (1998:332), borrowing Foucault's terminology, to celebrate skin, body and flesh as pure potential, as literally 'raw' material. Like Kathy Davis' view of cosmetic surgery as a negotiation of bodily agency within a framework of controlling cultural discourses concerning taste, style and beauty (1995), Morgan wishes to reclaim an ideological purpose in pursuing cosmetic surgery, to demonstrate that '*all* bodies are dialectically created artefacts' (1998:340). Skin is the surface where these dialectical forces are negotiated and inscribed, where for Westernized women 'dualities such as submission and resistance, excess and control' are played out (Farber 2006:247).

The surgeon's craft is often likened not to the feminine skill of the seamstress, sewing and suturing layers of fleshy fabric, but to the more masculine skill of the sculptor. We have previously encountered Herder's treatise on *Sculpture* (2002 [1778]), in German *Plastik*, the shaping of material according to dominant masculine classical ideas of form and beauty. Herder returns to the story of Pygmalion, who crafts the statue of perfect female beauty, Galatea, in Ovid's *Metamorphoses*. But this sculptural practice of perfecting female beauty by a male sculptor retains its resonance even now through aesthetic surgery. 'Many surgeons promote themselves as sculptors who fashion human flesh to create a body, which mimics the so-called perfect human form', confirms artist Leora Farber (2006:248). The surgeon as both sculptor and seamstress is explored in her videowork *Four Minor Renovations* (2000), which uses slow-motion, documentary-style footage to show the surgeon's hands 'cutting, stretching and stitching flesh' (2006:248), rendering usually hidden invasive procedures to the viewer on-screen. Aesthetic surgery as a visible, performed process is no longer limited to classical representations of idealized female beauty, realized in perfected forms of marble, stone or clay. Instead, the visible morphology of skin sculpture, exposing its underlying messy-fleshiness, becomes shown as process and performance. Those who approach the skin on-screen, in this way, respond with both horror and fascination.

From Skin to Screen: Orlan

Horror and fascination: these adjectives would suit the French performance artist Orlan, whose self-consciously staged performance-surgery demonstrates this ideological critique, and like Farber's work, additionally shows the interplay of skin-surface and screen-surface. These events almost hyperbolically celebrate technologies of skin reshaping and reconstruction in the ongoing construction of female beauty. Her skin undergoes almost continual modification, there being no discrete 'before' and 'after' photographs, as on the walls of a cosmetic-surgery practice, that might show a closure of figuration. She returns periodically to the theatre (simultaneously an operating theatre and site of performance), always to morph some more. The ongoing nature of her aesthetic performance-surgery means that, in the words of O'Bryan, Orlan becomes 'a live figure who unceasingly morphs into other forms of the same live figure' (1999:50).

One series of operations is entitled *The Reincarnation of Saint Orlan* (1990–present), the 'reincarnation' being the continual morphology of skin and flesh. It is what Grosz (1994) terms the 'incomplete body', in a state of perpetual becoming. The photographs shown alongside the exhibition are computer composites that place Orlan in poses familiar to historians of art, slyly alluding to classical depictions of feminine beauty by digitally superimposing ideals of beauty (Leonardo's *Mona Lisa*, Botticelli's *Venus* for example, themselves composites of idealized masculine conceptions of female beauty) onto Orlan's face before surgery. These photographic composites are 'as destabilized, transparent, and unfixed as her body seems to be (always in the process of) becoming', remarks O'Bryan (1999:51). They superimpose the fantastical over the material, layers of distortion over her physiognomy. How can there be a discrete 'before' and 'after' in this perpetually altering projection of fantasies of beauty upon her own elastic, morphing skin? Orlan herself questions the ideal of beauty, but also the lengths people go to achieve it. 'My work is not a stand against cosmetic surgery,' she declares, 'but against the standards of beauty, against the dictates of a dominant ideology that impresses itself more and more on feminine ... flesh' (in O'Bryan, 1997:52). Her comments resonate with Morgan's cited earlier on the dialectical nature of the construction of beauty and the ability to reclaim women's willing subjection to the knife as a continually morphing form of resistance. Not only is the actual skin continually being reshaped, but also the modes of mediation continually morph. From skin to screen the performance becomes distributed, being photographed, televised, video-taped and video-conferenced into public galleries. Then back to skin again, the superimposition of idealized beauty onto actual skin surface, as she returns to the aesthetic performance-surgery. Likewise, the digitally altered photographs extend the skin-surface and screen-surface morphology by revealing the gap between 'what is made by the body-machine' and 'what is made by the computer-machine', as Orlan herself distinguishes (1996:90). The morphology of the organic and the machinic becomes part of her aesthetic in these distributed performances, where actual jars of blood and body fat accompany the photographs in the performance.

So what of the surgery as performance? The surgeon's initial *inscriptions*, the planning and marking out by pen on the skin, are quickly replaced by *incisions*, incisions 'which yield lines of blood, open folds in the flesh, create shapes, even forms which exist for moments when the face is detached – disembodied to be reformulated' observes Moos (1996:70). The moments of incision, displayed on screen from the operating theatre, have an immediate, visceral effect on the audience. Orlan herself is anaesthetized with a spinal tap, remaining fully conscious and aware of incisions, of cutaneous foldings, but unable to feel them. The cutaneous surface of skin being particularly sensitive to touch, seeing the numb inertness of Orlan's skin undergoing cutting and reshaping leads to an uncanny feeling of dissociation in both spectator and performer. We feel more than she does, literally, because of her anaesthetized state. But there is something celebratory in her performance of inscription and re-inscription, where the memory of previous alterations is decorated over like a palimpsest. Dressing-up and oral readings are part of the event. Before her performance-operations she often quotes from the Lacanian psychoanalyst Eugenie Lemoine-Luccioni, who in *La Robe* (1983) rather naively discourses on the nature of skin:

> Skin is deceiving … in life, one only has one's skin … there is a bad exchange in human relations because one never is what one has … I have the skin of an angel, but I am a jackal … the skin of a crocodile, but I am a puppy, the skin of a black person, but I am white, the skin of a woman, but I am a man; I never have the skin of what I am. There is no exception to the rule because I am never what I have.

Rather than dwelling on this potentially dangerous misconception of skin and identity politics, naive wishes that help forge an attitude to cosmetic surgery as yet another form of consumption, reading this aloud is a preparatory element of Orlan's performance. While Orlan is reading Lemoine-Luccioni's inscription her skin has already been inscribed by the surgical marker pen, those delineations of her future physiognomy that serve as guides for the surgeon's actual incisions. This whole performance she calls 'Carnal Art' (*l'Art Charnel*), distinguishing it from the tradition of Body Art mainly from the 1960s, as Barbara Rose details (1993:101). Orlan describes it herself: 'Carnal Art is not interested in the plastic-surgery result, but in the process of surgery, the spectacle and discourse of the modified body which has become the place of a public debate' (Orlan, 2000). Yet it is not her *body* in actuality that undergoes a morphology, but her surface layers, 'at the surface of the body, at its interface with things' as Massumi (2002:25) describes skin. The surface surgical spectacles are 'carnal' in two senses. First, while advertisements and websites promoting cosmetic surgery stress the clinical neatness of their surgical procedures and downplay the possibility of scarring, Orlan's reconfiguring of skin exteriority as a live performance reveals glimpses of the fleshy, messy dermis beneath the epidermis, the brutishly carnal beneath the clinical aesthetic. Unlike the videogame *The Sims*, changing skin features is not as simple as clicking, dragging and dropping.[3] Secondly, the carnality of the audience is invoked in being party to the fleshy, visceral, distributed reception of the performance (the screens, the blood, the fat in jars, the readings). Abject bodily fluids, usually hidden discretely from view, again point to the messy vascularity, the dermis behind the folds and flaps of epidermis. This is a different kind of empathy (*Einfühlung*) than that of the previous chapter on aesthetic experience. Instead, the performance engages directly with bodily sensations, so that as 'reincarnation' of both Orlan and her audience, she says, it is a performance 'of blood' which does 'something bodily' to both performer and spectator (1996:91). Likewise, as we progress, the address to both performers and audience in the various artworks will become progressively more embodied, literally re-incarnated as we progress through the tangents of skin, flesh and finally the body.

Exteriority speaks to exteriority, from skin-surface to screen-surfaces, in the case of Orlan. But 'skin', apart from being superficially transformed and aesthetically adorned, remains a surface until folded and refolded. Then, becoming fleshy, it accrues depth. Orlan's multi-layered physiognomic refigurations go toward the identification of exterior with surface, and then surface into flesh. Although the skin-screen analogy is literally superficial, by watching the performance the audience glimpses the bloody dermis underneath. Therein lies the carnality. Live, on screen. From her face to in our face. As one reaction to the superficial male construction of female beauty, which encourages the warping and folding of skin surface, Orlan instead follows the nightmare reiterative logic of constant morphology, attempting literally to incarnate the masculine construct of the feminine ideal. An asymptotic exercise, it can never be fully realized. And within this process of skin-screen morphology, we are glimpsing and (almost) grasping what lies beneath. Associating morphology and carnality within a different context of feminine desire and identity, Irigaray rather cryptically pronounces: 'A *morphé* in continual gestation. Movements ceaselessly reshaping this incarnation' (1985:193). An apt description of Orlan's aesthetic performance-surgery in constant process, perhaps, the fluid morphologies of unconscious desires and superficial appearances never quite attaining full actualization. Now, our movement, from folding of skin to the folding of flesh, and toward different incarnations.

Prosthetics: Folding *Flesh*

[I]f you place the object on the *organ* it is not perceived, here if you place it on the flesh it *is* perceived; therefore flesh is not the organ but the *medium* of touch.

Aristotle, *De Anima* 423b

What is added to skin to make flesh? Both figuratively and physiologically? Perhaps it is a short etymological and conceptual distance between the 'vascular' and the 'visceral'. The 'visceral' relates to the internal organs, our interoception arising from the grouping of sensations deriving from nerve endings situated there. To talk of 'visceral reactions' or 'gut feelings' signifies deep inward feelings rather than intellect. The 'vascular' being the nerve-endings, fibres, veins and fluid transport mechanisms of the dermis, the fleshy skin that underlies and supports the surface skin, epidermis. As alluded to previously, the vascular, carnal dermis operates underneath the porous epidermis, 'rather as structural filaments [*des nervures*], as the axes of a corporeal system of activity and passivity' explains Merleau-Ponty (1964a:184), allied perhaps to that function of the homeostatic maintenance of interiority and exteriority. Deceptively, skin is both dead and alive. The composition of the dermis, consisting of nerve cells, lymph and sweat glands, hair follicles, oxygenated blood vessels and collagen-producing fibroblasts (e.g. Tobias 2002:45) entails a level of activity supportive of the epidermis. Although porous, the epidermis is mostly passive and 'consists of strata of cells that migrate towards the surface, where they compact into a layer of dead material' (ibid.:31), wherein lies its protective function. Appropriately enough, flesh arises for Irigaray in the sense that it is a 'fleshy layering' (1985:155), progressive strata or folds of skin, a theoretical correlate to Taylor's (1997) physiological explanation, smoothing out the relationship between skin and flesh. If Orlan's performance-surgery dealt predominantly with the topologies of skin surface, re-mapping and folding in order to link with the screen surface, the dermis that lies beneath the epidermis offers more vascular, more carnal opportunities for reconfigurability. Irigaray's notion of fleshy layering neatly fits the model of origami. Even if biologically not so neat, the relationship between skin and flesh can be intuitively grasped as a folding, the implication of cutaneous sensation (through skin) and interoception (through flesh). In everyday experience we rarely differentiate between skin and flesh, since – as Aristotle suggested – our embodied experience of touch occurs through the medium of flesh. As either precise cutaneous sensations on the skin surface, or less distinct sensations of contact and manipulation arising from muscular pressure and proprioception for example, tactility arises from a combination of these.

But when Vasseleu describes the 'transmutability of flesh' (1998:114), the idea of 'flesh' is not just skin, and not quite body. It involves fluid viscerality: like the dermis perhaps, something bloody, mucous, porous. Rather than the individuation of a body-subject that vision and distance implies, Tamsin Lorraine identifies the especially feminine yearning for an 'immanent, horizontal, intersubjective communication' (1999:103), a communicative state reminiscent of the womb. Skin offers cutaneous tactility. But it is the underlying flesh – with its chemical communication, muscular sensations and vascular transport – that offers deeper, more visceral feelings. So here we consider the morphology and extensions of the flesh unfolding and embracing a digital medium, being *prosthetic* flesh. To transmute from state to state, to perform morphology, common to all states of flesh is its radical, organic, porous, vascular reconfigurability. Flesh or meat, that 'zone of indiscernability' that Deleuze describes of Bacon's work: becoming-animal (2003:59), something prepersonal, neither quite subject nor quite object. This sense of flesh underlies the flesh/meat dichotomy that is absent in other non-Anglophone languages. *Fleisch* (German) and *la chair* (French) both communicate within a single word the sense of tender human flesh as well as of animal, edible meat. Flesh therefore exists as an undifferentiated yet material medium of morphological transformation, through which alterity may be enfolded.

Fractal Flesh: *Stelarc*

If Orlan is an example of the communication with and modification of *skin*, then the Australian performance artist Stelarc is an example of the transfiguration of *flesh*, something based on both internal and external physiology. His illustrious performance career commences with flesh, a series of hangings from flesh-hooks (1976–1989) that culminated in being suspended between two buildings in New York. The police intervened and stopped the performance after twelve minutes, the crowds beneath reacting viscerally to the suspension above them. His naked body hung from hooks, exposing its elastic fleshiness. The flesh extrudes, and in an interview he described how his 'skin squeaks' when hanging (*Tx: Pandaemonium*, 1995). Other performances involve prosthetic enhancements to the body, the interface of body and technology, and later playing with kinaesthetic elements that become choreographed into his own body movements. Throughout his increasingly technologically inventive and visceral performances, he repeatedly remarks on the limitations of our bodily physiology. For instance:

> Our actions and ideas are essentially determined by our physiology. We are at the limits of philosophy, not only because we are at the limits of language. Philosophy is fundamentally grounded in our physiology. (Stelarc, 1998:117)

If the body is obsolete, the flesh is to be celebrated, manipulated, metamorphosed. Continual translations and transductions, in fact, between flesh and data. He takes the prosthetic extension of bodily physiology and fleshy materiality into a staged theatrical event, allowing interaction and feedback directly into those prostheses from the audience and over the internet, including touchscreens. What results is often dramatic, and especially in *Fractal Flesh* (1995–96) and *Stomach Sculpture* (1992–99), absolutely visceral. Early versions of new works are often folded into other performances with established devices, so for example his *Third Hand* prosthesis (1990–95), an involuntary extension of his own hand, becomes part of the *Stimbod* and *Fractal Flesh* performances. Electrodes placed in certain specific muscle locations trigger movements in the prosthetic hand. This additional hand, attached to his forearm, also includes 'a tactile feedback system for a "sense of touch"' (Stelarc, 1991:593). *Fractal Flesh* involved plugging himself into muscle-stimulation circuitry, controlled by audience members. But what kind of touch is this? Not the straightforward cutaneous touch derived from pressure-sensitive mechanoreceptors on the skin, but proprioception, the sense of the muscles and ligaments, their position and movement in space. In Stelarc's case, proprioception is induced by audience gestures. By touching a segment of his body on a touchscreen, that muscular area is stimulated by an electric current. Involuntary muscular contractions result, so that an involuntary choreography is performed onstage. Watching him dance, with jerky spasmodic movements and accompanying glitchy electronic music, the effect is startling. In his dancing alongside a giant robotic arm there is a kind of kinaesthetic synergy between fleshy and machinic arms. Another incarnation of this performance, hooked up to the internet, the muscle-stimulation effects become more random and 'proprioception becomes net-induced', he explains (in Dery, 1996). Figuratively, as skin folds into flesh, a corresponding folding of sensation occurs, so that cutaneous tactility folds into proprioception. According to Massumi, that is:

> Tactility is the sensibility of the skin as surface of contact between the perceiving subject and the perceived object. Proprioception folds tactility into the body, enveloping the skin's contact with the external world in a dimension of medium depth: between epidermis and viscera... This asubjective and non-objective medium depth is one of the strata proper to the corporeal; it is a dimension of the *flesh*. (2002:58–9, original emphasis)

Plugging in to his flesh, the digital-machinic is inserted into the organic-vascular flesh, extending 'feeling' and 'touch' by infusing his proprioceptive sensations with an unpredictable element. In a pre-performance interview with Mark Dery, Stelarc explained the mechanics of *Fractal Flesh*:

> [We] predetermined that the biceps, for example, are going to be 'hot spots,' so if you touch or click those spots on the computer image of the body, it moves accordingly, displaying a simulation of the movement. Simultaneously, the system is sending signals to the muscle-stimulation circuitry, which initiates a channel of stimulation – zero to 60 volts, depending on the intensity of the stimulation I preset. That goes through electrodes on the skin to the nerve endings in the muscles, and the body moves accordingly. (in Dery, 1996)

Through technologies, through prosthetic extension, Stelarc performs vascular, fleshy experiments on the assumed fixity of the body. Baraibar questions such fixity, the 'rigidly defined, self-enveloped, bounded form that culminates in the production of an all too narrow economy of socially acceptable body projects' (1999:164).

Stelarc performs his body projects through a hybridized, technologized bodily aesthetic to expand the limits of this fixity, to literally perform metamorphosis. Stelarc's body is therefore mutable, the site of interchange between the organic and the machinic, blurring the distinction between where fleshy body ends and digital prosthesis begins. Simultaneously a sensory prosthesis, as in *Third Hand* and especially the whole-body *Fractal Flesh*, there is a double articulation whereby the habitual sense of one's bounded, proprioceptive body, self-directed and self-willed, maps onto an externally controlled body that dances and flexes according to involuntary impulses.

Stelarc's output has been prodigious, and later works such as *Exoskeleton: Event for Extended Body and Walking Machine* (1998–2004), and *Muscle Machine* (débuted in 2003), a self-styled 'motion prosthesis' with 'fluidic muscle actuators' (Stelarc 2003), are impressive in their kinaesthetic complexity and scope. But in a more directly visceral and physiological approach, *Stomach Sculpture* engages explicitly with his own flesh, dealing with internal body modification (inside) and its visibility (outside). Sensation folds again, as the proprioceptive sensations explored in *Fractal Flesh* become deeper, explicitly visceral sensation. In this piece, constructed for the third Sculptural Biennale in Melbourne, a mechanical sculpture with a camera probe proceeds via his mouth to his stomach, remaining simultaneously separated from him by the optical distance of display, as the interior space of his body is projected to the outside world on a screen. The sculpture itself he describes as a primitive beeping machine, a 'domed capsule shell containing a worm-screw and link-mechanism' (1994) that is inserted into the body by swallowing, guided by a flexible control cable with a control box that remains outside the body. Once the sculpture is inserted the stomach inflates with an endoscope, and excess body fluids are extracted. The control cable interfaces with the capsule, servomotors are activated, and the capsule unfolds within his stomach cavity into three sections emitting various lights and sounds. He describes it thus:

> Here technology invades and functions within the body, not as a prosthetic replacement for some medical necessity, but through artistic choice, as an aesthetic adornment. The hollow body becomes a host, not for a self, but simply for a sculpture – an alien, electronic object moving, flashing and beeping in a wet and vulnerable internal environment. The body reclines, pacified to accept the implant, but a machine mechanism dances within. (1994)

Stelarc describes the sculpture not as a prosthetic replacement of some organ or malfunctioning body part, but as an 'aesthetic adornment' within a 'hollow body' (1994). A hollow body is anaesthetized, emptied out of messy significance, a hybrid that connects its fleshiness to various prosthetics and has no meaningful distinctions between public, private and physiological spaces. His hollow body becomes an unusual enclosure for a metallic sculpture, which bleeps and flashes in a fleshy cavity, relaying images from inside the body to a public screen. Both *Fractal Flesh* and *Stomach Sculpture* seem to be an engagement with the messy tenderness of the flesh, contrasting the surgical metal precision of an artificial device with the chaotic, organic body and its excess fluids, chemically-induced desires and nervous palpitations. As performance it is felt as both visual and visceral, the audience's cathartic response dealing immediately with the messiness of flesh and the overcoming of organic-machinic boundaries. The *si*mulation and, in *Third Hand* and *Stimbod*, *stim*ulation of flesh produces the spectacle of its electro-vascular complexity and reconfigurability, seemingly from a few electro-mechanical rules and operations.

Other works are more direct exemplars of 'prosthesis', literally 'putting forward' or 'extension'. Greek *prosthenos*, as Stone (1995:12) reminds us, being the root; an assemblage of human-fleshy-machinic interaction. In this sense, *Stomach Sculpture* is clearly a prosthesis. Wills furthers the connection of prosthesis to alterity. 'By means of prosthesis the relation to the other becomes precisely and necessarily a relation to otherness, the otherness, for example, of artificiality attached to or found within the natural' (1995:44). Stelarc's great prosthetic virtue is not simply to extend himself through technology, then, but conversely to utilize his hollow body as receptacle, his flesh as test-tube, connecting at the middle depth of vascularity and viscerality to a device from outside. He uses technologies to actualize the artificial within the natural, to realize an aesthetic body in the Aristotelian sense: a feeling, proprioceptive, kinaesthetic body. Involuntary choreography, technological prosthesis. Just to see – but more importantly, to *feel* – the effects. From the prosthetics of glove, cane, stomach sculpture or third hand, next we consider a prosthetic sensorium.

Aesthetics: Folding Body

> The body is the first locus of intentionality, as pure presence to the world and openness upon its possibilities.
>
> Young, *Throwing Like a Girl*

It is all very well being a tactile surface, to sense an outside as opposed to an inside (skin). Or to be vascular fleshy objects, responding to electro-muscular stimulation (flesh). Folding in the cutaneous touch of the skin surface into the more visceral tactile-kinesic sense of the muscles and flesh, we fold again. This section deals with the 'felt' or sensorimotor body and the expansion of the sensorium. Our ponderous, weighty corporeality has its own distinct 'feel'. Iris Marion Young is interested in such questions, the 'tactile, motile, weighted, painful and pleasurable experience of an embodied subject', and additionally 'how this subject reaches out with and through this body; and how this subject feels about its embodiment' (1990:14). One way of exploring these questions is to address the sensory order, to perform other 'felt' phenomenologies. The techniques and technologies of immersion that occur in virtual reality directly address the sensorium, offering alternative ways of sensing the body and its relations to the outside. Through the use of virtual reality technologies, visceral experimentation can occur, playing with morphologies of feeling.

The sensorium, the sum of an organism's perception, becomes broadened, altered, and synergic with what Goldstein terms the 'motorium' (1995:124). Motility helps bind and cohere sensory experience, helps disclose a 'world' to us, as Merleau-Ponty argues (1992:137;234), and the body is already 'virtual', a set of possible actions that lurches and spills away from the 'real' body in the digital realm. So a definition of virtual reality (VR) should both involve the sensory and the motor and pose a virtual sensorium; and experiments in visceral philosophy can be performed with VR equipment to explore an interactive, continuous virtual world, a virtual environment (VE). Media theorist Achim Bühl describes VR as creating a man-machine interface 'that engages several human senses simultaneously, ... giving the user the impression that the computer environment is actually real' (in Jütte 2005:327). The second half of the definition is problematic. But the engagement of the senses is crucial, and the history of VR acknowledges this directly. In 1955 Morton Heilig imagined an 'Experience Theater' that addressed the five senses, immersing the viewer through multi-sensory onscreen activity (Heilig 1998). Around this time he also wrote of the 'Cinema of the Future', a curved screen that fully encompassed the entire visual field and which also addressed the senses of taste, smell and touch (Heilig 1992). In 1962 a prototype of this vision was built dubbed the Sensorama, a cabinet that involved projecting short films in stereoscopic 3D, with a filmtrack that dealt with sound, triggered aromas and even produced the sensation of wind. Predating digital computing, the Sensorama was a strictly mechanical and non-interactive device, finding its home in amusement arcades. According to Grau, Heilig acknowledged the artistic possibilities of such a device, since 'an artist's powers of expression would benefit considerably through knowledge of the human sensory apparatus and perception – a simple idea, yet remarkable for the period' (2003:157). This seems plausible considering bold advances in the psychology of perception would only take place subsequently, for example Gibson's theory of ecological perception (e.g. 1968; 1979). In 1968, the move from mechanical devices to digital technologies of sensory immersion took place in the first head-mounted display (HMD) devices of the flight-simulation pioneer Ivan Sutherland (see e.g. Hillis 1999), the interactive technology we most readily associate with VR.

Despite Bühl's assertion earlier that the user experiences a virtual world as 'actually real', there is no need for absolute verisimilitude, and participants bring their own somatic senses and states of rest, pain or pressure to the installation. The question therefore becomes how to integrate these haptic sensations into virtual reality. As will be established more concretely in the following chapter on haptic technologies, there is a correlation between touch and the feeling of presence, and this extends to VR:

> Virtual reality is never without touch since a person is always feeling the floor, the force
> of gravity... Without integration, touch degrades presence. With integration, touch is
> the most dominant form of presence ... so the moral is [that] haptics is the royal road to
> credibility, to presence in VR. (Bricken, in Lauria 2000)

While presence may be enhanced through technologies such as haptics, this need
not require complete sensory immersion. Interactions between bodies and technologies admit degrees of immersion, and while VR installations increasingly address
tactility through 'powergloves' or 'cybergloves', for example, touching objects and
people can be achieved in numerous ways in virtual environments.

There are numerous examples of analogue and digital performance pieces that
complicate this position, that explore levels of virtuality of the body. Briefly, one
such is Paul Sermon's *Telematic Dreaming* (1992), which placed Susan Kozel, a
dancer, with cameras and screens in one bedroom, and allowed an audience member
to interact in another. A videoconference link produced the impression that two
people, Kozel and an audience member, were sharing the same virtual bed. As Jütte
describes the effect, as spectators 'we see their eyes meet and their hands reach out in
search of each other, exactly as though they were together in a real space' (2005:327).
Touching without touching. Intimacy while remaining separated. The separate beds
became performance spaces, and although being and moving alone, Kozel saw the
virtual interaction on her monitor. She invested emotionally in her screen presence,
watching her virtual interactions as an avatar. Although purely optical, there was
indubitably a play with telepresence (the sense of presence at a distance) where
the setting of the bed fostered a simultaneous sense of intimacy and distance. The
status of 'real' and 'virtual' body becomes elided, since attacks or violations that
Kozel saw on the screen caused her to feel distance, but a tender, almost sexual
encounter made her closely identify with her on-screen body and human interaction
was stripped down to 'touch, trust, vulnerability' (Kozel 2005:440). The prolonged
nature of the installation, lasting for four weeks, meant constant reminders of the
body resurfaced due to pain, cramps and stiffness. Despite her own performance
being increasingly based on her movements as shown on the screen, her body came
through, reasserted itself:

> The more I ventured into the visual, virtual world the more my non-virtual body called
> attention to itself like an anchor, like ballast. I seemed to be pulled between the two
> extremes of an imaginary spectrum: the abjection of flesh and the sanitization of
> technology. (ibid.:441)

What Kozel experienced in that early interactive performance was a tension
between the virtual and the visceral, a tension present within any digital performance,
but to variously significant degrees in the case studies selected here. Tellingly Kozel
became convinced that 'the virtual body is entwined with the fleshly body', that the

experience was one of 'extending my body, not losing or substituting it' (ibid.:443). This form of phenomenological experimentation with the perceived boundaries of the body is what links phenomenological discussions of interoception and the somatic senses from before with the morphologies of feeling, the notions of intimacy and presence through technology, that have characterized the tangents here. This all comes together in the work of Char Davies.

The Thickening of Sensation: Char Davies

While there are numerous examples of the distributed multisensory body in performance, one artist who directly explores the possibilities of the digital sensorium and the limits of the virtual body is Char Davies.[4] Her interactive installation *Osmose* was exhibited initially at the *Musée D'art Contemporain de Montréal* in 1995, and *Éphémère* followed at the National Gallery of Canada in 1998. The virtual environment of *Osmose* is a full-body immersion with an unusual navigation system, involving a scuba-like bodysuit that responds to expansion of the diaphragm and tilt of the body. A head-mounted display renders a three-dimensional space with semi-transparent objects, and sounds of fluids are dynamically generated. Davies' preferred term for participants in these installations is 'immersant', because the combined effect is to alter the sensorium through immersion, being the digital equivalent of scuba-diving or a flotation tank, and hence to experiment with the phenomenology of the felt body. The immersant proceeds buoyantly through a series of beautifully rendered, multisensory worlds. Meanwhile, gallery visitors can watch the backlit silhouette of the immersant on a screen, a moving shadow with trailing wires, and the graphical rendering through the head-mounted display is reproduced on nearby monitors. In a review of *Éphémère*, which employs a navigation system similar to that of *Osmose*, Jennifer Fisher watches one immersant's silhouette and notes: 'the kinesthetic aspect of the haptic comes into play as the gestures of the person – hands open like antennae or grasped protectively before the body – can be studied' (1999:53).

Rather than the audience's third-person spectatorship of the aesthetic surgery of Orlan, or the fleshy-machinic prosthesis of Stelarc, or even a straightforward celebration of cutaneous touch or kinaesthesia, these Davies works are fully immersive multisensory worlds felt from a first-person perspective, altering the perceived boundaries of one's body and the realm of possible actions. It shifts the somatosensory context, and alters the immersant's sensibility. Fisher argues that this work has implications for a haptic aesthetics, impacting 'the sensational and relational aspects of touch, weight, balance, gesture and movement' (ibid.). Significantly, the hands are free. With pressure sensors on the vest, and vestibular sensors responding to tilt of the spinal axis, there are no tactile gloves. Nonetheless, this bodysuit is a haptic interface encouraging a full-body mode of navigation. Inhaling, you ascend;

exhaling, you sink. Leaning forward, one moves in that direction. And although a graphically intensive world is rendered, the work engages effectively with non-visual sensations, further implicating (that is, folding) sensations into the body of the immersant.

Trying to recreate the sensations of learning to scuba dive in the Caribbean (2001, personal communication), a self-described epiphany inspired Davies' painting and later VR installations. She came to believe, like the psychoanalytic and phenomenologically-influenced writer Gaston Bachelard, that the body's changing relationship to space was capable of 'transfiguring the participant' (Davies in Pesce, 2000:267). Fostering a fluid, dynamic sensory ambiguity in her installations she seeks to actualize Bachelard's belief that

> [by] changing space, by leaving the space of one's usual sensibilities, one enters into communication with a space that is psychically innovating. For we do not change place, we change our nature. (Bachelard 1994:206)

Davies' installations offer not only different sensibilities but also an altered sensorium. After experimenting with painting, her explorations with VR as an artistic medium employ a painterly aesthetic to an ongoing, interactive, immersive, multisensory virtual environment. Both *Osmose* and *Éphémère* attempt to blur boundaries between fluid environment and 'felt' bodily self. As Stone describes within a different context, what Davies intends is an 'elaboration and amplification of spatialization and presence' (1995:90) through this medium. An ephemeral, dynamic aesthetic that celebrates the ambiguity of interior and exterior, a fluid virtual environment involving transparent objects, the result is unnerving. 'There is a buoyant sense of movement in a world of partially dematerialized objects,' describes Fisher, who continues: 'Maneuvering beyond tangible forms, one enters a realm of affect that evokes an out-of-body experience' (1999:54). Adapting to this departure from habituated perception, of our usual sensibilities, can be an almost overwhelmingly affecting experience, as some comments by immersants reveal.

Once immersed in *Osmose* there is a fragmented narrative of sorts, each world osmotically transforming into the next. A three-dimensional Cartesian grid functions as ante-room and orientation space, and after the first few breaths with the unusual interface the grid recedes to reveal a forest clearing. From this space twelve other 'world-spaces' can be accessed, each focusing on a particular natural feature. Such features from the forest clearing that the immersant can visit include a Pond, a Tree (with a Leaf showing the osmotic fluid transport systems within), a Subterranean Earth, a Forest and an Abyss. These are all experienceable as three-dimensional, semitransparent worlds. Above them is another world, Text, that reproduces quotations from relevant texts on nature, technology and embodiment, and fragments from the artist herself, represented as two-dimensional text within a three-dimensional world that can be navigated around. Below the nature-based worlds is another textual level,

Code, which similarly represents the actual code used in the software. The textual levels work as parentheses, sandwiching the semi-realistic representations of nature in osmotic worlds.

The sense of immersion and bodily ambiguity is heightened through the production of a sense of enveloping, viscous space, 'thick' with sensation (see also Merleau-Ponty 1992:204). For example, Vivian Sobchack makes the distinction between 'thin' and 'thick' technological space in discussing cinema. The 'thin space of the machine' is transformed into a 'thickened and concrete world', she argues (in Stone 1991:115). Paradoxically, a thickened space of sensation is often achieved at the expense of the grounded sense of tactility that usually affirms the body's felt position in space. Dot Tuer maintains that the sense of immersion is actually enhanced in *Osmose* through the disconnection of actual bodily touch from the thickened, multi-sensory space of the installation:

> Unlike cinema, in which the audience sits in [a] darkened theater, their bodies grounded in the physical world, and watches the flickering projections of light on a screen, the enclosure of the self in a simulacrum is complete. Deprived of a tactile relationship to the outside world, one loses a perception of one's body as separate from the artificial environment it inhabits. (Tuer 1998)

Despite the almost hermetic illusion of sensory immersion in the work, the immersant is never completely cut off from the physical grounding of sensation, since the bodysuit and head-mounted display (HMD) constrain the actual body, have weight and constrict action. Nevertheless, the illusion of immersion is convincing enough, and an alternative sensibility results, a different morphology of feeling. The unusual mixture of natural imagery made fluid and ethereal makes *Osmose* 'both a solid mineral and a fluid intangible sphere, a non-Cartesian space', writes Grau (2003:195), involving a 'physically intimate synthesis of the technical and the organic' (ibid.:198) through the unusual interface. Unlike mimetic or hyper-representational VR that uses what Tikka describes as a 'joystick-phallus' (1994) to navigate, Davies wanted to change what the eye would see, make it non-mimetic, and alter the mode of navigation within this differently realized world. So the diaphragm and bodysuit promotes 'an embodying interface which tracks breath and shifting balance, grounding the immersive experience on the participant's own body' as Davies expresses it (2000). Tuer describes this sense of fluid immersion after experiencing the similar interface of *Ephémère*. 'Rather than experiencing the sensation of penetrating a mimetic realm,' she comments, 'one is gently suspended, floating and sinking in rhythm with the inhaling and exhaling of one's own breath' (1998). The worlds of *Ephémère* include organs of the body, bones and, following neatly from our discussions of fleshiness and vascularity, the circulatory system. Even navigation between different areas of the virtual environment occurs without abruptness as 'osmotic transitions', according to Grau (2003:195).

Reconfiguring of the Sensorium

Attempting to address the thorny question of where the body is in cyberspace, Sobchack (1987) criticizes the electronic space of the computer and video screen, describing it as 'a phenomenological structure of sensual and psychological experience that seems to belong to no-body' (in Stone 1991:114). But in a multidimensional, multisensory virtual space, being an immersant rather than a spectator, the body reappears through movement and action: 'it is the quality of direct physical and kinaesthetic engagement, the enrolling of hapticity in the service of both the drama and the dramatic' as Stone (ibid.:106) succinctly describes. The unusual interface and mode of navigation, and the sense of the thickness of an enveloping, de-solidified space, all contribute toward what Deikman calls the 'de-habituation of perception' (in Davies, 1998). This could be couched in terms of affect, the disordering of sensation; or as a disruption to the 'natural attitude' in phenomenological terms. Departing from the space of our usual sensibilities, the immersive space of *Osmose*, thinks Davies, provides

> a sense of bodily spatial envelopment, combined with virtuality and apparent three-dimensionality, as well as feelings of disembodiment with embodiment (given the use of an embodying interface), create an experiential context that is very different from the world of our habitual perceptions and behaviour. (1998)

It works as an alternative somatosensory context to explore our embodied consciousness in a thick, enveloping space of sensation where boundaries between inner and outer, mind and body, are immediately experienced as less distinct. As Hayles discusses in the context of another VR installation, Brenda Laurel and Rachel Strickland's *Placeholder* (1994), the ambiguous body and the subtle sensorium can be potentially either disorientating or liberating for the participant:

> When a user enters a VR simulation, body boundaries become ambiguous. Body motions affect what happens in the simulation, so that one is and is not present in the body and the simulation. The body marks one kind of presence; the point of view, or pov, that constructs the user's position within the simulation marks another (1996:13–14).

Additionally, there are different gendered responses to such immersion, and from anecdotal evidence from VR researchers she reports that women feel comparatively more disorientated and suffer more motion sickness, perhaps a result of the separation of the pov (point of view) and their actual body (ibid.:14). This separation is especially prominent in those works where the body is imagined and performed otherwise, where a morphology of the sensorium/motorium exists. In *Placeholder* for example, 'Smart Costumes' (bodysuits) enable the participant to take the form of four different animals, and the sensorimotor envelopes (the sensorium/motorium) are different for each. The snake for example can see into the infra-red spectrum. Hayles observes that these embodiments do not re-establish a natural connection between the user's point of view and their actual embodiment, since 'human beings do not naturally have sensoriums that process information in these ways', and instead the participant is a 'techno-bio-subject whose body has been resurfaced and reconfigured by its interface with the technology' (ibid.:17). These aspects are both acknowledged and exploited in Davies' work. She therefore brings her artistic approach to this new technological medium, allowing a form of phenomenological experimentation unparalleled in any other medium. While Cézanne had shown the tactile within the visible for Merleau-Ponty, the possibilities of immersion engage sensation and perception in more direct ways:

> I think of immersive virtual space as a spatio-temporal arena, wherein mental models or abstract constructs of the world can be given virtual embodiment in three dimensions, then kinaesthetically, synaesthetically explored through full-body immersion and interaction. No other space allows this, no other medium of human expression. (in Grau 2003:201)

The perception of a visually semi-transparent, de-solidified world where motile interactions are performed differently, paradoxically, thickens sensory space, helping to instil that ambiguously felt embodiment. In the words of Davies and Harrison (1996), immersants in *Osmose* 'feel both disembodied (because of the visual aesthetic, being able to float and pass through things) and embodied (due to a reliance on breath and balance) simultaneously.' Proprioception is usually automatic and unobtrusive, providing a sense of our bodily boundaries and the ability to navigate through complex spaces, but in this case the sensorimotor envelope is experienced differently. In extremely rare cases, such as that of Ian Waterman (Cole 1995), there is loss of proprioception through neurological damage, and patients feel they are manipulating their body with conscious effort from the outside, like a puppetmaster, and every movement must be preplanned. They have no sense of being inside their own bodies. The body's ambiguity in Davies' work therefore explores proprioception by altering perceived bodily boundaries and altering the mode of interaction with that world. While motility and interaction in the virtual world affect immersants' point of view as they float through a series of worlds, their actual bodies remain standing, their arms making sweeping or grasping movements, plugged into the installation. So what Tikka identifies as the more usual phallic mode of insertion into virtual space, with its associated need for mastery and control, now finds different expression. What Davies and Harrison are grasping toward in this ambiguous sensorimotor body, following from Fisher (1997), is a haptic aesthetic rather than simply a 'visual aesthetic'.

While neither *Osmose* nor *Ephémère* employs cutaneous tactility as such, Davies' installations and haptic interface engage with the vestibular and proprioceptive body, under-explored somatic sensations that now receive empirical, experimental treatment. It thereby alters the body's mode of insertion and potential actions in that world. The visual perception of a semi-transparent, de-solidified world, the use of bodily movements to navigate that world, fosters a de-habituated perception. In these works the felt boundaries of the body are blurred into a semitransparent environment, providing the sense of a thickness to space, and of an altered sensory orientation to the world. As such, these interactive performances are visceral experiments, a kind of practical phenomenology of the sensorimotor envelope, using non-tactile technologies to pursue a haptic aesthetics.

Conclusion: Tangents and Tangible Play

The digital performances associated with each 'tangent' have not been merely examples or illustrations. They have been ways of thinking through the body, a form of phenomenological experimentation. In this case, the opening out of the concept of tactility and sensation into a wider morphology of feeling, a haptic aesthetics mediated variously from skin to screen, flesh and stage, virtual body and virtual environment. These performances support the overarching conceptualization of an 'aesthetics as practice,' in the words of the architect John Rajchman, something that performs an 'affirmative play of conceptual experimentation and novelty' (2000:119). The visceral experiments discussed so far have certainly exemplified this, suffusing conceptual experimentation with a gendered politics, and exploring potential morphologies through the use of technologies which mould and refold skin and numb sensation, alter the flesh and play with proprioception, and expand the sensorium and alter our usual sensibilities. These three seemingly arbitrary 'tangents' of skin, flesh and body are merely instants in an ever-enfolding continuum. They signify particular cuts across this continuum, cuts that bleed out of containment and segmentation, but which reveal certain interconnections between experiential strata.

Feminist technophiles such as Stone (1991:87), Hayles (1996:1) and Senft (1996:34) argue that digital mediations are never truly, completely disembodied, and that identity play and gender slippage are potentially positive aspects of online or virtual negotiations. An 'aesthetics as practice' is not fixated on novelty, nor on the capabilities of the technology, the medium itself. And it is assuredly *not* an exercise in escapological politics, leaving grounded historical and culturally specific problems of gender and oppression behind in an absurd leap of faith toward disembodied, masculinist technology. Instead of eschewing politics, then, an aesthetics as practice can allow a further examination by visceral experimentation of the manifold relations between gender, sexuality, desire, embodiment, sensation and technology. The tangents selected show how particular sensibilities can be mediated and remediated, to articulate and even offer sympathetic experiences and empathic responses from a minoritarian perspective. 'Sensibilities' is such a catch-all term. Extending the skin, fleshing out understandings, and extending the sensorium beyond the subjective body, each of the tangents has conceptually experimented with the body, or as Baraibar puts it, 'realized' it differently:

> By taking the body, stretching it, and making it obsolete, we can gauge and conceptualize it 'as is' – in all its dispersed, multiplicitous glory... It is not so much about saving the human body, but about 'realizing it' in a different way, so that it is possible to relate to it, through it, and the world that surrounds it. (Baraibar, 1999:166)

An aesthetics as practice, indeed a haptic aesthetics as practice, can similarly realize the body, sensation and space in a different way. Performing visceral philosophy, or staging phenomenological experimentation.

Building on the collected insights concerning haptic aesthetics discussed so far, the following chapter will address touch and technology. New technologies can sometimes smack of barbarism, but Walter Benjamin thought there were redemptive aspects. They afford new possibilities for experience, indeed may shape or change the structure of experience, and new freedoms might arise (Caygill 1998:31). We have seen this in terms of tangible play, but in looking explicitly at haptic technologies we shift our attention from the evocation of tactility, the play with the somatic senses, to some mechanisms for engendering and engineering a sense of touch. Taussig (1993:26), writing at a time of rapid advances in computer-graphics technology, thought that mimetic machines still celebrate the power of the image, manipulating the 'real' to produce something better – or more intense – than the real. In the following exploration of the engineering of touch we examine the relationship between the image and engendering the presence, and the right 'feel', of a virtual object through non-visual means. Touch is a rapidly growing and exciting area of videogames, computing and robotics, and this area of technology is known as 'haptics'.

–7–

'Feel the Presence': the Technologies of Touch

'Going to the Feelies this evening, Henry?' enquired the Assistant Predestinator. 'I hear the new one at the Alhambra is first-rate. There's a love scene on a bearskin rug; they say it's marvellous. Every hair of the bear reproduced. The most amazing tactual effects.'

Aldous Huxley, *Brave New World*

Intimate Distances

Huxley's fanciful vision of a sensory cinema known as the 'Feelies', as opposed to the 'movies', would make an object not just look real, but feel real. It would have presence. The Feelies are unlikely to occur in that particular form, but elsewhere the technologies of touch, or what is known in engineering terminology simply as 'haptics', are moving into the mainstream. The astonishing success of Apple's iPod music player, with its innovative touch-sensitive scrollwheel designed by Synaptics Inc., has 'triggered a user-interface revolution for portable devices' thinks Yoshida (2005). The increasing employment of touch in the user interface, and the prevalence of touchscreens in consumer electronics is interesting enough, but in October 2002 newspapers reported the first 'virtual handshake', where researchers at Boston's MIT TouchLabs and London's UCL held virtual hands and manipulated objects together over the internet using more sophisticated haptic interfaces (Arthur 2002:7; BBCi 2002; Kim et al. 2004. These interfaces provide the sensation of touch by exerting accurately controlled forces on the fingers. By this means it is possible to simulate not only the feel of a virtual object, but also its texture and elasticity. Sharing these objects and properties over large distances, and being able to manipulate them virtually, encourages talk of 'presence'. The term 'telepresence', coined in the history of robotics to mean the sense of presence at a distance (Sheridan 1989), is exactly what the virtual handshake achieved, and Kim et al. (2004) adapt this term to speak of 'copresence', the ability to interact with another and feel their presence. But what exactly is this sense of 'presence' and 'copresence', and how is it facilitated by touch? In the case of the virtual handshake, what is felt through the interface as the presence of another person Haans and Ijsselsteijn refer to as 'mediated social touch' (2006:149), 'a sense of presence of a distant other' (ibid.:153) achieved through haptic technology. This chapter concerns how the spatially proximate sense of touch can be communicated and experienced over a distance. What are the associated sensory and spatial effects for the engineering of touch over distance? Such questions are addressed using a mixture of theoretical work concerning space, distance and presence, along with empirical work based on participant observation and interviews in research labs and technology demonstrations.

While the concept of multimedia has been trumpeted for years, usually this is equated merely with vision and sound. In the context of the human-computer interface, touch ranks third in the hierarchy of the senses (e.g. Downton and Leedham 1991:19). With smell devices currently in prototype at MIT and elsewhere (see Paterson, 2006d), haptics is a fast-growing aspect of multimedia (e.g. Hodges 1998; Furner, BT Martlesham Heath Laboratories, interview 8 September, 2000; Wall and Brewster 2006), evidenced by the emerging waves of engineering, human-computer interface and medical simulation literature. After many years of overemphasis on the visual elements of computing in personal computers and videogame consoles, then, other senses are being reasserted. Haptic technologies have made an appearance in high-end workstations for computer-aided design and manufacture (CAD/CAM) as well as lower-end home computers, and are standard in controllers for videogame consoles such as Sony's PlayStation 2, Microsoft's Xbox and Xbox 360, and Nintendo's GameCube. Effectively this means adding what Hayward (in Hodges 1998) calls a 'new mechanical channel', or 'an additional communications channel' (Cleaveland 2006:49) to aid in the visualization of data or to enhance human-computer interaction. Whereas the keyboard is a passive mechanical channel between the computer and user, haptics enables a more active exploration and allows the user not just to *see* three-dimensional shapes represented on the screen, but also to *feel* them and interact with them. The implications for enriched sensory experience, as we shall see, are not limited to playthings. Haptics devices are becoming cheap and ubiquitous, increasingly accessible via everyday technologies such as mobile phones. These unfolding technologies are a set of augmentations that begin to play with an emerging multisensory realm, one that talks of the engendering and engineering of 'immersion', of 'presence', of 'aura' through the addition of touch. While the phenomenon of haptic interaction with computing devices and the literal manipulation of information is interesting in itself, the main focus here concerns how this sense of presence at a distance is enhanced through haptic technologies. I will therefore roughly trace the arc between haptics as a proximal tactile interaction and the 'feeling at a distance' that haptic simulations allow: between the sense of copresence that fosters feelings of nearness and intimacy, and a sense of presence that is mediated and communicated through long-distance networks.

The first section, 'Proximal Touch', looks at the multisensory nature of the human-computer interface (HCI), our way of interacting with and accessing information through the computer. The addition of touch to the computer interface originally emerged to facilitate access to those with visual impairments. In this respect, haptics is one of a number of what Laurel calls 'enabling technologies' (in Rheingold 2000:340) that ease human-computer interaction. This theme of the proximity of interaction is examined further, in the section 'Taking Hold of an Object Close at Hand' which looks at the simulation of touch as a form of mimesis, and echoing comments by Walter Benjamin (1999 [1936]) on auratic properties of objects as a prelude to thinking what happens to aura over distance. The present immediacy of our interactions with virtual objects is enhanced by the collocation of vision and touch, and this is the subject of the following section, 'The Senses of Presence'. Subsequently, in 'Bringing Distance to Life' there is a more protracted discussion concerning the sense of immediacy and presence of an object over long distances, this telepresence being aided by haptic technologies. Here, I enter into more theoretically complex debates concerning technologies and distance, reworking some recent socio-spatial contributions concerning the senses, the body and technologies (e.g. Latham 1999; Thrift 2000; Laurier 2001; Laurier and Philo 2003) to better articulate the sense of presence at a distance, and allow us to reconnect with Merleau-Ponty's work, along with Dreyfus' (2000) phenomenological articulation of 'skilful coping'. Afterward, some conclusions will be drawn concerning the increasing ability to touch and be touched at a distance, and how haptic technologies are influencing our notions of touching, presence, communication and distance.

Proximal Touch: The Human-computer Interface

> The screen is a window through which one sees a virtual world. The challenge is to make that world look real, act real, sound real, and *feel real*.
>
> Sutherland 'The Ultimate Display', emphasis mine

With the reproduction of sound at a relatively advanced level, and the creation of artificial scents at the very beginning of its digital life (e.g. Mullins et al. 1998; Paterson 2006d), the role of touch in computing is becoming established and the various technologies of touch are becoming increasingly prevalent. Whether for research or for entertainment, these devices augment interaction with virtual objects. The user's 'sense of presence' (Yelistratov et al. 1999) in a virtual space is reciprocally constituted by the sense of an object's virtual presence. The goal then is to create the illusion of tangibility through mimetic machines, and the greater the fidelity of haptic sensation the greater the user's sense of presence in a virtual space. But mimesis is not representation. As Murphie notes, mimesis 'is always first and foremost a form of production' (2002:193). This distinction will become important as we move away from realistic representations of touch toward complex, creative operations that involve the tactile, both near and afar.

A Brief History of Haptics...

To chart the development of haptic technologies – from the earliest amusement rides, military simulators and experiments with the human-computer interface would be a fascinating story, and in *Digital Sensations* Hillis (1999) goes part-way toward this. Instead, this chapter distils some themes common to many of the technologies, whether mechanical or electronic. A prompt overview might situate the discussion. As Burdea (1996) and Srinivasan and Basdogan (1997) have shown, there is a history of force-feedback devices as augmentations to the near-space of the human-computer interface (HCI). Work on haptics at the University of North Carolina at Chapel Hill used the Argonne Remote Manipulator (ARM), a large mechanical arm in development since 1953 that augmented a three-dimensional visual display. This was used for nano-level molecular modelling and manipulation (Stone 2000:2). Haptic devices later developed to work at the finger, hand, arm and whole body levels. Both Immersion Corporation's Impulse Engine 2000 (1995) and the subsequent PHANToM work at fingertip level. The TeleTact pneumatic glove, which later appeared in W. Industries' *Virtuality* recreational VR devices in videogame arcades, was prototyped in 1989 and went through several generations until it became a hand-held device as opposed to a wearable glove. This development of haptics continues through to complete tactile bodysuits. While Stone recognizes the military origins of the majority of these devices, he also details current use of haptics technology in an industrial setting, such as training in surgery (also discussed by Amato 2001b), remote surgical operations, and training in landmine clearance. The literature on haptics for surgical simulation and laparoscopic and keyhole surgery training has exploded in the last few years. Writing for an engineering trade journal, for example, Cleaveland writes: 'Haptic medical training systems can reproduce with startling reality the sensations of inserting a needle or a laparoscope while viewing results on the screen – and hearing the patient complain if it's done incorrectly' (2006:48). This uncannily visceral sensation of inserting a needle into the skin of a virtual hand derives in part from the collocation of three-dimensional graphical representations with force feedback, in effect mapping a visual image onto a tactile image. This is discussed further in the section on visual-haptic collocation, 'The Senses of Presence', later in this chapter.

So these haptic sensations occur within the near-space of the human-computer interface. But there is the possibility of touching at a distance. While visual-haptic collocation is the basis for surgical simulations of complex procedures in medical training, it is also possible to conduct surgical operations across large distances through a network. These sensations are more usually associated with proximal interactions, yet technically they allow the possibility of long-distance operations in remote regions or even behind enemy lines (e.g. Hannaford 2000; Amato 2001b). Salisbury (1995), Hannaford (2000) and Stone (2000) also write about the history of force-feedback devices that originated from long-distance robot manipulation, or telemanipulation, for instance in the handling of nuclear material, submarine, military and space operations. 'Teleoperation and telerobotics are technologies that support physical action at a distance', is how Hannaford (2000:247) neutrally defines these. At first purely mechanical, later a combination of motors and sensors were combined so that a remote user would be able to literally manipulate an object. A vital way to get a sense of interacting with the object was through the recreation of forces and resistances of the object, however geographically distant. The goal of 'telemanipulation' or 'teleoperation', the remote operation of a device, was therefore achieved through force feedback, so the earliest haptics devices were force-feedback devices. The feeling engendered through this long-distance operation has been called 'telepresence', that is 'the experience of presence in an environment by means of a communication medium' (Steuer, in Hillis 1999:182).

While the hyperbolic rhetoric of virtual reality has diminished, the technologies of touch have been quietly proliferating, as we have seen, finding serious uses within military training and surgical simulation, for example, but also within recreational uses such as internet sex and, most commonly, videogames (e.g. Hannaford 2000; Stone 2000; Amato 2001b; Arthur 2002). One strand running throughout these technological developments is the engendering and engineering of a sense of 'presence' through the hitherto missing sensation of touch. A leading MIT telerobotics journal is even entitled *Presence*, and the notion of presence has pervaded engineering and telerobotics since its earliest days. The Links Corporation's first flight simulators were little more than wooden crates on mechanical stilts in the 1930s, as Hillis shows (1999). The need to recreate the haptic components of flight such as vibration, pitch and roll, playing with the body's balance senses, occurred through the mechanical production of sensations. Even now haptics technology remains largely mechanical, but the sense of presence is increasingly aided by electronics, engaging directly with the somatic senses of kinaesthesia, proprioception and the vestibular sense, greatly enhancing the sensations of being there. Speaking of the virtual handshake experiment, Slater noted that touch is the most difficult aspect of virtual environments to simulate, but that it 'enhances the sense of being together even though the physical distances involved are vast' (in BBCi 2002). To investigate presence and copresence through haptic technologies – in other words, mediated social touch – is to explore the effects of feeling proximity at a distance, from high-end computation in medical simulation and virtual environments through to low-end haptics in videogame consoles and computer mice. The significance of haptics therefore lies in its increasing popularity and ubiquity, both in home entertainment and in commercial product design, and its ability to enhance the sense of presence of an object in a gameworld or on the desktop. More importantly, it also lies in the ability for this sense of presence to be communicated at a distance, to literally feel the presence of another. After the notion of mediation and remediation in considering tangible play, previously, thinking of haptic technologies as mediated social touch is certainly apt.

Engineering the Feelies: Mimetic Machines of Touch

We return now to the notion of mimesis as a form of production. The vast majority of our everyday interactions with proximal objects in the physical world are taken for granted, and haptic technologies attempt to replicate such interaction in a virtual world. These are some of the problems that mimetic machines of touch must face, to give the sense of interacting with objects by supplying composite sensations that include the cutaneous, the vestibular, the proprioceptive and so on, to engender – and, indeed, engineer – the right 'feel'. In both physical, real-world interaction and interaction with digital sensation, then,

> A significant component of our ability to 'visualize', remember and establish cognitive models of the physical structure of our environment stems from haptic interactions with objects in the environment. Kinesthetic, force and cutaneous senses combined with motor capabilities permit us to probe, perceive and rearrange objects in the physical world. (Massie and Salisbury 1994:295)

This visualization of cognitive models is the case even without the micro-detailed touch stimulation of the fingertips and other sensitive areas. The forces and motions that are reported back to us from our fingers and limbs through the tactile-muscular system, Massie and Salisbury argue, generate 'significant information about the spatial map of our environment' (ibid.). As these engineers understand, the haptic system is more than the cutaneous sense of the skin surface. What is significant here is the user-oriented intention, trying to engender the right 'feel' to objects, whether it be a model of a gearshift mechanism, a virtual prototype of a car door, the feeling of weighted switches when turning on and off in the virtual world, and the ability 'for users to distinguish between massive and low-mass objects by feel alone' (ibid.:298). This discovery from a user-centred perspective in this case is one of ponderability – that is, reproducing or mimicking the sensation of weight and mass.

'Haptics' is always that larger human system of perception that deals with touch, and so the human haptic system consists of 'the entire sensory, motor and cognitive components of the body-brain system' (Oakley *et al.* 2000:416). But a key concept in the engineering of haptics technology is 'force feedback'. 'Devices use force feedback to present kinaesthetic stimuli and produce the feeling that the user is interacting with physical objects, such as a line cut into a virtual surface or a solid three-dimensional object', as Wall and Brewster (2006:95) explain. At one end of the spectrum, low-fidelity force feedback in videogame controllers produces vibrations and 'rumble' through the use of electric motors. An example is the Logitech 'Rumblepad' force-feedback controllers for PC, or the 'built-in rumble' of the Nintendo GameCube. Further up the spectrum, higher-fidelity force-feedback devices such as SensAble Corporation's PHANToM (Personal Haptic iNTerface Mechanism) can produce a credible illusion of a tangible object in virtual space, through a combination of resistances and free play produced by electric motors in a workspace. While the skin detects temperature through thermoreceptors, and extreme pressure, heat and pain through nociceptors, it is through mechanoreceptors that normal pressure is sensed (Dix et al. 1998:23).

Force feedback occurs through a combination of cutaneous mechanoreceptor sensation and kinaesthesia – in other words, pressure and movement in space for a determinable duration. In space and duration, its presentment to us is a feeling of solidity, which haptics devices emulate through the use of force feedback. In fact, the inherently spatial and temporal characteristics of touch are described by the English empiricist philosopher John Locke: 'The idea of *solidity* we receive by our touch; and it arises from the resistance which we find in body to the entrance of any other body into the place it possesses, till it has left it' (in Appelbaum 1988:20, original emphasis). As a set of artificial or illusory resistances in haptics devices, the tactile illusion of solidity is produced through electric motors in the device that work to selectively counter the movement of the user. With the variability of the electromotor force opposing that of the user, varying levels of hardness, softness or elasticity can be modelled. Haptics devices that use force feedback appear to attach physical sensations to virtual objects, and in the words of Mahoney (1997:42), the user's 'force is input and reflected via a physical interface device, which can be anything from a joystick or steering wheel to a thimble or an exoskeletal structure'.

This explains the technology, but the significance of haptics lies in the user's experience of a simulated object or environment. Like the 'Feelies' in Aldous Huxley's *Brave New World*, the use of touch for interface and entertainment purposes is premised on the idea that the sense of immersion in an artificial environment is augmented by touch in addition to vision and sound. Whether in virtual reality, virtual environments, or the burgeoning market of videogame controllers, haptics are going 'mainstream' (Rosenberg, in Hogan 1998). The addition of the haptic to the visual and aural enhances the experience of the user, and is commonly expressed in terms of 'immersion' or 'presence'. Solidifying some of the associations between touch and immersion first suggested in the previous chapter, for example, two leading haptics engineers declare:

> Being able to touch, feel and manipulate objects in an environment, in addition to seeing (and hearing) them, provides *a sense of immersion* in the environment that is otherwise not possible. It is quite likely that much greater immersion in a VE [Virtual Environment] can be achieved by the synchronous operation of even a simple haptic interface with a visual and auditory display, than by large improvements in, say, the fidelity of the visual display alone. (Srinivasan and Basdogan 1997:393, emphasis mine)

The addition of the sense of touch allows, in Johnson's words, a sense of the 'direct manipulation' of objects, where 'the user makes things happen in an immediate ... way' (1997:179), and therefore a sense of being immersed in, or engaged upon, the task at hand. If the various technologies involved in the provision of this sense of touch differ in terms of sophistication, then, we can say along with MacPherson and Keppell (1997) that there is a 'degree of immersion'. From inexpensive videogame haptics to 'fully immersive' VR, the perceived degree of immersion differs according to the fidelity of the technologies being deployed, and this itself affects the perceived separation between the tools of the human-computer interface and the actual task at hand. We will explore this further in terms of Merleau-Ponty's 'sharpness of perception', in this case haptic acuity or 'grip'.

Taking Hold of an Object Close at Hand

Following Walter Benjamin's notion of aura and its loss in reproducible images of photographs and cinema, Gržinić suggests that the new technologies of telerobotics represent 'a way to restore the aura, to restore the sense of *time* and *place* that the image conveys' (2000:220, emphasis mine). I want to pursue this theme and others in the exploration of haptic technologies, which are genealogically related to telerobotics (devices to aid the manipulation of objects at a distance) and telepresence (the evocation of a sense of presence of objects at a distance). Indeed, the virtual-handshake experiment is an example of telepresence as Manovich defines it, being 'representational technologies used to enable action, that is, allow the viewer to manipulate reality through representations' (2001:165). Disregarding his use of the term 'viewer', the participant arguably uses representations of an object that are not only visual but also haptic, through the use of force feedback.

Benjamin's discussion of the mimetic faculty, and Taussig's subsequent discussion of 'mimetic machines' that provide a 'new sensorium' (1993:24) thereby affecting the nature of experience, are potentially useful starting points from which to continue discussions of technologies of touch. This is not simply the straightforward expansion of the sensorium in the way that technologies are supposed to do, the machinic extensions of the senses of the human. Previously we acknowledged this play with the sensorium through technology. And, writing about the transformation of the sensorium in modernism, for example, Sara Danius describes the way that sensory technologies have gone from *prosthesis*, the 'essentially external relationship between the senses and their technological supplements', to *aisthesis*, the 'interiorization of technological modes of perceiving' (2002:194). Her argument is certainly applicable to those immediate haptic sensations such as videogame controllers or tactile mice, where repeated operations start to bind actions (shooting an alien, driving a car) with force feedback sensations (weapon recoil, the rumble when departing the road surface). However, the notions of presence and copresence at a distance complicate this, and I will argue that there is more to attend to than interiorizations of perception.

Writing of the transformations of experience that new technologies were capable of effecting, Benjamin famously discussed the desire to take something close at hand, 'to get hold of an object at very close range by ways of its likeness, its reproduction' (in Taussig 1993:32). By this he was referring to the aura, and we have already explored the notions of tactile appropriation and aura. The importance here lies in the mimetic nature of the haptic experience, recreated through digital means, being unambiguously illusory; a phantom-like presence. With teleoperation and telemanipulation (the ability to conduct operations with objects through mechanical means) able to be conducted over large distances, the need for something close at hand, the production of these tangible presences through artificial means, collapses the distance and makes an extremely distant, or even non-existent, object immediately present, actually manipulable or graspable. The ghostly, those virtual possibilities that become locally actualized, Valéry calls 'the active presence of absent things' (in Thrift 2000:222) and this is particularly apt in considering the naming of one of the most important haptic devices, the PHANToM. Given a high resolution of sensors and actuators in such a device, Hannaford explains:

> we create 'knots' or 'ports' in space through which we can see, hear, touch and manipulate distant objects or people as though they were present. Multiple locations can be brought together at such a port and effectively superimposed in space and time. (2000:274)

Hannaford goes on to ask, as we shall do, what this means in terms of a sense of presence. Thinking of this presence at a distance can be conjoined, however, with another definition of aura, that of Josipovici. 'Aura does not abolish distance, to adapt a wonderful phrase Benjamin once used..., *it brings distance to life*' (1996:10, emphasis mine). Before more detailed discussion of this in relation to the case study of the virtual handshake, I wish to remain within the near-space of the computer desktop. If the origin of force feedback was to bring those distances of telemanipulation to life, then the user's experience of haptics is the intimacy of touch, the prehensile and exploratory space of touch within reach. Haptic interfaces open up a tactile space on our desktop, too.

Appropriately enough, the majority of my analysis will concentrate on Massie and Salisbury's device, the PHANToM desktop haptic interface, invented at MIT in 1993. There are reasons for this. First, after several iterations it remains the most advanced haptic device, with far higher tactual resolution than any comparable device. Secondly, it is versatile, being employed in a variety of non-military applications such as design, medical simulation and rehabilitation. Thirdly, I personally experienced using the device, as various models were employed by academic institutions and corporations within the course of empirical research. In addition, it forms the basis of other devices such as the Reachin Desktop, used for design work and medical simulation, which I also experienced first-hand. Fourthly, its name is suggestive of a theme that recurs in haptics marketing literature, a phantasm being illusory, both absence and presence.[1] Lastly, it was the device involved in the 'virtual handshake' cited at the beginning of this chapter. Technically it is a point interaction device where users have a single point of contact with a virtual object using either the tip of a stylus or their fingertip. Wall and Brewster describe this model rather disparagingly as 'analogous to exploring the world with a stick' (2006:95). Yet, as Descartes showed in *Dioptrique* in 1637, the spatial perception of the blind is enhanced immeasurably by the single-point roaming contact of the cane, which he now familiarly likened to 'seeing with the hands'. The PHANToM is a machinic example of the intangible (digital data, the virtual) becoming tangible. It produces sensations, creates tactile effects. More than a set of tactile-muscular interactions, and especially in conjunction with a visual display, it provides a sense of presence of a virtual object. Like mimesis, haptics becomes a form of production, to enhance operations, to provide richer user experience, even to promote experimentation through free-flowing play and creativity. But primarily, haptics creates a whole set of forces and corresponding sensations, a fusion of feelings that are generated and retro-engineered from the perspective of the user, not imposed by programmers or coders themselves, in order to recreate the right 'feeling'. We engage directly with this in two examples, a virtual gearbox and a hypodermic injection simulation, later. For now, the inventors of the device provide a taste of the user experience:

> Users of the PHANToM provide evidence that our visual, haptic and auditory senses are closely linked and that all three sensory modes are required for navigation within virtual environments… Many users claim that they can 'see a sphere' after touching a virtual sphere with the PHANToM. (Massie and Salisbury 1994:299)

This is confirmed with my own experience of the interface, at MIT TouchLabs in Boston; at BT Labs at Martlesham Heath; at CERTEC (the Division of Rehabilitation Engineering Research) in Lund, Sweden; and at Reachin AB of Stockholm. The feeling elicited through force feedback in this 'thimble-gimbal' (Salisbury 1995) interface of virtual objects is one of solidity, of texture, sometimes of elasticity of a surface. All these sensations are reproduced through software algorithms in the applications program interface (API), appropriately enough called 'Ghost'. Mostly the haptic models of virtual objects accompany visual representations on a screen, so that one can both see and feel an object simultaneously, the haptic sensation confirming the visual impression or vice versa. But the decoupling of the haptic from the visual may also take place. For example, with no visual representation on screen the feeling of a switch that can remain on or off is still somehow 'visualized' as a haptic model. These sensations will be examined further in the following section.

The Senses of Presence: Visual and Haptic Collocation

The hand-based manipulation of virtual objects can occur with or without a visual component to aid the recognition of the object. Visual-haptic collocation, the correspondence between visual and haptic stimuli, is particularly desirable for a believable sense of interaction with a virtual object (Dionisio et al. 1997:465), and therefore enables more sophisticated training and medical simulation to take place. Haptics alone without visual rendering produces an unusual feeling, while the visual alone, despite being the primary method of 3D modelling and rendering, sometimes leads to ambiguities and is an unwieldy, non-intuitive method of computer-aided design and object manipulation. As is now familiar from the association of touch with verification ('seeing's believing, but feeling's the truth'), haptic technology therefore offers the verification of an object in space, to get a real sense of the presence of that object, in a way that vision alone cannot do. As Massie shows:

> Touching something with the Phantom resolves all of the ambiguities on the screen. For example, if you see a shaded, rendered sphere on screen, your brain is trying to interpret this 2D projection and reconstruct a 3D image from that without the advantage of binocular vision. So you're subconsciously making decisions like whether the sphere is concave or convex. As soon as you touch it, you know immediately what it is. (in Mahoney 2000:41)

Visual-haptic collocation therefore reduces visuospatial ambiguities, as well as augmenting the invisible haptic set of forces as experienced through the interface. Noyes and Mills, in distinguishing between 'immersive' and 'non-immersive' virtual reality, claim that to be truly immersive there needs to be 'some form of haptic input[,] so the user wears gloves or uses some other specially designed three-dimensional interactive device which is usually hand-held' (1999:124), and certainly we can class the PHANToM as such a device. The process of pointing and manipulating in a three-dimensional space is a complex set of coordinated perceptions and responses, and haptics helps to resolve those ambiguities, making a strictly 'non-immersive' workspace more 'immersive' as a result, they argue (ibid.:129). And, within the desktop-based workspace of the PHANToM, there is certainly a sense of 'presence' of the object for the user.

Engineering the Right 'Feel': Virtual Veins and a Simulated Gearbox

Reachin Technologies AB of Stockholm exemplify this visual-haptic collocation. Specializing in medical simulation, their Desktop is a graphic display that overlooks and obscures a small PHANToM, thereby producing a very 'real' sense of manipulating an object. As the computer display is reflected onto a screen, the visual element is superimposed directly onto the haptic, so that manipulation of the virtual object occurs in what appears, from above, to be a 'shared' space of vision and touch. By collocating representations of the haptic with the visual more effectively, this device allows a more realistic feeling of manipulating a virtual object, one that can better evoke the feelings of weight, mass, ponderability and other real-world behaviours. 'When the stylus [of the PHANToM] hits something displayed in the mirror, you find that the objects there have surfaces, weight, viscosity and all the other properties of real world objects that you can feel through a tool', they boast (Reachin.se, 2002). To manipulate a virtual object with the hand, and have the image change accordingly on the screen over the haptic device, produces a credible sensation of a tangible virtual object. So credible, in fact, that haptic interfaces like the PHANToM and the Reachin Desktop are being marketed in configurations that allow medical training such as an epidural simulator, a dental simulator, even a 'Bovine Rectal Palpation Simulator' (a.k.a. the 'haptic cow', Baillie et al. 2005). The superimposition of a visual display over a haptic set of forces is a more sophisticated form of visual-haptic collocation, although Reachin themselves more awkwardly call it 'visu-haptic' (Thurfjell, interview 13/9/00). The sense of realism is essential for medical and surgical training, and Immersion Corporation's visual-haptic medical simulations are marketed as 'vascular access platforms' (Cleaveland 2006:48). The vascularity and the viscerality discussed previously in terms of tangible play now has a decidedly serious and profitable use. A technology demonstration that I tried, the medical simulation of the injection of a hand with a hypodermic syringe, revealed the startlingly realistic sensations this device could provide. In the demonstration, now licensed as 'Virtual Veins' (Reachin.se 2006), the Reachin Desktop provided enough graphical detail to discern veins on a three-dimensional model of a hand. When the virtual needle was manoeuvred and inserted into the model, the skin-puncturing moment was reproduced through the force feedback in the PHANToM underneath the display. These sensations were not just felt as simply localized kinaesthetic forces by the fingertips alone, but engendered a visceral feeling, the synthesis of the visual and the haptic mimicking the sensation of injecting into the springiness and resistances of flesh. This is a very visceral sensation, a 'gut feeling':

> But when it comes to the visu-haptic what makes a big difference is the collocation, which is both ... but somehow this collocation thing of Reachin makes a big impact on the gut feeling. And we don't know why, but that's empirical! (Tomer, interview 13/9/00)

The visceral component that emerges from the visual-haptic collocation finds an application not only in the field of medical simulation but also in creating 'digital mock-ups' or virtual prototypes. Reachin has done work for automotive manufacturers such as Saab-Scania and Volvo.[2] Interviewed at their headquarters in Stockholm, European Sales Director Anneka Hofsten explained the way that the design of a purely hypothetical piece of engineering, in her example a gearbox, could be imbued with different sensory properties, and these sensations could be altered and experimented with using the Reachin Desktop. This is a user-centred approach to design, using the haptic interface to produce something as unquantifiable and indefinable as the right 'feel' for a piece of new technology – the satisfying 'thunk' of a gear shift, or a car door closing, arising simultaneously from auditory, visual and kinaesthetic stimuli, somehow visceral in nature. These visual-haptic sensations are imprecise, arising from repetitive experimentation with the conjunction of different forces and sensory stimuli, by 'playing with different feelings' as Hofsten herself explains:

> So just imagine you want to look, you want to find out what the feeling is when touching the instruments, or the gear shift for example. What do you want the feeling to be like when changing gears in the car? Do you want it to be the Scania feeling, you know, a lot of power ... you could do it just by pressing button, 1,2,3,4,5 [or] how many gears you have, but this is not the right feeling. And the old Scania drivers, they don't like it, they prefer to have the old feeling of changing gear, you know, and *this is a kind of playing with different feelings*, and they can still implement the new technology but keep the old feeling... (Hofsten, interview 13/9/00, emphasis mine)

Similarly with paper cartons, another piece of collaborative research has enabled them to try out the 'feel' of different paper types using the Reachin Desktop, thereby reducing the number of actual prototypes that must be produced (Hofsten, interview 13/9/00), shortening the development cycle. What is significant is the way a new language of haptic sensations is being articulated within a marketing and engineering context, so that these forces and sensory properties are mimicked, modelled, experimented with, reproduced through the interaction between hardware and software; and the collocation of the different forces and sensations is altered and combined in new ways. It is this attempt to reproduce and articulate new sensations, by a form of retro-engineering from the experience of the user, which is indicative of the 'new means of expression' that emerge from 'the expanding space of virtuality of the body and technology' (Thrift 2004:23). These emergent sensations and means of expression filter down into everyday devices and user interfaces, impacting on the aestheticisation of everyday life.[3] The admixture of sensory properties by haptic hardware and software, therefore, opens up a discussion of the right 'feel' of a virtual object and, significantly, has genuine impact on future design and the crafting of actual objects (e.g. Amato 2001a). The engendering of the 'feel' of a virtual object is impacting digital creativity and craft, where manual contact with the material can now be mediated by a haptic interface, for example actually manipulating 'virtual clay'. (For more extensive discussion of these aspects, see Paterson 2005c; 2006c; 2007; also McCullough 1998.) Bordegoni and Cugini (2006) also take a user-centred approach to design, looking at how designers create models with their hands and tools in order to subsequently create innovative and useful haptic tools. Whether the virtual is a set of somatic, kinaesthetic possibilities in dance, or virtual clay to be moulded on the desktop, it is a 'performative experiment' of play that 'encourages the discovery of new configurations and twists of ideas and experience' (Scheichner in Thrift 2000:221). Mimesis, it was remarked earlier, is about production rather than representation; this play of haptics produces sensation but also variation.

What is in effect a form of virtual prototyping affects the computer-aided design and manufacture (CAD/CAM) in the development process, adding the simulation of material properties of an object through haptic interactions. Although the present technology allows only an imprecise mimicking of the touch sensation, the combination of haptic sensations and visual representation – that is, visual-haptic collocation – can, as we have seen, produce startlingly visceral effects.

Bringing Distance to Life: Presence and Copresence

> For there to be a sense of presence in telepresence one would have to be involved in getting a grip on something at a distance.
>
> Dreyfus, 'Telepistemology'

Let us now bring distance into the discussion. By concentrating on the example of the 'virtual handshake' we can track the senses of proximity and distance engendered through haptics devices. This has the advantage of distilling some themes recurring throughout this book, while bypassing the always incomplete cataloguing of various technological developments. We therefore return to that first virtual handshake mentioned in the introduction, the transatlantic touching between PHANToM haptic interfaces at MIT in Boston and UCL in London in 2002. Discussed in newspapers and the popular press (e.g. Arthur 2002; BBCi 2002), the experiment was written up by researchers at both institutions in the telerobotics journal *Presence* (Kim et al., 2004). Along with a summary of the experiment the paper used questionnaires to elicit responses from the participants concerning 'the subjective levels of presence and copresence experienced' during performance of the task (ibid.:328). Having discussed the notions of 'presence' in the near-space of the human-computer interface, in this section I wish to address 'copresence' and the effects of space in particular.

We have discussed the sense of presence as manipulation of virtual objects on the computer desktop being enhanced by force feedback, and telepresence as the use of force feedback in the interaction with objects and virtual objects at a distance. The virtual handshake experiment utilized two sets of haptic devices, each with a human user, manipulating a virtual object. The aim was the collaboration between users on each side of the Atlantic to manipulate an object on the screen through a haptic interface. This involved feelings of 'copresence'. In their words, the 'fundamental aspect of shared experience is the sensory communication between geographically separated users that enables them to display their actions to each other through a connected network' (ibid.). The network in this case was WWW2, a fast internet backbone, in order to minimize system delay in the conveyance of tactile information to the user. For, as Noyes and Mills explain, 'the delay between a hand movement and a corresponding change on the display' (1999:132) would not only shatter the sense of real-time engagement with an object, but would also seriously challenge the ability to carry out useful tasks.

There are various ways of thinking these distributed tactile and spatial relations, one being so-called 'actor-network' theory, and there are advantages in variations of this approach. Bingham for example defines 'remote control' as the ability to 'act at a remove', to exert 'force at a distance with predictable and repeatable consequences' (1996:650). Thus we could talk of the virtual handshake experiment alongside such familiar examples as Portuguese shipping networks and the immutable mobiles of laboratory life, and something about the laboratory-based arrangements over networks lends itself to this. Indeed, one of Law's (1986) observations of shipping networks is the amount of work necessary to maintain the network, and minimizing the degeneration in communications between components within it. This is to reduce the 'noise' between the centre and the periphery, pertinent to the noise that Noyes (and Mills, 1999) described above concerning network delays in real-time haptic engagement. We could also follow Law and Mol (2001) in rethinking these networks along metaphors of fluidity or, more aptly concerning the flickering of presence and absence, of fire. Or we could combine approaches, to correlate a materialist semiotics with the media theory of Friedrich Kittler (1999), for example, where the establishment of order and the building of ergonomic pathways could be analysed in computer inputs and outputs, a way to think about the historical-material shaping of the mouse, the keyboard, the gamepad. Yet there is something more immediate and sensorily engaging occurring, as discussed on the section on visual-haptic collocation, and the notion of the feeling of the presence of an object and the copresence of another operator at a distance is experienced otherwise than as a stable maintenance of topologies. And here we start to ask about the role of a mediated telepresence as compared to direct perception, if the task requires the manipulation of a virtual object. As Dreyfus argues, 'what gives our sense of being in direct touch with reality is that we bring about changes in the world and get perceptual feedback concerning what we have done' (2000:57). Deceptively straightforward as this seems, some unforeseen implications emerge when we consider this occurring over protracted distances. One significant problem is network latency, delays and bottlenecks in the flows of digital data over a network that might interrupt the smoothness of the user's experience. Book and Swanson identify the 'destabilizing time delays' (2004:92) over the internet, with an unpredictable variation in time delay due to surges in traffic flow rather than to geographical distance. If network latency is kept to a manageable level, however, there is no perceived difference between being in direct touch with an object across the Atlantic and being in touch with a virtual model on a computer desktop. Benjamin's notion of aura collapses if the distances involved do not qualitatively affect the feeling of the manipulation process, the sense of presence of an object or copresence of another person.

The notion of 'copresence' in the virtual-handshake experiment is defined by Kim et al. in terms of 'human-human interaction' (2004:329) as opposed to human-computer interaction, aided by haptic devices at either end. The task involved lifting a virtual cube represented on the screen, requiring cooperation between the users by manipulating PHANToM devices, each respondent exerting pressure on the cube as a collaborative exercise in order to lift it off the ground for as long as possible. The task itself being straightforward, the real purpose of the experiment was to gauge the role of haptics in the sense of presence and copresence. Methodologically, this was measured statistically by Kim et al. through questionnaires for each respondent conducted after the experiment, asking rather naive questions to elicit responses on a score range of 1 to 7, such as:

(1) To what extent, if at all, did you have a sense of being with another person?

(2) To what extent were there times, if at all, during which the computer interface seemed to vanish, and you were directly working with the other person?...

(6) During the time of the experience, did you often think to yourself that you were just manipulating some screen images with a pen-type device, or did you have a sense of being with another person? (Kim et al. 2004:335)[4]

The results unsurprisingly showed a statistical correlation between haptics and the sense of copresence. Obviously, to gauge subjective experiences of copresence required a more qualitative approach, and while discussion of my haptic interactions is centred on the computer desktop, we could extrapolate from feelings of presence in the near-space of the desktop to feelings of copresence over the network-space of the internet. Tying in with my earlier observations on visual-haptic collocation, they conclude that: 'Visual immersion along with haptic immersion would greatly increase the collaboration over a vast physical distance' (ibid.:336).

Rather than the statistical survey Kim et al. conducted, having experienced using the PHANToM device to accomplish various tasks (playing with a ball, injecting a hand), we can speak almost phenomenologically of bringing the remote into nearness, into the near-space of proximal touch. Hence long-distance control, the exertion of force at a distance, simultaneously brings the distant into an almost phenomenologically felt near-space of proximity, while also maintaining that distance. In the words of Cooper, long-distance control is possible:

Through a sequence of short-distance achievements of remote control, all of which embodied the following steps: (1) the substitution of a symbol or technical device for direct human involvement; which led to (2) the curious effect of bringing the remote – that which is cut off by a limit or boundary – near, while at the same time keeping it at a remove. (in Bingham 1996:650) sensations of bringing the remote into nearness are more akin to Laurier's example of reaching for a mobile phone, being 'digitally accomplished in that place' (2001:493), itself an adaptation of Sudnow's (1993) famous example of observing a jazz pianist from the outside; a skilled absorption that does not require the separation of representation from the task at hand. As Dreyfus describes this, our active and involved body puts us directly in touch with perceived reality, and can be described as 'everyday coping', 'absorbed activity' or simply 'going with the flow' (2000:57). No inner mental representation is required to perform these activities, to become digitally accomplished in that place, whether it is the locale of the computer desktop or over a network.

Dreyfus' phenomenological approach to technology is helpful, and especially so in the case of haptic manipulation, where we may again invoke Merleau-Ponty's concept of 'maximum grip', the notion that in grasping something we do so in order to obtain the most satisfactory purchase on it, either on the parts or the whole. This is a perceptual attitude that translates from immediate practical contexts in 'virtual' and 'real' worlds alike, and therefore both in the immediate space of the desktop and at a distance. The minimization of network latency, the delay between performing an action and obtaining feedback through an interface and on the screen, increases the grip on the task at hand. In Merleau-Ponty's words this increases the 'sharpness of perception', being a continuation of the analysis of the kinaesthetic background of perception (hands and 'grip') we raised in chapter 2:

> This maximum sharpness of perception and action points clearly to a perceptual ground, a basis of my life, a general setting in which my body can co-exist with the world. (1992:250)

It is with this non-representational notion of getting a grip that Dreyfus can then argue, as at the beginning of this section: 'for there to be a sense of presence in tele-presence one would have to be involved in getting a grip on something at a distance' (2000:58). This is skilful coping with things and people, using several sensory dimensions in real time, an illusion that breaks as soon as network latency appears. But skilful coping with things is what invokes a sense of presence, and skilful coping with people that invokes the sense of copresence, where the sharpness of perception involves high-fidelity force feedback over a network without latency. With this haptic acuity over a distance, we can become digitally accomplished in a variety of places.

Conclusion: Haptics and Mediated Touch

> The computer molds the human even as the human builds the computer.
>
> Hayles, 'Virtual Bodies and Flickering Signifiers'

Although Huxley's 'Feelies' are unlikely to occur in the way he envisaged, haptic technologies are adding further sensory content to mediated communication, bringing what was distant into present proximity. For the sake of focus we have mostly concentrated on desktop haptics, even if the two desktops are geographically separated. Before making conclusions about touching, proximity and distance, however, I wish to consider very briefly a more distributed sense of haptics, moving away from the computer desktop or joystick. Some of the alternative ways that haptics are being employed have been suggested in terms of performance and play, but other relevant digital-arts installations include the multiple and distributed tangible 'widgets' used in Edinburgh's *Tacitus* project (e.g. Shillito et al. 2001) which have been displayed in publicly accessible spaces, and include haptic components.[5] Kangas (1999) has observed the uptake of haptics in games and the advent of wearable computing, and notes how this has affected the man-machine interface. From this she sees haptics devices becoming embedded in everyday objects such as tables and couches, using tactile stimuli as a communicative tool.[6] And, from a more utilitarian perspective, the use of haptic information to provide spatial information for the blind and visually impaired is an important consideration (see e.g. Paterson 2002; Jacobson et al. 2002).[7] In addition, future robots will incorporate a sense of touch in order to achieve necessary levels of dexterity for complex operations, since even the most advanced robotic hands cannot perform tasks that the average six-year-old accomplishes routinely. Crowder describes how high-fidelity touch sensors can be incorporated into a thin film (2006:1478). Effectively this would be a robotic 'skin' around a robotic 'hand' (for a posthuman interpretation see Castañeda, 2001).

Through discussion of a variety of haptic technologies, although primarily the example of the virtual handshake conducted in 2002 between London and Boston, there are a number of observations concerning experiences of touch, proximity and distance that I wished to make. First, while touch is often associated with near-space or even intimacy, it is obviously of concern in the human-computer interface because it effects, in Johnson's phrase, 'direct manipulation' (1997:179). Secondly, if haptic technologies can provide sensations of direct manipulation with a virtual object on the computer desktop, then in Benjamin's words, 'taking hold of an object close at hand' produces a sense of presence of the object through force-feedback sensations, the mimicking of sensations of solidity and spatial extension of an object. Especially through the collocation of the visual with the haptic, these produce a sense of presence whether the virtual object is produced on a local machine, or whether the data is relayed across the internet from another continent. The implication is that, given no noticeable network latency, the effects of distance are collapsed, and tasks or operations that are being conducted at great distance can theoretically be introduced into the proximate space of a local computer desktop. Haptics therefore reach out way beyond the human-computer interface itself. Thirdly, we have discussed copresence, the haptic manipulation of objects with other users. This is notable for the accomplishment of collaborative tasks, but will become increasingly significant for other human-human interactions, as suggested by MIT's ComTouch project and Samsung's production mobile phone that uses force feedback (see e.g. Biever, 2005).[8] So, fourthly, the expensive and specialized haptic devices utilized in the virtual-handshake experiment should not blind us to the near ubiquity that inexpensive force-feedback devices already enjoy through videogame console controllers, and will continue to do so in future communications devices.

My last points are interconnected and concern some of the underlying spatial assumptions behind much of this chapter and the haptics literature. When in 1936 Benjamin wrote about the hunger for the aura or presence of an original artwork increasing due to the proliferation of mechanical copies, the categories of 'original' and 'copy' were distinct (1999 [1936]). For Benjamin, only the original work had aura, and never its reproductions. Without even using the language of simulation and simulacra we have noticed that the distinction is elided, since objects can be virtual and still have a presence. This point is strengthened when we consider that these objects can be located at a distance but felt locally, and that this also applies to copresence, the presence of another. Like the telephone perhaps, only with the haptic modality, we proceed as if the person is actually 'there' – a convincing enough sense of copresence. In collaborative tasks such as the virtual handshake, then, this is the phenomenological extension of the task at hand over a network; being digitally accomplished here and elsewhere. As Johnson prophesies: 'We can be sure that the exploratory, spatial quality of the medium – the haptics of information-space – will be of enormous importance' (1997:221). Indeed it will.

After examining the relationship between vision and touch in the history of philosophy, and then the aesthetics and technologies of touch, next we move away from technological mediations of touch to consider the therapeutic aspects of touching. Arguably, touch is always already mediated through whatever means, haptic sensations arising through interaction and the cutaneous surface of the skin, the organ of touch. But the immediacy of contact and the direct sensations of manipulation, aspects of the final chapter, will return us to the phenomenological territory from whence the book started.

–8–

Affecting Touch: Flesh and Feeling-With

Touch is not a sense at all; it is in fact a metaphor for the impingement of the world as a whole upon subjectivity ... to touch is to comport oneself not in opposition to the given but in proximity with it.

Wyschogrod, 'Doing Before Hearing'

Touch as Metaphor

Is there *a* sense of touch, or are there in fact *many*? What is touch, after all? What if we consider touch as a metaphor, as Edith Wyschogrod does, as interpretive, enactive, expressive, as experiential framework and conceptual resource; bringing distant objects or people into proximity? The model not only for all other senses, as Democritus would have it, but a model for sympathy, of literally *feeling-with*? Here we develop one of the recurrent themes of this book, the relationship between touch and proximity. Drawing on work by Edith Wyschogrod (especially 1980, 1981) and the later work of Merleau-Ponty, and applying this to empirical work concerning therapeutic touching, we consider touching and being touched by others, relations between bodies, proximity and empathy. Without embarking on detailed explanations of energy fields and life forces, the complex interpersonal forms of touching involved in Reiki allows us to provide rich descriptions of touching and feeling. We revisit some of the historical and phenomenological resources hitherto invoked for interpreting touch, such as the phenomenologically felt bringing-near of what is distant, and the immediacy and presence of felt sensations. In addition, we augment the analysis with observations concerning the intertwining of touching and feeling, intercorporeity, and the exchange of affects between bodies. By itself this does not constitute a comprehensive programme for a 'felt' phenomenology. But actual experiences of touching within fieldwork settings exemplify an application of a 'felt' phenomenology within an empirical context, in this case a sensuous ethnography of the manifold experiences of touch within a therapeutic setting.

Therapeutic touching is an example of a previously unorthodox practice whose increasing popularity entails heightened visibility within contemporary cultures of wellbeing.[1] Van Dongen and Elema's plea for the consideration of the relations between the body, touch and the emotions in nursing (2001:153) is obviously relevant to other areas and academic concerns. This is not the place to reiterate arguments concerning affect (which we have touched upon already via Deleuze and Spinoza; see also Paterson 2005a), whereby the language of affect can be used as a theoretical framework for understanding somatic sensations between bodies. Following from Levinas' conceptualization of proximity within the ethical relation (1991 [1968]), Wyschogrod's (1980) metaphorical touch as a feeling of impingement upon and proximity to the world is helpful in considering therapeutic spaces. Just like affect, touch is ambiguous, and ambiguity pervades this book. To affect or be affected, to touch and be touched, is to bring aspects and forces of the world nearer to us. To think touch and tactility outside individual skin and between bodies, bodies understood to share energies at both a local and a cosmological level, we need to grasp the relation between touch and affective experience. And, further, we need a suitable method for describing such experience. If Descartes in his third *Meditation* strives notoriously for 'clear and distinct' perceptions, touching ethnographies (or 'felt' phenomenologies) engage with those *in*distinct and *un*clear perceptions, the manifold of somatic sensations.

We reach back to the beginning of this book, with the notions of a 'felt' phenomenology and the difficulty of articulating somatic sensations. That conceptual and historical work is consolidated here and bridges with ethnographic work and empirical findings. Slightly different emphases are revealed, oscillating around a central ambiguity, that of touching as feeling – as somatic sensation, ineffable feeling, almost indescribably felt in the body and outside it, an indistinct and unclear perception. So a 'felt' phenomenology achieves two things. First, a way of reclaiming some aspects of phenomenology as a potentially radical framework for understanding touch, affect and intersubjectivity through, and between, situated and emplaced bodies. Secondly, toward the end of the chapter, reflexive considerations of the problems of writing and representing unusual combinations of somatic sensations, involving potentially innovative ethnographic methods.

Commoditizing Touch: the 'New' Pleasures in the Body

Ever since Fredric Jameson characterized postmodernism as the 'cultural logic of late capitalism' (1995), we are noticing an increasing engagement with the senses and sensuous experience in popular media, advertising and marketing. With a nod to Jameson, this is what David Howes has called 'hyperesthesia' or 'the sensual logic of late capitalism' (2005). We are familiar with the way that the sensory appeal of commodities is accentuated, exaggerated and remediated through a variety of channels, whether through selling ice-cream or cars, often conflating sensation with sensuousness, and in turn sensuousness with sexuality. But one strand within the commoditization of tactility is noticeably concerned with the negotiation of intimacy, paying other people to touch us. Jütte identifies these forms of commoditized touching as part of a larger 'rediscovery of the senses' in consumer culture, a validation of 'the new pleasure in the body' (2005:238). Without concentrating primarily on the aspect of sensuous consumption here (although see Paterson, 2005b), we note that the growth in uptake of alternative therapies, including therapeutic touching and such kinaesthetically aware practices as Tai Chi, capoeira and body-mind centring (BMC), is a measure of the rediscovery of the innumerable possibilities of bodily pleasure thrown up by late capitalism. The difficulty remains of how to write or represent such felt pleasures. In addition there are many healing forms of touch, as Tiffany Field (2001:108) remarks, negotiated forms of touching, enabling intimacy, that proliferate even as our culture increases its restrictions on touching in public life. Undoubtedly, the proliferation of such embodied practices and therapies could not arise without the increased availability of leisure time, and the importation of non-Western, non-traditional practices into everyday life for a considerable portion of the populations of cosmopolitan cities attests to this.

Yet, away from the promises of new pleasures, there is the faint but unmistakable underlying need for connection, a yearning for contact and proximity in a potentially isolating and alienating world, perhaps exacerbated by the emphasis on hollow consumerism in late capitalism. Such a yearning for proximity and contact is itself fairly universal, as evidenced succinctly by the troubled female narrator of Margaret Atwood's novel set in the 1930s, *The Blind Assassin*:

> There was a period of excessive drinking... As for the men, there were some of those as well. It was never a question of love, it was more like a sort of periodic bandaging. I was cut off from everything around me, unable to reach, to touch; at the same time I felt scraped raw. I needed the comfort of another body. (Atwood 2001:625)

The deeply felt yearning for contact through touch is similarly evident within healthcare institutions, where research with psychotic patients in Sweden un-surprisingly advocates physical contact by staff to advance feelings of connection, kinship and belonging. 'The yearning for physical contact can become so strong that they reach out and touch other people in order to fulfil their own needs', observe the researchers Salzman-Erikson and Eriksson (2005:848). In order to gratify this need for touching, the patients seek it within a range of different social contexts, including dance halls and massage parlours. Thus while independence, bodily integrity and self-sufficiency are encouraged in Westernized, industrialized cultures, we also value a more personal, intimate, emotional care where touch is crucial yet sharply spatially differentiated. It is appropriate in some spatial contexts and body parts, but decidedly inappropriate for others. Therapeutic touching on the other hand is often linked with 'body work', ways in which the body is cared for and attended to in settings like medical institutions, or therapeutic practices like Swedish massage,

Reiki, Shiatsu, acupressure, acupuncture and recently haptotherapy, relating spaces, emotions and power. Despite the proliferation and increasing visibility of such activities, Constance Classen notes the ambiguity in translating Asian massage practices into Western settings, based on alien concepts of the body and its energies. 'They are not quite denounced as superstitious, yet not quite accepted as efficacious', she judges (2005:348).

Despite the widespread medieval practice throughout Europe of the 'laying on of hands' (e.g. Kertay and Reviere 1998; Hetherington 2003), massage as an ancient practice only comes to prominence in Western medicine at the turn of the twentieth century. Before that, the famous naval explorer and navigator Captain Cook's experience in Tahiti in the nineteenth century is typical of that era in conflating the touch of massage with desire, steeped in both exoticism and eroticism. For example, after commenting on the dusky features of the host's daughter, Cook writes in his journal:

> To relieve us of our fatigue, she stroked our arms and legs and gently kneaded our muscles with her hands. The sensation was extremely gratifying. I will not attempt to judge whether these manipulations encouraged the circulation of the blood in the finer vessels or were able to restore the elasticity of the tired and slackened muscles; suffice it to say that they restored our energies and banished our fatigue (Cook, in Jütte 2005:241).

The comment on revitalising and restoring their energies seems an appropriate point at which to consider other forms of therapeutic touching, and their ability to facilitate movements or translations of affects and energies between bodies. Having never experienced massage, and therefore with the eyes of a novice, Cook explicitly links the muscular and cutaneous contact with an anatomical imagination of the circulatory system, but the whole enterprise is motivated by the need to transform somatically felt fatigue. So later we join up the phenomenological, literally 'felt' experience of Reiki with reference to practitioners' understandings of the practice, their felt connections between bodies, mind and world. It should now be clear that a 'felt' phenomenology is a suitable method for describing encounters with touching as both individual cutaneous sensation, interpersonal affect, and other metaphorical aspects (proximity, feeling-with), and that this nexus of relations varies widely between particularized, gendered bodies and cultures. Later, some reflexive thoughts on my own engagement with a therapeutic touching treatment, in this case Reiki massage, are used to interrogate the effects of proximity and distance, of sensuous immediacy, of how touch folds and unfolds intersubjective relations within therapeutic spaces. In the process, some ethnographic questions concerning the use of rich description, phenomenological method, and the difficulties of writing about sensory experience will be raised.

Therapeutic Touching

Among the variety of therapies involving touch, Reiki involves *non*-touch as well as touch. Swedish massage employs cutaneous contact with the skin surface but also the deeper vascular increase of bloodflow through the manipulation of the muscle tissue. Reiki, with its touching and equally its non-touching, goes deeply into the affective realm, the interiorization of emotion and its subsequent exchange and release. Before a discussion focusing on Reiki massage, however, a brief overview of another form of therapeutic touching will help contextualize the practice as a form of therapy that employs notions of energy and life-force, but detaches them from cosmological-theological contexts. At this point it is important to differentiate between 'therapeutic touching' as a general term indicating a range of practices involving touch, and 'Therapeutic Touch' (consistently demarcated by capitalization, and sometimes abbreviated accordingly as 'TT') which is a particular form of therapy. The practice of Therapeutic Touch is defined as, among other things, 'a non-invasive, perfectly safe procedure for pain alleviation, acceleration of healing processes, and stress reduction' (Ramnarine-Singh 1999, in Stewart and Legatto-Stewart 2005:3). As a set of practices Therapeutic Touch was identified and reactivated within the world of nursing in 1975 by a professor of nursing at New York University, Delores Krieger, who deals explicitly with religious concepts of energy (*prana*) and healing. In its development as a set of practices, it does seem a direct extension of the ancient laying-on-of-hands. For example, noticing the effects of the treatment on the ill, Krieger herself explains: 'an exchange of vitality occurs when a healthy person purposefully touches an ill person with a strong intent to help or heal' (in Smith 1989:200). The practitioner places hands on (or *near*) the body of the recipient, and in the words of Smith, 'gently attunes to them, placing hands over areas of tension and redirecting those energies' (ibid.), arguably producing measurable physiological effects.

Krieger held that the 'functional basis of Therapeutic Touch lies in the intelligent direction of significant life energies from the person playing the role of the healer to the healee (the ill person)' (1979:23), and the ability to utilize pathways between bodies to actualize the patient's own healing mechanisms is common to many Complementary or Alternative Medicines (CAM), including touch-based therapies. We are not concerned here with Krieger's rather personal and idiosyncratic formulation of 'Therapeutic Touch' per se, but rather with more general notions of therapeutic touching practices. While we could analyse a variety of these practices, many share the same interest in tactility, attunement and the notion of the conductance of paths of energy between bodies effectuated through touching (and indeed non-touching) as Reiki massage. The academic reception of such ideas is, predictably, mixed. On the one hand, a strong tendency within nursing literature moves away from the positivist approach of context-independent truth more usual to medical practice and training. Alongside hard-edged critiques of the socio-historical formations of power/knowledge inherent within medical institutions, they also advocate more literally 'touchy-feely' approaches to care. For example, admitting the use and expression of touch as both sensation and feeling is another tendency in nursing, and Thompson for example advocates a 'phenomenological approach' that 'can help [nurses] practice in more compassionate ways' (in Stewart and Legatto-Stewart 2005:9). On the other hand, scepticism abounds. The authors of an article comparing Krieger's Therapeutic Touch to the Victorian practice of mesmerism, subjecting the therapeutic practice to analysis from a philosophy of science background, concludes that 'therapeutic touch practitioners and researchers must realize that any benefit they provide patients has nothing to do with [chi, the life-force or Human Energy Fields]; it's more likely associated with the time they spend with patients and the care and compassion they show them' (ibid.:12). This sentiment could apply equally to a variety of different therapies, whether body-oriented, such as Therapeutic Touch or Reiki, or verbal, as in psychotherapy. While obviously dismissive of non-scientific notions, the attribution of positive qualities to proximity, presence and compassion (feeling-with) in those therapeutic encounters is notable.

Sympathetic and Empathetic Touch: *Feeling-with*

As part of the emerging tendency within nursing literature to take touch seriously, we can usefully bisect the forms of touch employed. First, 'professional', 'procedural' or 'task-oriented' touch is used in the everyday handling of patients. Secondly, what Van Dongen and Elema refer to as 'expressive' touch (2001:154), a touch that is 'affective' or 'caring' (Edwards 1998:810). One key to considering expressive or affective touch is that, like other therapeutic and psychotherapeutic practices, empathy is invoked (e.g. see Fagan and Silverthorn 1998; Bondi 2003).[2] It is another form of comforting and contact for therapists and healthcare professionals, an assurance based on empathy. Patients are aware of the empathic element because they appreciate that the nurse or healer "'knows what it is like to feel as they do"' (Edwards, 1998:815). In this way, touching is *feeling-with*, involving another tactile body, wherein the tactile and the emotional arise within each other. Feelings get communicated in the act of touching, and as Salzmann-Erikson and Eriksson found in follow-up interviews with patients after conducting trials of physical contact with nursing professionals, 'feelings are bound in and intertwined with the actual touching' (2005:848). Likewise in psychotherapy, experiments with trainee psychotherapists explicitly identified the importance of 'communicating sympathetic presence through touch' (Fagan and Silverthorn 1998:62). Such feeling-with, in terms of the literal touching involved in massage as well as the empathic content arising from an encounter with another, has significant spatial effects. For Edith Wyschogrod, empathy and sympathy are both a 'bringing near', drawing others into proximity (1981:25). Edwards extends this definition through the particular modality of touch, so that 'Touch can be a way of transferring sympathy and empathy between individuals[,] changing the proximity of feeling into what is felt' (1998:810). Her pithy explanation neatly solidifies the relation between touching and felt proximity.

In summary, touching within therapeutic settings is potentially cathartic, expressive, and opens up a potentially non-verbal communicative pathway between bodies that brings them into proximity. Conversely, being touched inappropriately in therapeutic settings may produce instantaneous negative affects such as anxiety, fear, disgust, alongside a concomitant sense of transgression, and reveals the asymmetry of gender relations in a therapeutic context (e.g. Alyn 1988; Kertay and Reviere 1998). But a number of voluntary tactile experiences explore more acceptable physical-emotional, psycho-social engagements between bodies. Like other therapies, Reiki occurs within prescribed yet uninstitutionalized spaces, where no formal medical or physiotherapeutic training is necessary. Touching as both immediate sensation and interpersonal affect (sympathy, empathy and intercorporeity) will therefore be examined through a particular filter: as proximity. Proximity is apt since it connotes both the physical nearness of tactile contact as well as the metaphorical nearness of empathy. In 'Feel the Presence' we explored the engineering of presence over a distance, so that technologies of touch allowed the user to accomplish tasks in the near-space of the desktop although actually performed through long-distance networks. Here, following Levinas (1991), Wyschogrod (1980, 1981) and to some extent Irigaray (2000), the more metaphorical aspect of touching – as a bringing into proximal presence of another – is developed. In their research on touch in psychotherapy, for example, Fagan and Silverthorn acknowledge this sense of felt proximity, noting that 'when people touch, the distance between them decreases', so that effectively 'our world shrinks when we touch' (1998:60). The felt proximity of another works as the engine of empathy, feeling-with, gathering much larger cosmological forces (e.g. in Reiki) into the felt presence of the body. Before proceeding to a detailed empirical exploration of Reiki, we temporarily return to the development of a suitable phenomenological framework for the analysis of such experience.

Phenomenology, *Meaning* and *Feeling*

> We *feel* meanings. A term that indicates the intimate association between bodily senses and emotion.
>
> Game and Metcalfe, *Passionate Sociology*

The phenomenological analysis of bodily experience, the description and redescription of felt meanings, emotions and sensations, rests on the ability to signify sensations, the ability to express such experiences. As Merleau-Ponty says: 'In a sense the whole of philosophy, as Husserl says, consists in restoring a power to signify, a birth of meaning, or a wild meaning, an expression *of* experience *by* experience' (2000:155, my italics). Throughout this book the phenomenology of Husserl and Merleau-Ponty has been evaluated as a departure point from which to frame the range of first-person and interpersonal tactile experiences, and to enhance their articulation. The language of touch as scientific, psychological or philosophical phenomenon does not always correlate with our actual embodied experiences of touching, as we know or recognize them. Or, as Merleau-Ponty puts it, 'my body is at once phenomenal body and lived body' (ibid.:136). One of the challenges for a phenomenology of lived, tactile experience is therefore to dissociate touch as measurable, psychological or even simply sensory phenomena from the manifold meanings and implications of touching within lived experience. For example, back in the first chapter we noted how Edith Wyschogrod speaks of a recovery of tactility:

> The meaning of tactility has, however, been hidden both in the classical philosophical tradition, which forces touch into conformity with a general theory of sensation, and in the physiological reductionism of contemporary psychology, which interprets tactility as the complex of interactions among afferent receptors and kinaesthetic acts. If we are to recover the meaning of tactility we must search in familiar analyses of sensibility for the trace, for the break with the conventional schematization of tactility as a species of the genus sensation. (1981:193, punctuation added)

Now I will argue that it is phenomenology, through the rich description of sensory and affective experience, that may help perform the break with conventional schematizations of tactility, that is, the decoupling of tactility from mere sensation. As has been argued throughout this book, touch reaches beyond the immediacy of present cutaneous sensation, unfolding to encompass a range of affective, empathic, metaphorical and other meanings, and phenomenology provides some rich descriptive tools through which these other meanings may find expression. However, phenomenology has been discredited as a methodology in some areas, remains deeply suspicious to others, and has been overtaken by recent movements in critical theory and poststructuralism. So what can a 'felt' phenomenology of touching and feeling positively contribute in the arena of sensuous scholarship and ethnography?[3] In other words, can we take these ideas into the field? Briefly returning to the core of the second chapter on 'felt' phenomenology, but now with specific reference to forms of touching that occur within therapeutic settings, my contention is twofold:

1   The *phenomenological method* already allows rich descriptions of phenomena, and the descriptive element (although not Husserl's transcendental project of discovering underlying 'essences') remains pertinent in describing touching as both individual tactile sensation and interpersonal affective communication. A

rich description of sensuous phenomena and conscious events need not remain straightforwardly a re-description or transcription of immediate sensations. The filter of other subjectively felt experiences may be incorporated in such re-description. In other words, phenomenology enables a rich sensuous description of manifold tactile experience not only in the psychologically based terms of the immediacy of cutaneous sensations (pressure, heat, pain) or even the somatic sensations (such as kinaesthesia, proprioception, the vestibular sense). It also allows other qualitative factors such as the feeling of proximity or distance that accompanies touch experiences, the affective charge that prompts cathartic release through therapeutic touching, or the empathic component that arises within touching-as-feeling.

In addition, while therapeutic touching and massage usually involve cutaneous contact, my particular empirical example is Reiki, a therapy of non-touch as well as touch. This will further decouple tactility from sensation, since this form of therapy involves a lack of cutaneous sensation in order to maintain its effectiveness, to facilitate self-healing, and as a manifestation for the yearning for proximity and connection with others. In their article on touch in the care of psychotic patients, Salzman-Erikson and Eriksson summarize this desire for affinity: 'Touching can therefore be regarded as a link not only between oneself and [another] human, but more importantly as a way to feel a sense of togetherness with the world' usually enabled by 'concrete, corporeal contact' (2005:851). The yearning for proximal togetherness in the case of Reiki is directed away from this essentially cutaneous, corporeal contact, and is therefore an excellent illustration of the decoupling of tactility from mere sensation, and the resultant opening-out of metaphorical meanings of touch.

2   The *'natural attitude'* of Husserl and Merleau-Ponty, as a ground for the observation and description of phenomena as they unproblematically disclose themselves within consciousness (*Gegebenheit*), can be the ground or basis of such rich ethnographic descriptions of sensuous events in everyday life, as above. To remind ourselves, in the natural attitude 'I do not have *perceptions*, I do not posit this object as beside that one, along with their objective relationships, I have a flow of experiences which imply and explain each other both simultaneously and successively', says Merleau-Ponty (1992:281). It is the 'everyday interpretive stance that takes the world to be principally "out there", separate and distinct from any act of perception or interpretation', in the words of Holstein and Gubrium (1998:139). This everyday interpretive stance is the basis for analysing experience and the social world through scientific and social-scientific methods. It is the assumption that there is a social world that precedes and succeeds our individual existence, having some form of reality that transcends individual subjectivity. Notably, the sociologist Alfred Schutz advocated Husserl's notion of the 'bracketing' of the lifeworld, that is, temporarily setting aside one's taken-for-granted orientation to it. Surely it would be more useful and pragmatic to study social activity not as something individual actors simply 'do', but as something intersubjectively constituted and maintained through

forms of practical reasoning and common sense, a stock of knowledge that makes up the lifeworld for each individual, yet whose origin is in fact social. These stocks of knowledge – images, theories, ideas, values and attitudes – 'are resources with which persons interpret experience, grasp the intentions and motivations of others, achieve intersubjective understandings, and coordinate actions' (ibid.). Revealing some of the mechanisms that underlie the taken-for-granted everyday embodied stance can therefore be achieved through the bracketing of the lifeworld, whether this concerns what is perceived to be intersubjectively 'real' entities within the sphere of social activity (such as queues, social hierarchies, class systems) or within individually embodied experience (such as appropriate or inappropriate touch). For Schutz, we take our subjectivity for granted and presume that we intersubjectively share the same reality, whereas in fact intersubjectivity is what Holstein and Gubrium describe as an 'ongoing accomplishment' (ibid.:140). The virtue of temporary bracketing in the case of tactile experience is that various individual and social levels of tactile experience may simultaneously be investigated, revealing the importance of the place of individual touch within larger social and historical practices of touching (for example as communication, as appropriate or inappropriate, as affirmatory, as empathic). Individual actions and experiences therefore take place within a specific cultural history that validates certain forms of touching but invalidates others.

Merleau-Ponty's writings on embodied perception have been accused by feminists such as Young (1990), Irigaray (1993), Weiss (1999) and Sullivan (2001) of being solipsistic and ill-attuned to bodily difference or cultural experience, underlining the facticity or givenness of embodied experience as something universally and unproblematically shared. Despite writing floridly and with introspective insight about flesh and our embodied encounters with the world, Merleau-Ponty's subject remains indubitably abstract, singularly white, adult, able-bodied and male. His first-person generalizations only seem to perpetuate and reaffirm this generalized, individualistic subjectivity, and although insights into touch and tangibility recur throughout his writing, they are often posed or framed within visualistic terms. The abstracted, generalized bodies posited by Husserl and Merleau-Ponty, then, tend to reinforce the binary of the 'normal' and the 'pathological'. However, although Iris Marion Young berates Merleau-Ponty for his continued absence of difference, her own autobiographical essay on the phenomenology of the specifically female, and later pregnant body (Young 1990, 1999), is inspired by Merleau-Ponty's approach while revealing an alternative to his supposed 'norm'. Furthermore, sensory impairments such as blindness offer alternative ways of conceptualizing the 'natural attitude', rendering the 'horizon' beyond the immediate milieu of the body as differently encountered and alternatively structured. As we have seen, the cultural history of blindness, along with autobiographical and philosophical treatments, demonstrates a revealing and powerful alternative mode of engagement with embodied experience, especially in terms of the relationship between vision and touch, eyes and hands (see also e.g. Paterson, 2006a, 2006b). This reconceptualization of the norm through pregnancy or blindness need not be considered as thought-experiments for unusual pathologies, but actually reaffirms the validity of the 'norm' as able-bodied, sighted, non-pregnant male. In other words, unlike Diderot's investigations of blindness, these are not 'special cases' that tell us more about human cognition and perception in general. Instead, the specificity of these cases offer pragmatic implications for policies of public transport, urban navigation or spatial access, as for example Rod Michalko (2002) explores. In terms of therapeutic touching, the medical-scientific validity or otherwise of such treatments is irrelevant to the perceived effectiveness of those practices, so that a phenomenology of therapeutic touching need not be concerned with scientifically measurable and verifiable results, nor with the empirically testable psychophysics of cutaneous sensation (the concern of Katz's *Der Aufbau von Tastwelt* of 1925, for example). Rather, the perceived significance of subjectively felt but unquantifiable aspects of therapeutic touching may be incorporated into descriptive accounts, such as feelings of empathy or cathartic release that accompany the physical acts of touching and being touched.

Flesh and Feeling Others

Aristotle believed flesh to be the *medium* of touch but not actually the *organ* of touch, as we saw. But another aspect of touch for Aristotle, distance and proximity, prefigures later phenomenological observations by Merleau-Ponty and Levinas, so we briefly return to Aristotle to seek insight into this inclination. Touch is a special case, its associated functions seated inside the body, connate with the heart, making touch the most inward of the senses (*De Anima* 423b). Whereas touch and taste require contact with the object, the other senses do not. And, despite there being no singular sense organ that corresponds to tactility, there is a distance between sensory medium – i.e. flesh – and object. Aristotle concludes that proximity is a special factor in touch, since the proximity of the object of touch in its everydayness obscures the fact that we perceive through a fleshy medium. Indeed, Wyschogrod argues that Aristotle finds the matter of proximity in touch so 'vexing' that he breaks with the usual model of the senses and adds something unusual, allocating 'vulnerability' to the medium of touch (Wyschogrod 1980:194). This vulnerability is the consequence of the immediate proximity of contact between object and medium (flesh) in tactility. A passage in *De Anima* reveals this special status of touch and proximity, although it is incidental to his wider theory of the sensory faculty: 'But there remains this difference between what can be touched and what can be seen or can sound; in the latter two cases we perceive because the medium produces a certain effect upon us, whereas in the perception of objects of touch we are not affected *by* but *along with* the medium' (443b, emphasis added). To illustrate this crucial difference he offers the example of a man carrying a shield. If the shield is struck forcefully the blow is felt immediately, not as the successive blow of sword on shield and then of shield to man. The intermediary nature of the shield recedes as the blow is felt, just as the intermediary of flesh is forgotten in tactile experience. This is potentially troubling for Aristotle. For, in sound and sight there is no awareness of the medium, yet our flesh, the medium of tactile contact, is itself felt when touched. If in reaching out, touching, or manipulating an object we register such tactile contact through the medium of flesh, whence comes the illusion that there is no intermediary? Through Aristotelian eyes this seems inconsistent. A parallel example partly answers this. In wearing clothes we are not constantly aware of the tactile sensation unless we become constricted or are extremely sunburnt. We become tactually aware if someone caresses or grips us through the material, but the intermediary of clothes as well as flesh seems insignificant to consciousness. Of course, in psychological terms this is explained by the habituation of certain tactile thresholds (e.g. Weber 1978). Nevertheless, what is central to Aristotle's account of tactility, thinks Wyschogrod, is that 'flesh is lived as vulnerability in every tactile encounter while the perception of tactile qualities, hardness, roughness, etc., is ancillary to this lived vulnerability and follows from it' (1980:194). Whether or not we agree with Wyschogrod's rather idiosyncratic view, the themes of flesh, proximity, vulnerability and contact raised by Aristotle remain conceptually pertinent and are developed presently.

Flesh has been discussed extensively in 'Tangible Play', working mostly as a metaphor for the messy carnality at play within performances of the body. The aspect of the radical reconfigurability of flesh is of concern here in terms of feeling-with other bodies, of the interchange of corporeal affects, of intercorporeity. But we share Merleau-Ponty's crucial caveat that 'flesh' here does not equate with 'matter' (2000:146). The openness and receptivity of touching and being touched by another betrays another potential form of vulnerability. We are familiar with critiques of visuality, and the relationship between vision and touch has been central throughout this book. But within the trope of the physiological and phenomen-ological interdependence of touch and vision there are ways to rethink tactile relations between bodies. If, ostensibly, vision affirms and reproduces boundaries, exaggerating the atomistic and the individual, then it is arguably *touch* and *tactility* that can explore relations *between* subjects, between bodies. Merleau-Ponty rarely writes explicitly of intersubjectivity per se (although in *Working Notes* there is evidence of the gestation of 'inter-subjectivity' from Husserl; see e.g. 2000:165). More usually he writes of 'intercorporeity' (2000:141, *passim*), which is the term adopted here, being less fraught with unrelated intellectual legacies or misleading assumptions concerning 'subjectivity'. The posthumously published *The Visible and the Invisible* (2000 [1964]) has an extensive discussion of vision, tactility and flesh as mutually imbricated in a remarkable chapter entitled 'The Intertwining – The Chiasm'. The sinuous interconnections between touch and vision are depicted through the trope of the 'tactile within the visible', which recurs throughout. One instance occurs within the following passage, where the fetishization of what he calls the 'visible' is manifest:

The visible about us seems to rest in itself. It is as though our vision were formed in the heart of the visible, or as though there were between it and us an intimacy as close as between the sea and the strand. (2000:130–1).

This passage, also picked up by Irigaray (1993:152), seems on first reading to indicate a departure from the careful investigation of the non-visual of Merleau-Ponty's earlier *Phenomenology of Perception* (1992), instead crowning the visual modality as the paradigmatic sense through which our other senses become filtered. In that work he argues for example that the 'natural attitude' implies not having separate sensory data but a flow of experiences (1992:281), and that 'synaesthetic perception is the rule' (ibid.:229). It is true that throughout his oeuvre he often falls back into visualistic metaphors, looking at painting, visual art, and visual examples of the gestalt in order to seek clarification, as in his famous essay 'Eye and Mind' (1964). But on further examination we find that 'visibility' denotes something far more complex and involved than mere 'vision', and that the openness and receptivity of flesh is symptomatic of a more 'generalised incarnate principle' inherent in any living being (2000:139). This will form the basis for intercorporeity, a way of understanding fleshly feeling and relations between bodies, and will allow us to rethink distance and proximity once again.

Further accusations against Merleau-Ponty include the charge that he often returns to a sense of the primordial, and is too often solipsistic (see e.g. Irigaray 1993:183ff). Both the primordiality and the solipsism are necessary constituents of what Merleau-Ponty terms 'anonymous existence', for example:

As the parts of my body together [comprise] a system, so my body and the other's are one whole, two sides of one and the same phenomenon, and the anonymous existence of which my body is the ever-renewed trace henceforth inhabits both bodies simultaneously. (1992:354)

Yet on this point feminist philosopher Shannon Sullivan works to reclaim the very possibility of intercorporeal communication. Anonymous existence is a pre-personal level of existence, that is, beneath the personal level of existence where I can distinguish my body from yours, a level 'in which there is a commonality between and a quasi-differentiation from other bodies' (Sullivan 2001:69). The wholeness that precedes individuation provides the very possibility of communication between bodies. Through trials, failures and sympathetic interactions, we can learn to 'grasp' another person's intentionality as they project themselves into the world. It is this more than anything, says Sullivan, that teaches me of the existence of others (ibid.:70). But the concretely phenomenological explanations of Merleau-Ponty's earlier work are reframed in *The Visible and the Invisible*, and the more abstract notion of 'flesh' achieves prominence, becoming the condition for the very possibility of intercorporeity. As Merleau-Ponty formulates it, flesh is neither matter nor substance (2000:146), but lies prior to the subject-object divide, a generalized 'incarnate principle' inherent within being (ibid.:139). It is an 'element' of being that is 'the formative medium of the object and the subject' (ibid.:147). As prepersonal and not simply material or corpuscular, it is prior to the recognizable division of subject and object. Flesh therefore implies the intertwining and exchange between subject and object, between the sensate and the sensible, which is the 'chiasm' of his title, resulting in an underlying ambiguity and possible reciprocity between them – hence his notion of reversibility, illustrated with the example of one hand touching the other, of each hand both touching and being touched. It is this concept of reversibility that most immediately challenges the usual notion of intentionality, which involves an act and an object. Instead, the reversibility of subject and object, of sensate and sensible, of toucher and touched, can be thought through the figure of the *hinge* (2000:148) or the *fold* (2000:146). Of course, this revisitation of the flesh and the fold will specifically involve the specific effects of touch, distance and intercorporeity through Merleau-Ponty.

One of Merleau-Ponty's goals, therefore, is to provide an insightful account of corporeal experience and intercorporeality without recourse to the transcendental ego of Husserl, or to the dualistic legacy of Descartes' meditative 'I'. Such a project is compatible with a form of corporeal feminism, as Young (1990) and Grosz (1994) especially show. Or, in Sullivan's words, feminists 'can and should benefit from a phenomenological focus on the situated, habitual, lived experience of human corporeal existence' (2001:87), but should not include the concepts of anonymous existence. With this attunement to situated experience in mind, phenomenological focus may be given to the tactile transactions and intercorporeal exchanges within the therapeutic encounter.

Proximity

The relationship between vision and touch is developed and revisited throughout Merleau-Ponty's works. What is embodied perception without touching and being touched? How is a reciprocal relation between another body and our own embodied consciousness established? Although not equated with matter, flesh is described at one stage in terms more akin to a fold of sensation that occurs within incarnate beings, as a 'sensible for-itself' that draws in or incorporates the outside (2000:135), and later as 'the coiling over of the visible upon the seeing body, of the tangible upon the touching body' (ibid.:146). This means that this sensible for-itself, the touching, seeing body is not a transcendental ego separated from the world, but reflexively implicated in the world it touches and sees, and takes its part in it:

> The body sees itself, touches itself seeing and touching the things, such that,
> simultaneously, *as* tangible it descends among them, *as* touching it demonstrates them all

and draws this relationship and even this double relationship from itself, by dehiscence or fission of its own mass. (ibid.)

Dehiscence, the gaping open or bursting forth like in a seedpod, is a figure that expresses something of the dynamic opening-out into the world of which it is a part. The presence of the fleshy body as a sensible for-itself simultaneously able to see and feel itself is a relation of reversibility, and reversibility has characterized the previously discussed example of the one hand touching the other, which becomes tangible for the other hence opens up into tangible being, and has already been invoked :

> Through this criss-crossing within it of the touching and the tangible, its own movements incorporate themselves into the universe they interrogate, are recorded on the same map as it; the two systems are applied upon one another, as the two halves of an orange. (ibid.:133)

Each of my hands is both touching and being touched, ambiguously and simult-aneously both subject and object, reversing their positions as subject-touching and object-touched. However, these separate maps never quite coincide. Reversibility is indeed 'always imminent' but never actually happens, it slips away before being fully realized: 'My left hand is always on the verge of touching my right hand touch-ing the things, but I never reach coincidence' (ibid.:147). This is not a failure, if the superposition is never exact, if reversibility recedes. There is always a gap, a 'hiatus' where 'the touching of the things by my right hand and the touching of this right hand by my left hand' (ibid.:148) never exactly overlaps. And this hiatus between the hand touched and the same hand touching, between my voice as heard and my voice as uttered, indicates a kind of blind-spot or zero-point of perception that remains unmistakably bodily. Merleau-Ponty describes this as 'the hinge' between these different experiences of reversibility, one which remains solid but 'irremediably hidden from me' (ibid.). It is a mechanism which generates differentiation rather than identity since there is a divergence (*écart*) within the body's own imminent experience of itself and an outside, an internal fissure within sensible experience. But the phenomenon of flesh admits special consideration through tactility, courtesy of Aristotle's observation of flesh as the medium of touch. While we cannot see our own retinas, as Merleau-Ponty puts it, there is a continuity of feeling between the flesh of our hand and the texture of an object: 'The flesh (of the world or my own) is not contingency, chaos, but *a texture* that returns to itself and conforms to itself' (ibid.:146, emphasis added). Like the saccadic movements of the eyes that follow the contours and movements of things, the kinaesthetic body responding to the movements, textures and rhythms of its surrounds, the dehiscence (the bursting forth of the massy body into the material world) suggests that flesh has a resonance, a vibration, a texture of its own that responds to the textures of the world. It 'makes a vibration of my skin become the sleek and the rough', he says (ibid.).

The hinge, the fold that lies behind the reversibility, is portrayed here as concerned with the immediacy and presence of one's own body. So, what of intercorporeity, of bringing another body into a relation of continuity, of resonance? How does another body enter into relations of reversibility, of felt proximity and distance? Merleau-Ponty has addressed the question by way of the operation of one's own body, 'my landscape', whereas 'the problem is to institute another landscape' (ibid.:141). The coiling over of the visible and the invisible, of the tangible and the intangible, 'can traverse, can animate other bodies as well as my own' (ibid.:140), he acknowledges. So far, the reversibility of flesh has assumed a single consciousness, a unitary, centrifugal 'consciousness of', the usual mode of phenomenological analysis familiar from Husserl and the earlier Merleau-Ponty of *Structure of Behaviour* (1984) and *Phenomenology of Perception* (1992). But here, instead of a single consciousness within a single body having experiences of a single world, Merleau-Ponty posits an assemblage of many consciousnesses (informed by e.g. eyes, hands, proprioceptors), where private, individual consciousnesses are not in juxtaposition but surround each other. Like the flesh, a general incarnate principle that underpins individual bodies, there is here a suggestion of a similarly reversible principle in terms of feeling: a 'Sentient in general' (capacity for *feeling*), and a 'Sensible in general' (perceptible by the senses, i.e. able to be *felt*). 'Now why would this generality, which constitutes the unity of my body, not open it to other bodies?' (2000:142) he asks rhetorically. Although this seems a circuitous exposition, it is clear that Merleau-Ponty's ideas concerning flesh and feeling are amenable to an analysis of tangibility, proximity and intercorporeity. 'What is open to us, therefore, with the reversibility of the visible and the tangible is ... an intercorporeal being, a presumptive domain of the visible and the tangible, which extends further than the things I touch and see at present', he says (ibid.:143). And while this seems absolutely intuitive and unproblematic, even commonsensical, we have followed through from Merleau-Ponty's earlier psychological phenomenology to a far more metaphorical attitude to visibility and tangibility, one that escapes the immediacy of sensation and the assumption of a separate realm of objects within intentionality, that decouples 'touch' from mere 'sensation', and that reaches out from the analysis of a singular consciousness to accommodate other bodies through his notion of 'intercorporeity'. Conceptually, we have arrived at a point somewhere near Wyschogrod's metaphorical notion of touch as metaphor, which started this chapter.

Tangibility, therefore, brings other bodies into nearness, may open quite literally onto something *other*. There is a relation of proximity. But it is not simply to reaffirm another binary in the cultural history of the senses – touch and taste as senses of proximity but vision, smell and audition as those of distance. Instead, we consider tangibility not as a sense but a model of proximity, something that modernist meta-phors of visuality clearly are not. Perhaps it is appropriate to consider a tactile rather than a visual subject in certain encounters, in order to ponder those felt spatial effects of proximity and distance. For, as Wyschogrod argues, 'Since empathy and sympathy are phenomena of proximity, they can only be understood as feeling-acts of a tactile rather than a visual subject' (1981:32). The phenomenological psychology of the later Husserl and Merleau-Ponty, especially *The Visible and the Invisible*, commendably attempts to break from naturalism (scientism), re-implicating mind, body and world, and gives touch a prominent role in this. However, most likely we agree with Wyschogrod when she argues that phenomenology is insufficiently radical when it comes to tactility (1980:198). Just what would a more radical phenomenology of touch consist in?

The Caress

Despite a generosity to 'non-philosophy' which allowed Merleau-Ponty to accommodate scientific data, and especially findings in experimental psychology into his phenomenology of perception, in terms of language and metaphor the tactile is inextricable from vision, and in this dyad the emphasis remains indubitably on the visual. There is no shortage of potential multisensory metaphors from which he could draw, and at times he intersperses his texts with rather poetic phrases that celebrate the ambiguity or intermodality of sensory experience, such as 'the palpation of the eye' (2000:133). As we saw, it was up to Dreyfus to formulate an actual haptic metaphor of gestalt perception and kinaesthetic orientation from Merleau-Ponty, that of maintaining a 'grip' (2004). So now let us briefly consider an alternative metaphor for a tactile, feeling engagement with others, that of the 'caress'.

In much the same way as Derrida can devote an entire book to Jean-Luc Nancy's treatment of touching (Derrida, 2005), Levinas' notion of 'the caress' is similarly rich, and potentially subject to lengthy exegesis. Space does not allow such treatment here (see e.g. Paterson, 2004), but nonetheless the central focus of both the theoretical framework and the empirical findings are cast here as relations of proximity and distance, and Levinas' phenomenologically inspired writings on proximity are indispensable here. Phenomenology has taught us that objects come into prominence and recede from consciousness as a result of the way our intentionality shifts from object to object. A kinaesthetic body with its saccadic eye movements and gripping hands concentrates on those objects at hand in the pursuit of a particular task, for example. But, as Wyschogrod observes,

> Distance is an important component of sight: no matter how proximate, objects are always given across an intervening space. Seeing acknowledges distance even while compensating for it by bringing what is far off into visibility. Thus true proximity, a phenomenology of ethical space[,] can never be founded upon vision. (1981:187–8, punctuation modified)

Sound instead can become a model for proximity, the way it impinges upon the hearer and bypasses the difficulties of vision and the separation of representation. But this passage acknowledges that the pathway to 'true' proximity is non-visual, and further that such proximity is an ethical relation. This is developed earlier by Levinas, who proposes an intimate relation between the One and the Other that is generative of subjectivity itself. The subject is called, invoked in relation to the Other, and the becoming of both One and Other is mutually interrelated. Levinas characterizes this interrelationship as a radical proximity, hence Wyschogrod's questioning of a radical phenomenology of touch. Proximity is therefore discounted as any form of quantifiable distance, but as a primary ethical responsibility to the Other. 'The relationship of proximity cannot be reduced to any modality of distance or geometrical contiguity,' he explains, and 'not to the simple 'representation' of a neighbour; it is already an assignation, an extremely urgent assignation – an obligation, anachronously prior to any commitment' (1996:90). A potentially radical phenomenology of touch might dwell on the ethical relation, or lead us into a discussion of Irigaray's response, to posit a dual subjectivity that is permeable and relational (2000). Without dismissing the importance of the ethics of proximity, the focus should remain on tactility, empathy and felt proximity. So we return to touch and follow a related strand.

Touch engages with alterity by entering into a relation with another affective, empathic body. Wyschogrod defines empathy as 'the feeling-act through which a self grasps the affective act of another through an affective act of its own' (1981:28). Her thinking of empathy through affect in this manner is an important way to think about the 'grasping', the entering into relations and the translations of affects that occur in therapeutic practices. However, rather than talking of a 'feeling-act', which suggests an individuated self performing an isolated act – the model of vision that allows the 'repetitive affirmation of a closed ipseity' in the words of Vasseleu (1998:107) – as part of a 'felt' phenomenology, we can talk of 'feeling-with', invoking intercorporeity, tactile empathy in a more unfolding, processual way. How this transpires within the particular embodied and spatial context of Reiki is now considered.

'Something will Shift': Touch as Feeling-with

Prelude.   *My first Reiki massage, ever. Anxious because of deadlines, a hundred things whizzing through the head. Talking with the Reiki master, trying to get a sense of what will happen. Then the massage begins, a curious mixture of touch and non-touch. As this is going on, something strange and unexpected starts to occur, then starts to surge uncontrollably, a welling-up that suddenly becomes an outpouring. Along with a feeling of incredible release, I start to cry and find I cannot stop.*

Here occurs the congruence of the psychological phenomenology of flesh and feeling-with, along with more metaphorical treatments of touch and tangibility. It is through the encounter with a form of therapeutic touching that ideas of intercorporeity and empathy, as feelings of proximity and distance, are revisited. On one level in Reiki there is empathic touching, a 'feeling-with', touch as reassurance and comfort, an interchange of affects. As much *non*-touch as touch, yet always feeling. On another level, the primacy of touching is a short circuit to feeling a deeper connection, feeling attuned to larger forces and energies. Such feelings are significant in being experienced as phenomenologically given, yet refer beyond the individual tactile body. For example, Constance Classen reminds us that sensory orders are also already *cosmic orders*. They are not 'read' but 'lived' through the body (1993:127), referring beyond the actual site of the body in its concrete, sensed particularity. A sensory order is therefore not given as such, but culturally ordered. By connecting up with a cosmic order or Human Energy Field in Reiki, the immediacy of touching opens out onto a much larger imaginary, one that accommodates the translations of forces and energies within an individual body into the vast networks of energy patterns that surround us. Obviously, for the majority of Reiki practitioners and recipients the contact, non-contact and the conception of cosmological forces (as either *Chi*, *Ki* or the Human Energetic Field) are inextricably intertwined.

By marrying up the phenomenologically descriptive method to an ethnographic encounter with touching, we are concerned less with a detailed explanation of cosmological forces than with a rich description of *feeling*. A key moment experienced within a Reiki encounter amplifies the inextricable link between touching and feeling, of tactile sensation and emotional release (catharsis). The observations detailed here involved my felt experience within Reiki sessions, as well as interviews and dialogues with Reiki practitioners. While Reiki involves tactile encounter, importantly it includes non-contact aspects. The *Rei-ki* – 'universal life force' in Japanese – traverses people through touch, making therapy an amalgam of tactile contact and non-contact, an intercorporeal energetics, an exchange of affective intensities. Like acupressure and acupuncture, Reiki follows the principle of the internal life force as a form of internal 'aqueduct' system of flows, necessary for the body to function (e.g. Kaptchuk and Croucher, 1986:40). This life force or energy ('chi', or 'ki' in Japanese) is used for acupressure, acupuncture and tai-chi in Chinese medicine, and both Shiatsu and Reiki in Japanese medicine bind the healer's energies with those of the recipient's through touch. These different traditions assume an energetic system which refers to 'the organizing factors that underlie what we call the life process', observes Montagu (1986:404) who, as a medical practitioner, acknowledges that non-contact in therapeutic touch can decrease anxiety. Reiki is perhaps more revealing than other touch therapies because of the very significance of this non-touch, the interaction with the body's energies arising both with and without actual cutaneous contact, and a concomitant emotional release. Attempting to understand this relation between contact and non-contact, massage and energy was central in my questioning of the practitioners. Touch becomes an irruptive, intercorporeal experience that, like Merleau-Ponty's notion of tangibility, traverses individual skin and flesh and suggests something of the generalized incarnate principle of flesh, or what Massumi describes as 'a prepersonal intensity corresponding to the passage from one experiential state to another and implying an augmentation or diminution of that body's capacity to act' (in Deleuze and Guattari, 1988:xvi). In fact this is his definition of 'affect', underlining the suitability of the term for conceptualizing relations between individual bodies and larger energetic frameworks.

These themes of individual, empathic touch and the connection with a cosmic order are worked out through the stories of two Reiki therapists who practice in Bristol, 'Rachel' and 'Louis'.[4] These two practitioners represent two corresponding aspects of interest in this study, for while Louis talked more about the intensities and energetic pathways, articulating something of the imaginary of cosmic forces, Rachel was more concerned with the emotive content of the Reiki experience, and talked of her emotional motivation to learn Reiki in the first place. Nevertheless, both themes are amenable to an interpretation in terms of touch and felt proximity, and are inextricable from each other in Reiki practice. For the sake of conceptual neatness, however, these themes have been assigned to different subsections.

Felt Cosmological Proximity

Louis is a healer who also teaches Reiki in workshops, commonly using Reiki as an introduction to more complexly codified massage such as Shiatsu. He articulates some of the themes mentioned, the notion of Reiki dealing within an affective economy that spills over and outside the body, irreducible to individual emotional states. Repeatedly in conversations and interviews he conveyed the fact that in Reiki the 'aura', or what he calls the 'bio-energetic field', is something that can literally be felt, something actualized in a particular body but exchangeable between and beyond them. Such exchange and transfer are facilitated through the touch and non-touch of the therapist. Interaction between bodies was not explained straightforwardly in terms of a more powerful body and a weaker body. Instead the impression was more akin to that of a Spinozist body of energies and intensities, facilitated by exchanges between the healer's body and the recipient: 'So ... it's not a directive treatment, it's almost like you're turning a tap on for someone else to drink from,' he explained, indicating a much larger set of surrounding forces and energies (Louis, interview 19/09/02). The way that the body refers beyond itself implies that it functions primarily as a conduit, in his language a 'vessel', within a vast cosmological imaginary of forces and energies, of which the individual body is significant only inasmuch as it participates in, and facilitates, transfer and exchange: 'it's very much empowering the receiver, without having any sort of ego, which is one of the beautiful things about Reiki', he said (ibid.). Occasionally there are unintended results in the exchange of energies between bodies. At one point Louis confessed that in early self-teaching of Reiki techniques, the energetic transfer flowed in an unintended direction. He took on the headaches and pains of the recipients, revealing that he conceptualized these energetic pathways as bidirectional, and confirming that the development of the practice required development, mastery and self-knowledge. In learning and experiencing Yoga, Luce Irigaray also recognizes and remarks upon the energetic transfer between bodies as potentially healing, but also acknowledging an asymmetric order when she says 'Each, faithful to him- or herself, would bring to the other his or her own energy and his or her manner of cultivating it' (2000:55).

The exchange of affects or intensities is facilitated by the drawing of Reiki symbols on the body, working within a larger symbolic and cosmic order, as both Louis and Rachel described. In their explanations and in the therapeutic encounter there was the sense of connecting with something much more extensive, of proximity with larger forces. Although herself a practitioner, Rachel clearly remembered her first experience as a Reiki recipient, and described how symbols were 'written' or inscribed onto the skin of her back by the practitioner:

> I just lay down and this woman just started to put her hands in all different positions over my body, and I was feeling this tingling sort of feeling. And there was something magical going on here, I couldn't quite put my finger on it, I thought there's something going on here, something special. And she was drawing these little symbols into my back, these Reiki symbols, I didn't know what she was doing at the time but I could feel she was somehow almost *programming my body*, like this *de de de de* [gesturing symbols in the air]. And I felt that there was a part of me that understood, even if the rest of me was not really sure... [Rachel, interview 16/09/02]

Rachel's description of her first Reiki experience hints at symbolic gestures and movements that open up paths for both energetic and emotional transfer. She understands it as a coherent, interconnected system of symbols, of movements, gestures, and energies. The symbols serve as markers to channel *ki* energy, a literal drawing-out that need not be inscribed *upon* the skin surface. A series of gestures, sweeps, motions, what Rachel showed me through sweeps of the hands ('*de de de de*'), that participate in a mapping of energy through, around and between bodies. Use of symbols was integral to the therapy for both practitioners. While the symbol has an explicit and 'correct' meaning when translated into English, for most the gesture-symbol remains invisible, unreadable. It simultaneously suggests a-signifying content, having 'magical' power; it reaches back to, refers to something barely articulable through language, and like Merleau-Ponty's notion of flesh (a 'generalized incarnate principle' (2000:139)), a set of pre-personal, pre-verbal intensities thought of in Reiki as prior to being embodied. A more metaphorical sense of touching results from this conceptualization of energies and intensity. Louis for example describes the Reiki symbols as 'a vehicle for transfer' of energies:

So the idea of prayer in ancient religions would be in bio-energetic terms a projecting of your energy field to *touch* somebody, to touch a situation – praying for world peace, praying for that – and in the same way distance healing or Reiki symbols or even if you're doing a hands-off feeling so you're giving Reiki but your hands are maybe six inches above the body, you're projecting your intention, the energy, you're visualizing or using your 'intent' is the best word, to intend that that energy is going to be transferred or is going to be made available to that person if they want it. And the Reiki symbols ... are kind of like a vehicle, it's a vehicle for transfer let's say [Louis, interview 19/09/02]

In a portion of the interview concerned with the relation between touching and non-touching, similar ideas were expressed, further solidifying the interconnection between touch, cosmic energies, proximity and distance. Different analysts have attempted to quantify how far the projection of the aura or bio-energetic field goes, but according to Louis 'it goes as far as you want it to, as far as you send it' (interview, 19/09/02). He mentioned projecting one's aura specifically in terms of 'touching' someone else. But the distinction between physical touching and non-touching in Reiki was explained unequivocally as a metaphorical form of touching. Along with Wyschogrod, we have previously identified metaphorical touching with the decoupling of tactility and sensation, and the felt collapse of distance into proximity. For Louis, this metaphorical touching is conceptualized not dissimilarly as a sort of willed projection across distances:

Well touch is ... very interesting, even though we're not touching each other sitting here now, we are sort of touching each other, you can touch someone with your eyes, or you can touch someone ... but might not actually feel a physical touching. (ibid.)

Yet equally this form of non-physical touching is recognizable in the immediacy of mundane encounters, an angry glance or a lusty look. While fascinated by the practitioners' conceptualization of touching as a mobilization of forces over a distance, my emphasis remains on feelings of proximity interpretable as the co-implication and presence of touch and affect, of touching as feeling.

Felt Emotional Proximity

Within the exchanges and transfers of energy, channelled through diagrams and symbols, there is affective charge. Along with the physicality of (non-)touching, there is often catharsis, release, sometimes crying. Rachel's first encounter with Reiki happened in her early twenties at Glastonbury, shortly after her father died. She identified Reiki as a therapeutic practice with an explicit emotional content on numerous occasions. Explaining what would happen within the impending Reiki session, for example, she said:

I'll put my hands in positions *on* your body, and also *off* the body, working on your aura, the sort of energy which is all around you, and I can feel that quite strongly... Sometimes you come out feeling a bit heavy, a bit disorientated, as if waking up from a deep sleep, but that's because it's aroused deep feelings and things, and people will go off and have a good cry or have a think, they'll just feel quite energized. *Something will shift*, then I'll just say drink plenty of water and take it easy, that sort of thing. [Rachel, interview 16/09/02]

Likewise, Louis had identified the emotional content of Reiki experience early in our conversations, linking it explicitly with touch and the energies involved between bodies. But he explicitly identifies the cathartic properties of the tactile exchange, indicating that touching involves emotional as well as energetic aspects. Most recipients experience a sense of relaxation, calm and nurturing feelings, thought Louis, arising directly out of touch. It's a 'subjective, non-invasive touch, but it's also a supportive touch' (Louis, interview 19/09/02), he clarified, which still has a potentially cathartic component:

as a result of the transfer of energy some people might experience a very beautiful, relaxing subsequent time, and *some people might have things stirred up, some kind of cathartic experience or emotional release*, depending on how they chose to respond or how they chose either at a conscious or unconscious level to use the energy that's been made available to them. (ibid., emphasis added)

From both practitioners' remarks there is an implicit notion of Reiki as being a form of touching that is not only immediate and physical, entwined with the particularity of the lived body, but also uses touch in a deeply affective way that reaches toward other bodies (intercorporeity). In the imaginary of practitioners and recipients, personal intent and the conscious manipulation of forces brought into proximity can be explicitly used to 'touch' a person or a situation. Reiki is exemplary therefore in involving both physical and metaphorical touching: as affective, intensive and concerned with the feeling and sensation of the individual subject; and as metaphorical, extensive, occurring as intercorporeity, within an overarching and pervasive conceptual framework of energies and events. Spaces of therapeutic touching allow what is distant and remote, these imaginations of larger frameworks, into the proximal immediacy of the encounter between tactile and non-tactile bodies, and with it sympathy, empathy, the mutuality of feeling-with.

The way that a tactile and, at times, non-tactile therapy can arouse deep feelings was surprising and unexpectedly powerful, as experienced first-hand in my initial Reiki session. Halfway through my first massage, as indicated in the Prelude, there was an almost palpable sense of release. With my back toward the practitioner and without actual tactile contact, those movements, gestures and symbols proceeded without my directly sensing them. An uncanny feeling, a series of sensations paradoxically resulting from the absence of direct cutaneous sensation, progressively became manifested as a mounting energy, a felt intensity. Over time this increased, eventually spilling over into physically-felt catharsis. As Rachel had correctly identified, as felt physically and emotionally, '*Something will shift*' in that moment. Partway through the session, suddenly and spontaneously an irresistible urge welled up, could be contained no longer, and at a key moment I burst into tears. Therapy continued with this uncannily warm sensation of release, a physical response to an emotional outpouring. Even as the weeping persisted there was little accompanying feeling of shame or embarrassment. For practitioners, such catharses are a familiar occurrence.

Outwardly observable factors such as poise, gesture, the actions of touching and non-touching, and the display of tactile techniques that occur within a therapeutic encounter could be transcribed. Correspondingly, so could the subjectively felt sensations of being touched, the anticipation in non-touch, as well as other somatic sensations. But it is the *shift* that comprises the key unutterable moment, ineffable feeling, that key moment, the physically felt unity of touch and affect. While the empathic content of touch implies co-presence, mutuality or feeling-with, the extraordinary moment of catharsis was experienced as a surge of intensity, an individually-occurring set of somatic sensations and emotional release. That moment, the *shift*, caused a disruption in my perception, a subsequent feeling of light-headedness and disorientation, and re-engaging with the outside world afterward was difficult. Louis had identified not only the disruptive yet potentially cathartic element of the practice but another possibility, a 'beautiful, relaxing' time resulting from the energy transfer, a sensation of receptivity and acquiescence that I also experienced following the cathartic moment. The shift occurs literally in more senses than one.

Returning to the opening words of Wyschogrod, we have rapidly departed from touch as naturalized, as measurable, as simply cutaneous. Following the notion that touching is impingement, as bringing into nearness: spaces of therapeutic touching allow what is distant and remote, these imaginations of larger frameworks, into the proximal immediacy of the encounter between bodies. We have described this as a mutuality of feeling-with, the empathic component of touching and feeling. Wyschogrod's definition of empathy, as 'the feeling-act through which a self grasps the affective act of another through an affective act of its own' (1981:28), certainly applies to the employment of touch (and non-touch) within therapeutic practices, feeling and grasping another and drawing them into proximity. However, rather than a 'feeling-act', which suggests an individuated self performing an isolated act, my notion of 'feeling-with' invokes the metaphorical idea of touching as empathy in a more processual, unfolding way.

The Textures of Touch: Concluding Thoughts

Thinking, as does Wyschogrod (1980), of touch as a feeling of impingement upon and proximity to the world has been helpful in thinking about therapeutic touching. To be affected, to be touched, is to bring aspects and forces of the world nearer to us. To think tactility outside the skin surface, to incorporate others (as intercorporeity), has involved empathy, feeling-with, the acknowledgement of the inextricability or co-presence of touch and affect. Or, in keeping with our discussions of empathy and intercorporeity, Michael Taussig declares: 'Sentience takes us outside ourselves' (1993:38). This has added resonance when we consider the etymology of 'sentience', the Latin word *sentire* meaning 'to feel'. Feeling within, between and across bodies. The ambiguity of touching, as physical and affective, as literal and metaphorical, reaching across space from the toucher to the touched, grasping them and drawing them into proximity. In Reiki, feeling does indeed take us outside ourselves, in terms of the empathy involved in therapeutic touching, of intercorporeity, but also in terms of connection with cosmic forces and energies. In empathic touching, feeling-with, and especially the surge of cathartic release, touch can lead to the externalization of an emotion, an exchange of affective intensities between bodies within a therapeutic space. On one level the encounter between practitioner and recipient in Reiki refers to a shared understanding of a cosmological imaginary of auratic energies; on another level the sheer empathic experience of feeling-with was enough to trigger the exteriorization of emotion, an intense physical and emotional feeling of cathartic release within the immediacy of that therapeutic space.

If you started reading this book from the beginning, as an exasperated reader you may be asking: Where is the subject? Where is subjectivity? Notable for their absence, at times skirted around, mentioned briefly in passing, or redescribed in other terms. Even though Wyschogrod began this chapter with the notion of touch as a metaphor for an impingement upon 'subjectivity', the core notion of the 'subject' remains unexamined for Wyschogrod, as here. One reason for this is the intellectual legacy surrounding subjectivity and intersubjectivity, one that presupposes a knowledge and a literature specifically addressing these problems. We have touched on opportunities for this, including Irigaray's notion of dual subjectivity in *To Be Two* (2000), a particularly apt formulation given the focus here. However, we have continually returned to certain key concepts within touching such as flesh, feeling, proximity and empathy and found something that exceeds individual subjectivity. When we decouple touch from sensation, other senses or meanings of touch start to be liberated.

One task of thinking through the long historical reach of a concept like touch, examining its cultural, psychological, philosophical formations within particular geographical areas during specific cultural-historical epochs, is that the 'subject' alters greatly over time, becomes fragmented and dispersed. Even in the empirical aspects of tactile research, touch has been dissociated from individual sensation, and there is awareness that 'touch' affects individual bodies in manifold ways. The admission of the lack of subjectivity is not an admission of culpability, then. The project of the decoupling of tactility from sensation, which pervades this book has framed this not as an impingement upon subjectivity as such, but as part of a complex folding of somatic sensations within particular bodies. Touch as metaphor, as impingement of the world, as shared experience, as the ability to rouse affects and catharsis, as a series of interconnected somatic sensations, as the conscious background behind embodied experience. All these are concerned not with subjectivity per se but with bodies and their capacities. And this only sediments the phenomenological, in fact post-phenomenological (after Ihde, 1995) enframing of touch throughout the book, whether it concerns for example the history of measurement, the mediation of tactile experience through haptic technologies, the attempt to articulate novel somatic sensations in unfamiliar ways, or the ability to touch and be touched by others.

Notes

Chapter 1 The Primacy of Touch

1. For Aristotle's texts I refer to the Bekker numbers (e.g. 429a in the margins) rather than page numbers, as this convention is used to overcome the difficulties of using different translations.
2. See Glossary for a series of more comprehensive definitions.

Chapter 2 Toward a 'Felt' Phenomenology

1. The text 'De Sensu et Sensibilibus' is variously translated as 'On Sense and the Sensible' (in the J.I. Beare translation) and 'Sense and Sensibilia' (in the W.D. Ross edited collections). The essay 'De Sensu ...' is part of a larger work by Aristotle edited by Ross, from which it is usually taken: *Parva Naturalia* (Aristotle 1955), and takes up some themes from *De Anima*, developing them unsystematically.
2. He also mentions the 'ascidians' (an ancient species noted by Aristotle but of unconfirmed veracity).
3. Notwithstanding Marx: if philosophy so far has only explained the world (abstraction), the point of phenomenology is to describe it (everydayness).
4. To be is to be felt. This of course is adapting George Berkeley's famous explanation of immaterialism in *A Treatise Concerning the Principles of Human Knowledge* (1710), where to be is to be perceived ('*esse est percipi*').

Chapter 3 Seeing with the Hands

1. There are two alternative spellings which were not standardized at the time. 'Molyneux' is sometimes spelt 'Molineux' (e.g. in Monbeck, 1973) or the Latinized 'Molinaeus' (in D'Alembert, 1772)
2. Congenital blindness refers to those born blind, whereas adventitious blindness refers to those who become blind at some later stage, usually through disease or accident.
3. The phrase 'tabula rasa' is not originally in Locke's *Essay* but is in Aristotle's *De Anima* (430a); Locke in 1690 uses the phrase 'white paper' which is later translated in the French (1700) as *tabula rasa*.

Chapter 4 The Forgetting of Touch

1. *Eidos* (idea, image) and *theoria* meaning 'viewing, a sight, spectacle' – 'mental view, contemplation' or mental schema (*Oxford English Dictionary*, 2nd edn, 1989) especially show this connection.
2. This visualistic history of geometry has been written by Frege, Carnap, Hilbert, Russell, Cassirer, Husserl and Serres, among others.
3. παντο (*panto*, all) + μετσον (*metron*, measure): universal measure. See e.g. Crosby 1997:21ff.
4. For example, this is evinced by Petit writing in 1797, who says: 'One must, as far as possible, make science ocular' (in Welton 1999:38).
5. Galileo writes: 'Philosophy is written in this grand book, the universe, which stands continually open to our gaze, but the book cannot be understood unless one first learns to comprehend the language and read the letters in which it is composed. It is written in the language of mathematics, and its characters are triangles, circles, and other geometric figures without which it is humanly impossible to understand a single word of it; without these, one wanders about in a dark labyrinth' (cited in Crosby 1997:240).
6. For example, Beck comments, 'Sensual qualities as well are reduced to motions and shapes that can be calculated mathematically' (1941:480).
7. On this increasing inscription after Boyle, Ivins writes: 'Science and technology have advanced in more than direct ratio to the ability of men to contrive methods by which the phenomena which otherwise could be known only through the senses of touch, hearing, taste and smell, have been brought within the range of visual recognition and measurements and then become subject to that logical symbolization without which rational thought and analysis are impossible' (1973:20).
8. However, subsequent experiments such as those of Rock and Harris tried to prove the opposite, that haptic sensation was modified when vision was distorted through prisms (Rock and Harris 1967:97).
9. 'Phoronomy' being the geometrical theory of motion, i.e. kinematics (from *Shorter Oxford English Dictionary*, Vol. 2 (2nd edn, Oxford: Clarendon, 1936).

Chapter 5 How the World Touches Us

1. J.H. Bernard's 1892 English translation of Kant's *Critique of Judgement*, published originally in German in 1790.
2. 'Sculpture' in German is *Plastik*, hence Herder's book (2002. See especially footnote 5, p.125).
3. Ponderability from Latin *ponderābilis*, that may be weighed (*Oxford English Dictionary* 1989, 2nd edn).

4. For example the Vision Australia building in Kooyong, outside Melbourne, uses different-coloured carpets as optical cues for low-level vision, along with a central water feature that provides a continual acoustic background for spatial location so that a visitor can hear where in relation to the central reception area they currently are. I am grateful to Francesca Davenport of Health Science Planning Consultants in Melbourne for arranging a visit in February 2006.

Chapter 6 Tangible Play

1. 'Tangent' being derived from Latin *tangere*, to touch.
2. Although often used interchangeably, technically 'plastic surgery' relates to reconstructive surgery, or the repair of deforms or defects, whereas 'cosmetic surgery' applies to procedures used simply to improve appearance.
3. Of course, there is a long tradition of making custom 'skins' for videogame characters, the textured envelopes around 3D models as they are represented on screen. Space does not permit detailed treatment, but the user-based modification of game-character skins is certainly conceptually aligned with this section's exploration of skin and screen.
4. Examples include David Rokeby's *Very Nervous System* (1986–1990) and Marcel-lí Antúnez's fascinating project *Réquiem* (1999).

Chapter 7 Feel the Presence

1. 'Phantom' and 'phantasm' meaning 'Something that appears to the sight or other sense, but has no material substance; an apparition, a spectre; a spirit, a ghost', or 'Something having the form or appearance, but not the substance, of some other thing; a (material or optical) image *of* something' (*Oxford English Dictionary*, 2nd edn, 1989).
2. For another discussion about the engineering of sensations, see e.g. Latham and McCormack's discussion of 'automobility' (2004).
3. The Nintendo Wii promises new ways of interacting with the videogame console, using a revolutionary controller which uses motion and orientation sensors that respond to tilting. Using the wireless controller as a virtual sword, for example, or a pair of handlebars are among the most interesting possibilities, and will be of appeal outside the traditional gaming audience. See http://en.wikipedia.org/wiki/Wii_Remote for further details (last accessed 21/10/06).
4. Obviously, such questions are undoubtedly naive from a methodological viewpoint, and the statistical analysis of what the paper's authors themselves describe as the 'subjective sense of presence and copresence' (Kim et al.: 2004:328) is better served by other methods; nevertheless, the interest in this paper lies in its not

only being a technology demonstration, but also attempting to define and evaluate novel feelings and sensations.

5. Multimedia installations that use presence and movement in innovative ways away from the computer desktop include David Rokeby's *Very Nervous System* (1991), Marcus Novak's *transArchitecture: Transmitting the Spaces of Consciousness* (1995) and *Sensor Space* (1997/98), and the IO-Dencies series (1997–1999). Also of note is Strömberg et al.'s (2002) *Nautilus* project which deals with social gaming and the detection of movement as a collective in order to navigate space. These works and others show that presence and co-presence has been investigated in informational space for some time.

6. MacLean and Roderick (1999) also depart from the desktop in their haptic doorknob project, using the doorknob as a communication device to provide instantaneous temperature feedback, based on certain prescribed ambient conditions, for example if an important meeting is happening.

7. Dan Jacobson (Calgary) and Reg Golledge (UCSB) have been collaborating for years on spatial information and mapping systems for the visually impaired, and their virtual collaborations are at http://www.hapticsoundscapes.org [last accessed: 11/01/05]

8. MIT Tangible Media Group's project at http://tangible.media.mit.edu/projects/ comtouch/comtouch.htm [last accessed: 11/01/05]. A similar technology was utilized in Samsung's mobile phones released in February, 2004.

Chapter 8 Affecting Touch

1. The phrase 'therapeutic touching' is used throughout this chapter to encompass a variety of touch-based therapies, including Swedish massage, Reiki, Shiatsu and others. 'Therapeutic Touch' is a particular form of touch-based therapy formulated by Dolores Krieger.

2. Although sympathy is related to empathy, the usual definition of empathy involves a form of emotional resonance, the ability to put oneself in another's shoes, to recognize, perceive and actually experientially feel the emotion of another. Sympathy is the feeling of compassion for another, the wish to see them better or happier, often described as 'feeling sorry' for someone.

3. For example, the special issue of journal *Ethnography* 3(4), 2003, on 'Phenomenology and Ethnography'. Also see Holstein and Gubrium (1998) for the influence of Husserl's phenomenology on Garfinkel's ethnomethodology, via Alfred Schutz.

4. As is standard, the names of the participants have been changed to protect confidentiality.

References

Broadcasts

Horizon (1997) 'The Man Who Lost His Body', BBC2. Rosetta Pictures. Originally aired 17 October 1997, 50 mins.

Rice, G. (2001) 'Programme 1: The First Sense', *Touch*. BBC Radio 4. Originally broadcast Monday 9 July, 9.00 p.m.

Tx: Pandaemonium. BBC 2. 50 minutes. Broadcast 30 December 1995. Directed and produced by Richard Curson Smith and Leslie Asako Gladsjo.

Bibliography

Alyn, J. (1988) 'The Politics of Touch in Therapy: A reply to Willison and Masson', *Journal of Counselling and Development* 66: 432–3.

Amato, I. (2001a) 'Touchy Subjects: From Digital Clay to the "nanoManipulator"', *Technology Review*, April 2001: 70–1.

Amato, I. (2001b) 'Helping Doctors Feel Better', *Technology Review*, April 2001: 64–70.

Angell, J.R. (1906) *Psychology: An Introductory Study of the Structure and Function of Human Consciousness* (New York: Henry Holt).

Appelbaum, D. (1988) *The Interpenetrating Reality: Bringing the Body to Touch* (New York: Peter Lang).

Aristotle (1955) *Parva Naturalia*, ed. W.D. Ross (Oxford: Clarendon).

Aristotle (1976) *Ethics* [*Nicomachean Ethics*], trans. J.A.K. Thomson (London: Penguin).

Aristotle (1982) *De Generatione et Corruptione*, trans. C.J.F. Williams (Oxford: Clarendon).

Aristotle (1984) 'Sense and Sensibilia' [*De Sensu*], trans. J.I. Beare, in W.D. Ross (ed.), *Aristotle: Works* Volume II (Princeton: Princeton University Press), pp. 693–713.

Aristotle (1986) *De Anima (On the Soul)*, trans. H. Lawson-Tancred (London: Penguin).

Aristotle (2001) *Historia Animalium*, ed. D.M. Balme (Cambridge: Cambridge University Press).

Armstrong, C. (2002) 'This Photography Which Is Not One: In the Gray Zone with Tina Modotti', *October* 101: 19–52.

Armstrong, D.M. (1962) *Bodily Sensations* (London: Routledge & Kegan Paul).

Arnheim, R. (1966) *Towards a Psychology of Art: Collected Essays* (London: Faber & Faber).

Arthur, C. (2002) 'Touching Moment 3,000 Miles Apart Becomes a Virtual Reality', *Independent* (Home News), 30 October 2002, p.7.

Atwood, M. (2001) *The Blind Assassin* (London: Virago).

Bachelard, G. (1994) *The Poetics of Space*, trans. M. Jolas (Boston: Beacon).

Baddely, A.D. (1986) *Working Memory* (Oxford: Oxford University Press).

Baddely, A.D. (1992) 'Working memory', *Science* 255: 256–9.

Baillie, S., Crossan, A., Brewster, S., Mellor, D. and Reid, S. (2005) 'Validation of a Bovine Rectal Palpation Simulator for Training Veterinary Students', *Studies in Health Technology and Informatics* 111: 33–6.

Baraibar, A. (1999) 'Stelarc's Post-Evolutionary Performance Art: Exposing Collisions Between the Body and Technology', *Women and Performance 21*, 11(1): 157–68.

Barasch, M. (2001) *Blindness: The History of a Mental Image in Western Thought* (London: Routledge).

Bate, M. (1974) 'The Phenomenologist as Art Critic: Merleau-Ponty and Cézanne,' *British Journal of Aesthetics* 14(4): 344–50.

BBCi. (2002) 'Virtual Hands Reach across the Ocean', 30 October 2002 13:08 GMT http://news.bbc.co.uk/2/hi/technology/2371103.stm [Accessed 04/11/02].

Beck, M. (1941) "The Last Phase of Husserl's Phenomenology: An Exposition and a Criticism", *Philosophy and Phenomenological Research* 1(4) (1941): 470–91.

Benjamin, W. (1977 [1931]) 'A Short History of Photography', trans. P. Patton, *Artforum* 15(6): 46–51.

Benjamin, W. (1999 [1936]) *Illuminations*, trans. H. Zorn, ed. H. Arendt (London: Pimlico).

Berenson, B. (1906) *The Florentine Painters of the Renaissance*, 3rd edn (London: G.P. Putnam's Sons).

Berkeley, G. (1983). *Philosophical Works including the Works on Vision* (London: Dent).

Biever, C. (2005) 'The Touchy-feely Side of Telecoms: from Vibrating Game Pads to TouchSense Phones', *New Scientist* 185(2488), 28 February.

Bingham, N. (1996) 'Object-ions: from Technological Determinism Towards Geographies of Relations', *Environment and Planning D: Society and Space* 14(4): 635–57.

Bloomer, K.C. and Moore, C.W. (1978) *Body, Memory and Architecture* (London: Yale University Press).

Boden, M.A. (2000) 'Crafts, Perception and the Possibilities of the Body,' *British Journal of Aesthetics* 40(3): 289–301.

Bolter, J.D. and Grusin, R. (2000) *Remediation: Understanding New Media* (London: MIT Press).

Bondi, L. (2003) 'Empathy and Identification: Conceptual Resources for Feminist Fieldwork', *ACME: An International E-Journal for Critical Geographies* 2(1): 64–76. Online at http://www.acme-journal.org/vol2/Bondi.pdf [Last accessed: 14/06/04].

Book, W.J. and Swanson, D.K. (2004) 'Reach out and Touch Someone: Controlling Haptic Manipulators Near and Far', *Annual Reviews in Control* 28(1): 87–95.

Bordegoni, M and Cugini, U. (2006) 'Haptic Modeling in the Conceptual Phases of Product Design', *Virtual Reality* 9(2–3): 192–202.

Bourdieu, P. (2000) *Pascalian Meditations*, trans. R. Nice (Stanford University Press: Stanford, CA).

Bronner, S.J. (1982) 'The Haptic Experience of Culture', *Anthropos* 77(3) 351–62.

Burdea, G.C. (1996) *Force and Touch Feedback for Virtual Reality* (London: John Wiley & Sons).

Cache, B. (1995) *Earth Moves: The Furnishing of Territories*, trans. A. Boyman (Cambridge, MA: MIT Press).

Carman, T. (1999) 'The Body in Husserl and Merleau-Ponty', *Philosophical Topics* 27(2): 205–26.

Carr, J.L. (1960) 'Pygmalion and the *Philosophes*: The Animated Statue in Eighteenth-century France', *Journal of the Warburg and Courtauld Institutes* 23(3/4): 239–55.

Carreiras, M. and Codina, B. (1992) 'Spatial Cognition of the Blind and Sighted – Visual and Amodal Hypotheses', *Cahiers de Psychologie Cognitive/Current Psychology of Cognition* 12(1): 51–78.

Cassirer, E. (1950) *The Problem of Knowledge: Philosophy, Science and History since Hegel*, trans. W.H. Woglom and C.W. Hendel (London: Yale University Press).

Cassirer, E. (1985) *The Philosophy of Symbolic Forms*, Vol. 3: *The Phenomenology of Knowledge*, trans. R. Manheim (London: Yale University Press).

Castañeda, C. (2001) 'Robotic Skin: the Future of Touch?' in S. Ahmed and J. Stacey (eds), *Thinking Through the Skin* (London: Routledge), pp. 223–36.

Causey, A. (1998) *Sculpture Since 1945* (Oxford: Oxford University Press).

Caygill, H. (1998) *Walter Benjamin: The Colour of Experience* (London: Routledge).

Cézanne, P. (1995) *Paul Cézanne: Letters*, ed. J. Rewald (New York: Da Capo Press).

Cheselden, W. (1728) 'An account of some observations made by a young gentleman, who was born blind, or lost his sight so early, that he had no Remembrance of ever having seen, and was couch'd between 13 and 14 years of age', *Philosophical Transactions of the Royal Society of London* 35: 447–50.

Chrétien, J.-L. (2004) *The Call and the Response*, trans. A.A. Davenport (New York: Fordham University Press).

Classen, C. (1993) *Worlds of Sense: Exploring the Senses in History and Across Cultures* (London: Routledge).

Classen, C. (1997) 'Foundations for an Anthropology of the Senses', *International Social Science Journal* 153: 401–12.

Classen, C. (2005) 'Tactile Therapies', in C. Classen (ed.), *The Book of Touch* (Oxford: Berg Publishers), pp. 347–51.

Cleaveland, P. (2006) 'Haptic Controls: A Touching Experience', *Control Engineering,* 1 March: 48–50.

Cole, J. (1995) *Pride and a Daily Marathon* (London: MIT Press).

Colebrook, C. (2002) *Gilles Deleuze* (London: Routledge).

Condillac, É.B. de (1930). *Treatise on the Sensations,* trans. G. Carr (London: Favil).

Cranston, J. (2002) 'The Touch of the Blind Man: The Phenomenology of Vividness in Italian Renaissance Art', in E.D. Harvey (ed.), *Sensible Flesh: On Touch in Early Modern Culture* (London: University of Pennsylvania Press) pp. 224–42.

Crary, J. (1990) *Techniques of the Observer: On Vision and Modernity in the Nineteenth Century* (London: MIT Press).

Crary, J. (1999) *Suspensions of Perception: Attention, Spectacle, and Modern Culture* (London: MIT Press).

Creech, J. (1986) *Diderot: Thresholds of Representation* (Columbus: Ohio State University Press).

Crosby, A.W. (1997) *The Measure of Reality: Quantification and Western Society, 1250–1600* (Cambridge: Cambridge University Press).

Crowder, R. (2006) 'Towards Robots That Can Sense Texture By Touch', *Science* 312, 9 June: 1478–9.

Crowther, P. (1993) *Art and Embodiment: From Aesthetics to Self-consciousness* (Oxford: Clarendon Press).

D'Alembert, J.L.R. (1772) 'Blindness', in *Selected Essays from the Enclyopedy* (translator unknown, London: Samuel Leacroft), pp.132–47.

Damasio, A.D. (2000) *The Feeling of What Happens: Body, Emotion and the Making of Consciousness* (London: Vintage). B F 3 11 . D33 1999

Danius, S. (2002) *The Senses of Modernism: Technology, Perception and Aesthetics* (London: Cornell University Press).

Davies, C. (1998) '*Osmose*: Notes on Being in an Immersive Space', *Digital Creativity* 9(2): 65–74.

Davies, C. (2000) 'On Osmose' at http://www.immersence.com [Last accessed 9/6/2001].

Davies, C. and Harrison, J. (1996) 'Osmose: Towards Broadening the Aesthetics of Virtual Reality' at http://www.softimage.com/Projects/Osmose/broadening.htm [Last accessed 28/08/2001].

Davis, K. (1995) *Reshaping the Female Body: The Dilemma of Cosmetic Surgery* (London: Routledge).

De Fontenay, E. (1982) *Diderot: Reason and Resonance* (New York: George Braziller).

Deleuze, G. (1986) *Cinema 1: The Movement Image*, trans. H. Tomlinson and B. Habberjam (London: Athlone Press).

Deleuze, G. (1988) *Spinoza: Practical Philosophy*, trans. R. Hurley (San Francisco: City Light Books).

Deleuze, G. (1989) *Cinema 2: The Time Image*, trans. H. Tomlinson (London: Athlone).

Deleuze, G. (1993) *The Fold: Leibniz and The Baroque*, trans. T. Conley (London: Athlone).

Deleuze, G. (1995) *Negotiations, 1972–1990*, trans. M. Joughin (New York: Columbia University Press).

Deleuze, G. (2003) *Francis Bacon: The Logic of Sensation*, trans. D.W. Smith (London: Continuum).

Deleuze, G. and Guattari, F. (1988) *A Thousand Plateaus: Capitalism and Schizophrenia* (London: Athlone).

Deleuze, G. and Guattari, F. (1994) *What Is Philosophy?* trans. G. Burchell and H. Tomlinson (London: Verso).

Derrida, J. (1989) *Edmund Husserl's 'Origin of Geometry': An Introduction*, trans. J.P. Leavey (London: Bison Books).

Derrida, J. (2005) *On Touching – Jean-Luc Nancy*, trans. C. Irizarry (Stanford, CA: Stanford University Press).

Dery, M. (1996) 'Fractal Flesh: Stelarc's Aesthetic of Prosthetics' at http://www.levity.com/markdery/ESCAPE/VELOCITY/author/stelarc.html [Last accessed 26/01/2002]

Descartes, R. (1968 [1641]) *Discourse on Method and the Meditations*, trans. F.E. Sutcliffe (London: Penguin).

Descartes, R. (1972) *Treatise of Man*, trans. T.S. Hall (Cambridge MA: Harvard University Press).

Diderot, D. (1916) *Diderot's Early Philosophical Works*, ed. M. Jourdain (Chicago: The Open Court Publishing Co.).

Diderot, D. (1977) 'Letter on the Blind, for the Benefit of Those who See', trans. M.J. Morgan, in M.J. Morgan, *Molyneux's Question: Vision, Touch and the Philosophy of Perception* (Cambridge: Cambridge University Press).

Dionisio, J., Henrich, V., Jakob, U., Rettig, A. and Ziegler, R. (1997) 'The Virtual Touch: Haptic Interfaces in Virtual Environments', *Computers & Graphics* 21: 459–68.

Dix, A., Finlay, J., Abowd, G. and Beale, R. (1998) *Human-Computer Interaction*, 2nd edn (London: Prentice Hall).

Dixon, R. (1995) *The Baumgarten Corruption: From Sense to Nonsense in Art and Philosophy* (London: Pluto).

Doel, M. (1999) *Poststructuralist Geographies: The Diabolical Art of Spatial Science* (Edinburgh: Edinburgh University Press).

Downton, A and Leedham, G. (1991) 'Human Aspects of Human-Computer Interaction', in A. Downton (ed.), *Engineering the Human-Computer Interface* (London: McGraw-Hill), pp. 13–26.

Dreyfus, H. (2000) 'Telepistemology: Descartes' Last Stand', in K. Goldberg (ed.), *The Robot in the Garden: Telerobotics and Telepistemology in the Age of the Internet* (London: MIT Press), pp. 48–63.

Dreyfus, H. (2004) 'Merleau-Ponty and recent cognitive science' in T. Carman and M.B.N. Hansen (eds), *The Cambridge Companion to Merleau-Ponty* (Cambridge: Cambridge University Press).

Drobnick, J. (ed.) (2006) *The Smell Culture Reader* (Oxford: Berg).

Durie, B. (2005) 'Doors of Perception', *New Scientist* 185(2484), 29 January: 33–6.

Edwards, S.C. (1998) 'An Anthropological Interpretation of Nurses' and Patients' Perceptions of the Use of Space and Touch', *Journal of Advanced Nursing* 28(4): 809–17.

Eilan, N. (1993) 'Molyneux's Question and the Idea of an External World', in N. Eilan (ed.), *Spatial Representation: Problems in Philosophy and Psychology* (Oxford: Blackwell).

Fagan, J. and Silverthorn, A.S. (1998) 'Research on Communication by Touch' in E. W.L. Smith, P.R. Clance, S. Imes (eds), *Touch in Psychotherapy: Theory, Research, and Practice* (New York: Guilford Press), pp. 59–73.

Farber, L. (2006) 'Skin Aesthetics', *Theory, Culture & Society* 23(2–3): 247–9.

Farrell, G. (1956) *The Story of Blindness* (Cambridge, MA: Harvard University Press).

Feld, S. (2005) 'Places Sensed, Senses Placed: Towards a Sensuous Epistemology of Environments', in D. Howes (ed.), *Empire of the Senses* (Oxford: Berg), pp. 179–91.

Field, T. (2001) *Touch* (Cambridge, MA: MIT Press).

Fine, A. (1973) 'Reflections on a Relational Theory of Space', in P. Suppes (ed.), *Space Time and Geometry* (Boston: D. Reidel).

Fisher, J. (1997) 'Relational Sense: Towards a Haptic Aesthetics', *Parachute* 87(1): 4–11.

Fisher, J. (1999) 'Char Davies', *Parachute* 94: 53–4.

Focillon, H. (1989) *The Life of Forms in Art*, trans. C.B. Hogan and G. Kubler (London: Zone).

Freeland, C. (1992) 'Aristotle on the Sense of Touch', in M.C. Nussbaum and A.O. Rorty (eds), *Essays on Aristotle's De Anima* (Oxford: Clarendon), pp. 227–48.

Friel, B. (1994) *Molly Sweeney, A Play* (London: Penguin).

Gallagher, S. (2005) *How The Body Shapes the Mind* (Oxford: Clarendon).

Game, A. and Metcalfe, A. (1996) *Passionate Sociology* (London: Sage).

Gärdenfors, P. (2000) *Conceptual Spaces: The Geometry of Thought* (London: MIT Press).

Garfinkel, H. (1967) *Studies in Ethnomethodology* (Englewood Cliffs, NJ: Prentice-Hall).

Geurts, K.L. (2002) *Culture and the Senses: Bodily Ways of Knowing in an African Community* (Berkeley: University of California Press).

Geurts, K.L. (2005) 'Consciousness as "Feeling in the Body"', in D. Howes (ed.), *Empire of the Senses: The Sensual Culture Reader* (Oxford: Berg), pp. 164–78.

Gibson, J.J. (1950) *The Perception of the Visual World* (London: George Allen & Unwin).

Gibson, J.J. (1968). *The Senses Considered as Perceptual Systems* (London: George Allan & Unwin).

Gibson, J.J. (1979) *The Ecological Approach to Visual Perception* (London: Houghton Mifflin).

Goldstein, K. (1995) *The Organism: A Holistic Approach to Biology Derived From Pathological Data in Man* (New York: Zone).

Gombrich, E.H. (1991) *Art and Illusion: A Study in the Psychology of Pictorial Representation* (Oxford: Phaidon).

Grau, O. (2003) *Virtual Art: From Illusion to Immersion*, trans. G. Custance (Cambridge, MA: MIT Press).

Graven, T. (2003) 'Aspects of Object Recognition: When Touch Replaces Vision as the Dominant Sense Modality', *Visual Impairment Research* 5(2): 101–12.

Gregory, R.L. (1967) *Eye and Brain: The Psychology of Seeing* (London: World University Library).

Gregory, R.L. (2004) 'The Blind Leading the Sighted: An Eye-opening Experience of the Wonders of Perception', *Nature* 430, 19 August: 836.

Gregory, R.L. and Wallace, J. (1963) *Recovery From Early Blindness: A Case Study*. Experimental Psychology Society Monograph No. 2 (Cambridge: Heffers), pp. 65–129.

Grosz, E. (1994) *Volatile Bodies: Towards a Corporeal Feminism* (Indianapolis: Indiana University Press).

Gržinić, M. (2000) 'Exposure Time, the Aura, and Telerobotics' in K. Goldberg (ed.), *The Robot in the Garden: Telerobotics and Telepistemology in the Age of the Internet* (London: MIT Press), pp. 215–24.

Haans, A. and Ijsselsteijn, W. (2006) 'Mediated Social Touch: a Review of Current Research and Future Directions', *Virtual Reality* 9: 149–59.

Hamlyn, D.W. (1959) 'Aristotle's Account of Aesthesis in the *De Anima*', *Classical Quarterly* (New Series) 9(1): 6–16.

Hannaford, B. (2000) 'Feeling is Believing: A History of Telerobotics' in K. Goldberg (ed.), *The Robot in the Garden: Telerobotics and Telepistemology in the Age of the Internet* (London: MIT Press), pp. 246–75.

Harries, K. (1997) *The Ethical Function of Architecture* (London: MIT Press).

Hatwell, Y. (2003) 'Introduction: Touch and Cognition', in Y. Hatwell, A. Streri and E. Gentaz (eds), *Touching for Knowing: Cognitive Psychology of Tactile Manual Perception* (Amsterdam: John Benjamins), pp. 1–14.

Hayles, N.K. (1993) 'Virtual Bodies and Flickering Signifiers', *October* 66: 69–91.

Hayles, N.K. (1996) 'Embodied Virtuality: Or How to Put Bodies Back Into the Picture', in M.A. Moser and D. MacLeod (eds), *Immersed in Technology: Art and Virtual Environments* (London: MIT Press), pp. 1–28.

Heilig, M.L. (1992) 'El Cine del Futuro: The Cinema of the Future', *Presence* 1(3): 294–7.

Heilig, M.L. (1998) 'Beginnings: Sensorama and the Telesphere Mask', in C. Dodsworth Jr. (ed.), *Digital Illusion* (New York: ACM Press), pp. 343–51.

Heller, M.A. (1991) 'Haptic Perception in Blind People', in M.A. Heller and W. Schiff (eds), *The Psychology of Touch* (London: Lawrence Erlbaum), pp. 239–61.

Helmholtz, H. (1962) 'On the Origin and Significance of Geometrical Axioms', *Popular Scientific Lectures*, trans. E. Atkinson, ed. M. Kline (New York: Dover).

Helmholtz, H. (1971) 'The Facts of Perception', *Selected Writings of Hermann Helmholtz*, ed. R. Kahl (Middletown CT: Wesleyan University Press).

Herder, J.G. (2002 [1778]) *Sculpture: Some Observations on Shape and Form from Pygmalion's Creative Dream*, trans. J. Gaiger (London: University of Chicago Press).

Hetherington, K.I. (2003) 'Spatial Textures: Place, Touch, and Praesentia', *Environment and Planning A*, 35(11): 1933–44.

Hillis, K. (1999) *Digital Sensations: Space, Identity and Embodiment in Virtual Reality* (London: University of Minnesota Press).

Hodges, M. (1998) 'It Just Feels Right', *Computer Graphics World* 21(10): 48–56.

Hogan, H. (1998) 'Virtual Touch', at HighTechCareers.com: http://www.hightechcareers.com/doc697/virtualtouch697.html [Last accessed: 16/5/2000]

Holstein, J.A. and Gubrium, J.F. (1998) 'Phenomenology, Ethnomethodology and Interpretive Practice', in N.K. Denzin and Y.S. Lincoln (eds), *Strategies of Qualitative Inquiry* (London: Sage), pp. 137–57.

Howes, D. (2003) *Sensual Relations: Engaging the Senses in Culture and Social Theory* (Ann Arbor: University of Michigan Press).

Howes, D. (2005) 'Hyperesthesia, or The Sensual Logic of Late Capitalism' in D. Howes (ed.), *Empire of the Senses* (Oxford: Berg), pp. 281–303.

Hull, J.M. (1991) *Touching the Rock: An Experience of Blindness* (London: Arrow).

Hume, D. (1978) *A Treatise of Human Nature*, 2nd edn (Oxford: Clarendon).

Husserl, E. (1960) *Cartesian Meditations: An Introduction to Phenomenology*, trans. D. Cairns (The Hague: Martinus Nijhoff).

Husserl, E. (1970a) *The Crisis of European Sciences and Transcendental Phenomenology: An Introduction to Phenomenological Philosophy*, trans. D. Carr (Evanston IL: Northwestern University Press).

Husserl, E. (1970b) *Logical Investigations*, Vol. 1, trans. J.N. Findlay (London: Routledge & Kegan Paul).

Husserl, E. (1973) *Experience and Judgement*, trans. J.S. Churchill and K. Ameriks (London: Routledge).

Husserl, E. (1981) 'Pure Phenomenology, Its Method and Its Field of Investigation', trans. R.W. Jordan, in P. McCormick and F.A. Elliston (eds), *Husserl: Shorter Works* (Notre Dame, IN: University of Notre Dame Press).

Husserl, E. (1989a) *Ideas Pertaining to a Pure Phenomenology and a Phenomenological Philosophy, Book 2: Studies in the Philosophy of Constitution*, in *Collected Works*, Vol. 3 (Dordrecht: Kluwer).

Husserl, E. (1989b) 'The Origin of Geometry', in *Edmund Husserl's 'Origin of Geometry': An Introduction*, trans. J.P. Leavey (London: University of Nebraska Press).

Husserl, E. (1998) *Thing and Space: Lectures of 1907* (Edmund Husserl *Collected Works*, Vol. 7) (New York: Springer).

Husserl, E. (1999) 'Material Things in their Relation to the Aesthetic Body', in D. Welton (ed.), *The Body: Classic and Contemporary Readings* (Oxford: Blackwell Publishers), pp. 11–22.

Huxley, A. (1984) *Brave New World* and *Brave New World Revisited* (London: Chatto & Windus).

Ihde, D. (1986) *Experimental Phenomenology: An Introduction* (Albany: State University of New York Press).

Ihde, D. (1995) *Postphenomenology: Essays in the Postmodern Context* (Evanston, IL: Northwestern University Press).

Imrie, R. (2003) 'Architects' conceptions of the human body', *Environment and Planning D: Society and Space* 21(1): 47–65.

Ingold, T. (1995) "Building, Dwelling, Living: How Animals and People Make Themselves at Home in the World', in M. Strathern (ed.), *Shifting Contexts: Transformations in Anthropological Knowledge* (London: Routledge).

Ione, A. (2000) 'An Inquiry into Paul Cézanne: Defining the Role of the Artist in Studies of Perception and Consciousness', *Journal of Consciousness Studies* 7(8–9): 57–74.

Irigaray, L. (1985) *This Sex Which is not One*, trans. C. Porter and C. Burke (London: Cornell University Press).

Irigaray, L. (1991) *The Irigaray Reader*, ed. M. Whitford (Cambridge: Basil Blackwell).

Irigaray, L. (1993) *An Ethics of Sexual Difference*, trans. C. Burke and G.C. Gill (London: Cornell University Press).

Irigaray, L. (2000) *To Be Two*, trans. M.M. Rhodes and M.F. Cocito-Mondoc (London: Athlone).

Ivins, W.M. (1964) *Art and Geometry: A Study in Spatial Intuitions* (New York: Dover).

Ivins, W.M. (1973) *On the Rationalization of Sight* (New York: Plenum).

Jablonski, N.G. (2006) *Skin: A Natural History* (London: University of California Press).

Jacobson, R.D. and Kitchin, R.M. (1997) 'Techniques to Analyze the Cognitive Map Knowledge of Persons with Visual Impairment or Blindness: Issues of Validity', *Journal of Visual Impairment and Blindness* 91: 360–76.

Jacobson, R.D., Kitchin, R.M., and Golledge R.G. (2002) 'Multimodal Virtual Reality for Presenting Geographic Information', in P. Fisher and D. Unwin (eds), *Virtual Reality in Geography* (London: Taylor & Francis), pp. 382–400.

Jacomuzzi, A.C., Kobau, P. and Bruno, N. (2003) 'Molyneux's Question Redux', *Phenomenology and the Cognitive Sciences* 2: 255–80.

Jameson, F. (1995) *Postmodernism, or The Cultural Logic of Late Capitalism* (London: Verso).

Jay, M. (1994) *Downcast Eyes: The Denigration of Vision in Twentieth-Century French Thought* (London: University of California Press).

Johnson, G. (1993) 'Introduction', in G. Johnson and M. Smith (eds), *The Merleau-Ponty Aesthetics Reader* (Evanston, IL: Northwestern University Press).

Johnson, G.A. (2002) 'Touch, Tactility and the Reception of Sculpture in early modern Italy' in C. Wilde and P. Smith (eds), *A Companion to Art Theory* (Oxford: Blackwell), pp. 61–74.

Johnson, S. (1997) *Interface Culture: How New Technology Transforms the Way We Create and Communicate* (New York: Basic).

Jonas, H. (1954) 'The Nobility of Sight: A Study in the Phenomenology of the Senses', *Philosophy and Phenomenological Research* 14(4): 507–19.

Jones, B. (1975) 'Spatial Perception in the Blind', *British Journal of Psychology* 66(4): 461–72.

Josipovici, G. (1996) *Touch: An Essay* (London: Yale University Press).

Jütte, R. (2005) *A History of the Senses: From Antiquity to Cyberspace*, trans. J. Lynn (Cambridge: Polity).

Kangas, S. (1999) 'From Haptic Interfaces to Man-Machine Symbiosis', *M/C: A Journal of Media and Culture* 2(6), http://journal.media-culture.org.au/journal/past_vol_2.php [Date accessed: 22/08/06]

Kant, I. (1990) *Critique of Pure Reason*, trans. N. Kemp-Smith (London: Macmillan).

Kaptchuk, T. and Croucher, M. (1986) *The Healing Arts: A Journey Through the Faces of Medicine* (London: Guild).

Karlsson, G. and Magnusson, A.-K. (1994) 'A Phenomenological-Psychological Investigation of Blind People's Orientation and Mobility', Report 783 from Department of Psychology, Stockholm University, pp.1–22.

Kennedy, J.M., Gabias, P. and Heller, M.A. (1992) 'Space, Haptics and the Blind', *Geoforum* 23(2): 175–89.

Kertay, L. and Reviere, S.L. (1998) 'Touch in Context', in E.W.L. Smith, P.R. Clance and S. Imes (eds), *Touch in Psychotherapy: Theory, Research, and Practice* (New York: Guilford), pp. 16–35.

Khatchadourian, H. (1974) 'On the Nature of Painting and Sculpture,' *British Journal of Aesthetics* 14(4): 326–43.

Kim, J., Kim, H, Tay, B.K., Muniyandi, M., Srinivasan, M.A., Jordan, J., Mortensen, J., Oliveira, M., Slater, M. (2004) 'Transatlantic Touch: A Study of Haptic Collaboration over Long Distance', *Presence: Teleoperators and Virtual Environments* 13(3): 328–37.

Kitchin, R.M., Blades, M. and Golledge, R.G. (1997) 'Understanding Spatial Concepts at the Geographic Scale without the Use of Vision,' *Progress in Human Geography* 21(2): 225–42.

Kittler, F.A. (1999) *Gramophone, Film, Typewriter*, trans. G.W. Young (Stanford CA: Stanford University Press).

Klatzky, R., Lederman, S.J. and Reed, C. (1987) 'There's More to Touch than Meets the Eye: The Salience of Object Attributes for Haptics With and Without Vision,' *Journal of Experimental Psychology: General* 116(4): 356–69.

Kleege, G. (1999) *Sight Unseen* (London: Yale University Press).

Knight, I. (1968) *The Geometric Spirit: The Abbé de Condillac and the French Enlightenment* (London: Yale University Press).

Kozel, S. (2005) 'Spacemaking: Experiences of a Virtual Body', in C. Classen (ed.), *The Book of Touch* (Oxford: Berg), pp. 439–46.

Kreuger, L.E. (1982) 'Tactual Perception in Historical Perspective: David Katz's World of Touch', in W. Schiff and E. Foulke (eds), *Tactual Perception: A Source Book* (Cambridge: Cambridge University Press), pp. 1–54.

Krieger, D. (1979) *The Therapeutic Touch: How to Use your Hands to Help or Heal* (Englewood Cliffs, NJ: Prentice-Hall).

Kyburg, H.E. (1984) *Theory and Measurement* (Cambridge: Cambridge University Press).

Lachterman, D.R. (1989) *The Ethics of Geometry: A Genealogy of Modernity* (London: Routledge).

Landgrebe, L. (1981) *The Phenomenology of Edmund Husserl: Six Essays*, ed. D. Welton (London: Cornell University Press).

Lant, A. (1995) 'Haptical Cinema', *October* 74: 45–73.

Latham, A. and McCormack, D.M. (2004) 'Moving Cities: Rethinking the Materialities of Urban Geography', *Progress in Human Geography* 28(6): 701–24.

Latham, A. (1999) 'The Power of Distraction: Distraction, Tactility, and Habit in the Work of Walter Benjamin', *Environment and Planning D: Society and Space* 17: 451–73.

Latour, B. (1986) 'Visualization and Cognition: Thinking with Eyes and Hands', *Knowledge and Society: Studies in the Sociology of Culture Past and Present.* 6(1): 1–40.

Latour, B. (1987) *Science in Action: How to Follow Scientists and Engineers Through Society* (Cambridge MA: Harvard University Press).

Lauria, R. (2000) 'electric poetic space: full sensory immersion', *Spark Online* 6.0 at http://www.spark-online.com/march00/discourse/lauria.html [Last accessed 23/07/2006].

Laurier, E. (2001) 'Why People Say where they are during Mobile Phone Calls', *Environment & Planning D: Society and Space* 19(1): 485–504.

Laurier, E. and Philo, C. (2003) 'The Region in the Boot: Lone Subjects and Multiple Objects', *Environment and Planning D: Society and Space* 21(1): 85–106.

Law, J. (1986) 'On the Methods of Long Distance Control: Vessels, Navigation and the Portuguese Route to India', in John Law (ed.), *Power, Action and Belief: a New Sociology of Knowledge?* (London: Routledge & Kegan Paul), pp. 234–63.

Law, J. and Mol, A.M. (2001) 'Situating Technoscience: an Inquiry into Spatialities', *Environment and Planning D: Society and Space* 19(1): 609–21.

Le Corbusier (1925) *The Decorative Art of Today* (London: Architectural Press).

Leder, D. (1990) *The Absent Body* (London: University Of Chicago Press).

Lemoine-Luccioni, E. (1983) *La Robe: Essai psychanalytique sur le vêtement* (Paris: Seuil).

Levinas, E. (1991 [1968]) *Otherwise Than Being or Beyond Essence*, trans. A. Lingis (Boston: Kluwer Academic Publishers).

Levinas, E. (1996) 'Substitution', in S. Hand (ed.), *The Levinas Reader* (Oxford: Blackwell), pp. 88–126.

Lipps, T. (1903) 'Einfühlung, innere Nachahmung und Organempfindung', *Archiv für die gesamte Psychologie* 1, pp. 465–519.

Locke, J. (1991) *An Essay Concerning Human Understanding* [abridged] (London: Everyman's Library).

Lorraine, T. (1999) *Irigaray and Deleuze: Experiments in Visceral Philosophy* (London: Cornell University Press).

Lucas, J.R. (1973) *A Treatise on Time and Space* (London: Methuen).

Luckmann, T. (1973) 'Philosophy, Science, and Everyday Life', in M. Natanson (ed.), *Phenomenology and the Social Sciences* (Evanston, IL: Northwestern University Press), pp. 143–58.

Lupton, E. (ed.)(2002) *Skin: Surface, Substance and Design* (New York: Princeton Architectural Press).

MacLean, K.E. and J.B. Roderick (1999) 'Smart Tangible Displays in the Everyday World: a Haptic Door Knob', *The IEEE/ASME Intl Conf on Advanced Intelligent Mechatronics* (AIM'99), September 1999, Atlanta, GA. Online at http://www.cs.ubc.ca/~maclean/publics/aim99–HapticDoorknob.PDF [last accessed: 25/10/05]

Macpherson, C. and Keppell M. (1997) 'Is the Elephant Really There? Virtual Reality in Education', conference presentation document online at: http://www.infocom.cqu.edu.au/Units/aut99/00101/00101/RESOURCE/TUTORIAL/VR-PRES.PDF [last accessed: 11/01/05]

Magee, B. and Milligan, M. (1998) *Sight Unseen: Letters Between Bryan Magee and Martin Mulligan* (London: Phoenix).

Mahoney, D.P. (1997) 'The Power of Touch', *Computer Graphics World* 20(8), August: 41–8.

Mahoney, D.P. (2000) 'Innovative interfaces', *Computer Graphics World* 23(2), February: 39–44.

Manovich, L. (2001) *The Language of New Media* (London: MIT Press).

Marks, L.E. (1978) *The Unity of the Senses: Interrelations Among the Modalities* (London: Academic Press).

Marks, L.U. (2000) *The Skin of the Film: Intercultural Cinema, Embodiment, and the Senses* (Durham, NC: Duke University Press).

Marks, L.U. (2004) *Touch: Sensuous Theory and Multisensory Media* (London: University of Minnesota Press).

Martin, F.D. (1981) *Sculpture and Enlivened Space: Aesthetics and History* (Lexington: University Press Of Kentucky).

Massie, T. and Salisbury, J.K. (1994) 'The PHANToM haptic interface: a device for probing virtual objects', Proc. ASME Winter Annual Meeting, Dynamic Systems and Control, Chicago, vol. 55, DSC, pp. 295–301. Available at http://www.sensable.com/products/datafiles/phantom_ghost/ASME94.pdf [last accessed: 25/10/05]

Massumi, B. (2002) *Parables for the Virtual: Movement, Affect, Sensation* (Durham: Duke University Press).

Maull, N.L. (1978) 'Cartesian Optics and the Geometrization of Nature', *Review of Metaphysics* 32(2): 253–73.

McCullough, M. (1998) *Abstracting Craft : The Practiced Digital Hand* (London: MIT Press).

McLuhan, M. (1964) *Understanding Media* (London: Routledge & Kegan Paul).

Merleau-Ponty, M. (1964a) *The Primacy of Perception and Other Essays on Phenomenological Psychology, the Philosophy of Art, History and Politics*, trans C. Dallery, ed. J.M. Edie (Evanston IL: Northwestern University Press).

Merleau-Ponty, M. (1964b) *Sense and Non-Sense* (Evanston IL: Northwestern University Press).

Merleau-Ponty, M. (1969) 'Cézanne's Doubt', in A.L. Fisher (ed.), *The Essential Writings of Merleau-Ponty* (New York: Harcourt, Brace & World).

Merleau-Ponty, M. (1984) *The Structure of Behaviour*, trans. A.L. Fisher (Pittsburgh, PA: Duquesne University Press).

Merleau-Ponty, M. (1992) *The Phenomenology of Perception*, trans. C. Smith (London: Routledge).

Merleau-Ponty, M. (2000) *The Visible and the Invisible*, 7th edn, trans. A. Lingis, ed. C. Lefort (Evanston, IL: Northwestern University Press).

Michalko, R. (2002) *The Difference That Disability Makes* (Philadelphia: Temple University Press).

Millar, S. (1994) *Understanding and Representing Space: Theory and Evidence from Studies with Blind and Sighted Children* (Oxford: Oxford University Press).

Molnar, J.M. and Vodvarka, F. (2004) *Sensory Design* (Minneapolis: University of Minnesota Press).

Monbeck, M.E. (1973) *The Meaning of Blindness: Attitudes Towards Blindness and Blind People* (London: Indiana University Press).

Montagu, A. (1986) *Touching: The Human Significance of the Skin*, 3rd edn (London: Harper and Row).

Moorhouse, P. (1991) *Anthony Caro: Sculpture towards Architecture* (London: Tate Gallery).

Moos, D. (1996) 'Memories of Being: Orlan's Theater of the Self', *Art + Text* 54: 67–72.

Moran, D. (2000) *Introduction to Phenomenology* (London: Routledge).

Morgan, K.P. (1998) 'Women and the Knife: Cosmetic Surgery and the Colonization of Women's Bodies', in D. Welton (ed.), *Body and Flesh: A Philosophical Reader* (Oxford: Blackwell) pp. 325–47.

Morgan, M.J. (1977) *Molyneux's Question: Vision, Touch and the Philosophy of Perception* (Cambridge: Cambridge University Press).

Motluk, A. (2005) 'The Art of Seeing without Sight', *New Scientist* 2484, 29 January: 37.

Mulligan, K. (1995) 'Perception', in B. Smith and D. Woodruff Smith (eds), *The Cambridge Companion to Husserl* (Cambridge: Cambridge University Press), pp. 168–238.

Mullins, J. (1998) 'Hear me, See me, Touch me', *New Scientist* 2109, 7 November: 36–8.

Murphie, Andrew (2002) 'Putting the Virtual back into VR', in B. Massumi (ed.), *A Shock to Thought: Expression after Deleuze and Gauttari* (London: Routledge), pp. 188–214.

Natanson, M. (ed.) (1973) *Phenomenology and the Social Sciences* (Evanston, IL: Northwestern University Press).

Natanson, M. (1985) 'Descriptive Phenomenology', in D. Ihde and H.J. Silverman (eds), *Descriptions* (Selected Studies in Phenomenology and Existential Philosophy, Vol. 11) (Albany, NY: State University of New York Press), pp. 2–13.

Norberg-Schultz, C. (1971). *Existence, Space and Architecture* (London: Studio Vista).

Noyes, J. and Mills, S. (1999) 'Virtual Reality', in J.M. Noyes and M. Cook (eds), *Interface Technology: The Leading Edge* (Baldock: Research Studies Press), pp. 123–33.

Oakley, I., McGee, M.R., Brewster, S. and Gray, P. (2000) 'Putting the Feel in "Look and Feel"', *Transactions of ACM CHI 2000* (The Hague: ACM Press), pp. 415–22.

O'Bryan, J. (1997) 'Saint Orlan Faces Resurrection', *Art Journal* 56(4): 50–6.

O'Bryan, J. (1999) 'Penetrating Layers of Flesh: Carving in/out the Bodies of Orlan and Medusa, Artaud and Marsyas', *Women and Performance* 21: Bodywork 11(1): 49–63.

O'Neill, M.E. (2001) 'Corporeal Experience: A Haptic Way of Knowing,' *Journal of Architectural Education* 55(1): 3–12.

Olkowski, D. (2002) 'Flesh to Desire: Merleau-Ponty, Bergson, Deleuze', in *Strategies* 15(1): 11–24.

Orlan (1996) 'Conférence, in D. McCorquodale (ed.), *This is My Body, This is my Software* (London: Black Dog).

Orlan (2000) 'Carnal Art Manifesto' (Manifeste d'art charnel) at http://www.orlan. net/ [last accessed 28/05/2007]

Ovid (1976) *Ovid's Metamorphoses. In Latin and English. Two Volumes*, trans. Garth, Dryden et al. (London: Garth).

Pallasmaa, J. (2000) 'Hapticity and Time: Notes on Fragile Architecture', *Architectural Review* 207(1239), May: 78–84.

Pallasmaa, J. (2005) *The Eyes of the Skin: Architecture and the Senses* (London: Academy Editions).

Paterson, M. (2002) *Haptic Spaces*. Doctoral Thesis, School of Geographical Sciences, University of Bristol.

Paterson, M. (2004) 'Caresses, Excesses, Intimacies and Estrangements', *Angelaki: Journal of the Theoretical Humanities* 9(1): 165–77.

Paterson, M. (2005a) 'Affecting Touch: Towards a Felt Phenomenology of Therapeutic Touch', in: J. Davidson, L. Bondi and M. Smith (eds), *Emotional Geographies* (Aldershot: Ashgate), pp 161–76.

Paterson, M. (2005b) *Consumption and Everyday Life* (London: Routledge).

Paterson, M. (2005c) 'Digital Touch', in C. Classen (ed.), *The Book of Touch* (Oxford: Berg), pp. 431–6.

Paterson, M. (2006a) '"Seeing with the Hands": Blindness, Touch and the Enlightenment Spatial Imaginary', *British Journal of Visual Impairment* 24(2): 52–60.

Paterson, M. (2006b) 'Seeing with the Hands, Touching with the Eyes: Vision, Touch and the Enlightenment Spatial Imaginary', *Senses and Society* 1(2): 224–42.

Paterson, M. (2006c) 'Feel the Presence: The Technologies of Touch', *Environment and Planning D: Society and Space* 24(5): 691–708.

Paterson, M. (2006d) 'Digital Scratch and Virtual Sniff: Articulating a Language of Smell through iSmell', in J. Drobnick (ed.), *The Smell Culture Reader* (Oxford: Berg), pp. 358–70.

Paterson, M. (In Press, 2007) 'Digital Craft, Digital Touch: Haptics and Design', in B. Hawk, D. Rieder, and O. Oviedo (eds), *Digital Tools in Cultural Contexts: Assessing the Implications of New Media* (Minneapolis: University of Minnesota Press).

Pesce, M. (2000) *The Playful World: How Technology is Transforming Our Imagination* (New York: Ballantine).

Petit, J.-L. (2003) 'On the Relation between Recent Neurological Data on Perception (and Action) and the Husserlian theory of constitution', *Phenomenology and the Cognitive Sciences* 2(4): 281–98.

Piaget, J. (1955) *The Child's Construction of Reality* (London: Routledge & Kegan Paul.

Piaget, J. and Inhelder, B. (1956) *The Child's Conception of Space* (London: Routledge & Kegan Paul).

Piaget, J. and Inhelder, B. (1969) *The Psychology of the Child* (New York: Basic).

Plato (1986) *Republic*, 2nd rev. edn, trans. H.D.P. Lee (Harmondsworth: Penguin).

Plato (1987) *Thaetetus*, trans. R.A.H. Waterfield (Harmondsworth: Penguin).

Politz, A. (1979). 'On the Origin of Space Perception', *Philosophy and Phenomenological Research* 40: 258–64.

Probyn, E. (2001) 'Dis/connect: Space, Affect, Writing.' Spatial Cultures Conference, The University of Newcastle, Australia 2–3 June 2001, University of Newcastle. Paper at http://home.iprimus.com.au/painless/space/elspeth.html [Last accessed: 07/06/2006].

Rajchman, J. (1998) *Constructions* (London: MIT Press).

Rajchman, J. (2000) *The Deleuze Connections* (London: MIT Press).

Ramachandran, V.S. and Blakeslee, S. (1999) *Phantoms in the Brain: Human Nature and the Architecture of the Mind* (London: Fourth Estate).

Reachin.se (2002) 'The feeling of the Reach In interface', http://www.led.br/~tissiani/arquivos/ePapers/papers_VRUI/chalmersMediaLab/haptic_interfaces/Chalmers%20Medialab%20–%20The%20Reach-In%20concept.htm [last accessed 28/10/05].

Reachin.se (2006) Press Release, Stockholm, 5 April 2006. Available at http://www.reachin.se/pressroom/news/ [Last accessed: 28/08/06].

Read, H. (1961) *The Art of Sculpture* (London: Faber).

Révész, G. (1937) 'The Problem of Space with Particular Emphasis on Specific Sensory Spaces', *American Journal of Psychology* 50: 429–44.

Révész, G. (1950) *The Psychology and Art of the Blind* (London: Longmans Green).

Révész, G. (1958) *The Human Hand: A Psychological Study*, trans. J. Cohen (London: Routledge & Kegan Paul).

Rheingold, H. (1991) *Virtual Reality* (New York: Touchstone).

Rheingold, H. (2000) *Tools for Thought: The History and Future of Mind-Expanding Technology*, 2nd edn (London: MIT Press).

Riegl, A. (1995 [1901]) 'Late Roman Art Industry', trans. R. Winkes, in E. Fernie (ed.), *Art History and Its Methods: A Critical Anthology* (London: Phaidon), pp. 116–26.

Riskin, J. (2002) *Science in the Age of Sensibility: The Sentimental Empiricists of the French Enlightenment* (London: University of Chicago Press).

Roberts, M. (1998) 'The Ends of Pictorial Representation: Merleau-Ponty and Lyotard', in H.J. Silverman (ed.), *Cultural Semiosis: Tracing the Signifier* (London: Routledge), pp. 129–39.

Rock, I. and Harris, C.S. (1967) 'Vision and Touch', *Scientific American* 216: 96–104.

Rodaway, P. (1994) *Sensuous Geographies: Body Sense and Place* (London: Routledge).

Rogers, L.R. (1962) 'Sculptural Thinking', *British Journal of Aesthetics* 2(4): 291–300.

Rose, B. (1993) 'Orlan: Is it Art? Orlan and the Transgressive Act', *Art in America* 81 (2): 83–125.

Rose, S.A. (1994) 'From Hand to Eye: Findings and Issues in Infant Cross-Modal Transfer', in D.J. Lewkowicz and R Lickliter (eds), *The Development of Intersensory Perception: Comparative Perspectives* (Hove: Lawrence Erlbaum), pp. 265–84.

Sacks, O.W. (1986) *The Man who Mistook his Wife for a Hat* (London: Picador).

Sacks, O.W. (1993) 'To See and Not See', *New Yorker*, 10 May: 59–73.

Sacks, O.W. (1995) *An Anthropologist on Mars: Seven Paradoxical Tales* (London: Picador).

Sacks, O.W. (2003) 'A Neurologist's Notebook: The Mind's Eye – What the Blind See', *New Yorker*, 28 July: 48–59.

Salisbury, K. (1995) 'Haptics: The Technology of Touch', at SensAble.com: sensable.org/products/datafiles/ phantom_ghost/Salisbury_Haptics95.pdf [Last accessed: 22/08/06].

Sallis, J. (1994) *Stone* (Bloomington: Indiana University Press).

Salzmann-Erikson, M. and Eriksson, H. (2005) 'Encountering Touch: A Path to Affinity in Psychiatric Care', *Issues in Mental Health Nursing* 26: 843–52.

Schutz, A. (1967) *The Phenomenology of the Social World*, trans. G. Walsh and F. Lehnert (Evanston, IL: Northwestern University Press).

Schutz, A. (1970) *On Phenomenology and Social Relations: Selected Writings*, ed. H. Wagner (Chicago: University of Chicago Press).

Scott, G. (1914) *The Architecture of Humanism: A Study in the History of Taste* (London: Architectural Press).

Senft, T.M. (1996) 'Introduction: Performing the Digital Body – A Ghost Story', *Women and Performance* 17: *Sexuality and Cyberspace* 9(1): 9–34.

Seremetakis, C.N. (ed.) (1994) *The Senses Still: Perception and Memory as Material Culture in Modernity* (Oxford: Westview).

Serres, M. (1982) *Hermes: Literature Science and Philosophy* (Baltimore: Johns Hopkins University Press).

Serres, M. (1995) 'Gnomon: The Beginnings of Geometry in Greece', in M. Serres (ed.), *A History of Scientific Thought* (Oxford: Blackwell).

Shakespeare, W. (1993 [1608]) *King Lear*, Arden Edition, ed. K. Muir (London: Routledge).

Shaviro, S. (1993) *The Cinematic Body* (London: University of Minnesota Press).

Sheridan, T.B. (1989) 'Telerobotics', *Automatica* 25(4): 487–507.

Sherrington, C. (1947 [1906]) *The Integrative Action of the Nervous System* (New Haven, CT: Yale University Press).

Shiff, R. (1991) 'Cézanne's Physicality: the Politics of Touch', in S. Kamal and I. Gaskell (eds), *The Language of Art History* (Cambridge: Cambridge University Press), pp. 129–80.

Shiff, R. (1997) 'Breath of Modernism (Metonymic Drift)', in T. Smith (ed.), *In Visible Touch: Modernism and Masculinity* (Chicago: University of Chicago Press), pp. 184–213.

Shillito, A.M., Paynter, K., Wall, S. and Wright, M. (2001) 'Tacitus Project: Identifying Multi-Sensory Perceptions in Creative 3D Practice for Development of a Haptic Computing System for Applied Artists', *Digital Creativity* 12(1): 195–204.

Shusterman, R. (2006) 'The Aesthetic', *Theory, Culture and Society* 23(2–3): 237–52.

Smith, B. (2000) 'Truth and the Visual Field', in J. Petitot, F.J. Varela, B. Pachoud and J.-M. Roy (eds), *Naturalizing Phenomenology: Issues in Contemporary Phenomenology and Cognitive Science* (Stanford, CA: Stanford University Press).

Smith, D.W. (2003) *Deleuze on Bacon: Three Conceptual Trajectories in the Logic of Sensation* (Minneapolis: University of Minnesota Press).

Smith, J. (1989) *Senses and Sensibilities* (Chichester: John Wiley & Sons).

Sobchack, V. (1992) *The Address of the Eye: A Phenomenology of Film Experience* (Princeton, NJ: Princeton University Press).

Sobchack, V. (1995) 'Beating the Meat/Surviving the Text, or How to Get Out of this Century Alive', in M. Featherstone and R. Burrows (eds), *Cyberspace, Cyberbodies, Cyberpunk* (London: Sage).

Solokowski, R. (1985) 'The Theory of Phenomenological Description', in D. Ihde and H.J. Silverman (eds), *Descriptions* (Selected Studies in Phenomenology and Existential Philosophy, Vol. 11) (Albany, NY: State University of New York Press), pp. 14–24.

Solokowski, R. (2000) *Introduction to Phenomenology* (Cambridge: Cambridge University Press).

Sorabji, R. (1992) 'Intentionality and Physiological Processes: Aristotle's Theory of Sense-perception', in M.C. Nussbaum and A.O. Rorty (eds), *Essays on Aristotle's De Anima* (Oxford: Clarendon), pp. 195–225.

Spiegelberg, H. (1982) *The Phenomenological Movement: A Historical Introduction*, 3rd edn (London: Martinus Nijhoff).

Spolsky, E. (1994) 'Doubting Thomas and the Senses of Knowing', *Common Knowledge* 3(2): 111–29.

Srinivasan, M.A. and Basdogan, C. (1997) 'Haptics in Virtual Environments: Taxonomy, Research Status, and Challenges', *Computers & Graphics* 21: 393–404.

Stelarc (1991) 'Symposium Paper – Prosthetics, Robotics and Remote Existence: Postevolutionary Strategies', *Leonardo* 24 (5): 591–5.

Stelarc (1994) 'Hollow Body, Host Space', *Proceedings of ISEA '94* (International Symposium on Electronic Arts) at http://www.isea.qc.ca/symposium/archives/ isea94/pr405.html [Last accessed 30/4/2001].

Stelarc (1998) 'From Psycho-body to Cyber-systems: Images as Post-human Entities', in J.B. Dixon and E.J. Cassidy (eds) *Virtual Futures: Cyberotics, Technology and Post-human Pragmatism* (London: Routledge), pp. 116–23.

Stelarc (2003) 'Fractal Flesh' at http://www.stelarc.va.com.au/fractal/index.html [Last accessed 18/08/2006].

Stewart, R.S. and Legatto-Stewart, B. (2005) 'Modern Mesmerism or Postmodern Science? The Case of Therapeutic Touch', *Contemporary Philosophy* 25(3/4): 3–14.

Stoller, P. (1997) *Sensuous Scholarship* (Philadelphia: University of Philadelphia Press).

Stone, A.R. (1991) 'Will the Real Body Please Stand Up?: Boundary Stories about Virtual Cultures', in M. Benedikt (ed.), *Cyberspace: First Steps* (London: MIT Press), pp. 81–118.

Stone, A.R. (1995) *The War of Desire and Technology at the Close of the Mechanical Age* (London: MIT Press).

Stone, R. (2000) 'Haptic Feedback: A Potted History, from Telepresence to Virtual Reality', *The First International Workshop on Haptic Human-Computer Interaction*, Glasgow, UK (Amsterdam: Springer-Verlag Lecture Notes in Computer Science), pp. 1–7. Available at http://www.dcs.gla.ac.uk/~stephen/ workshops/haptic/papers/stone.pdf [last accessed 28/10/05].

Streri, A. (1993) *Seeing, Reaching, Touching: the Relations between Vision and Touch in Infancy* (Hemel Hemstead: Harvester Wheatsheaf).

Streri, A. (2005) 'Touching for Knowing in Infancy: The Development of Manual Abilities in Very Young Infants', *European Journal of Developmental Psychology* 2(4): 325–43.

Strömberg, H., Väätäinen, A. and Räty, V.P. (2002) 'A Group Game Played in Interactive Virtual Space – Design and Evaluation', *Proceedings of DIS2002: Designing Interactive Systems*, London, 25–28 June (London: ACM Press), pp. 56–63.

Sudnow, D. (1993) *The Ways of the Hand: The Organisation of Improvised Conduct* (London: MIT Press).

Sullivan, S. (2001) *Living Across and Through Skin: Transactional Bodies, Pragmatism and Feminism* (Bloomington: Indiana University Press).

Suppes, P., Krantz, D.M., Luce, R.D., and Tversky, A. (1989) *Foundations of Measurement*, Vol. 2, *Geometrical Threshold and Probabilistic Representations* (London: Academic Press).

Sutherland, I.E. (1965) 'The Ultimate Display', *Proceedings of the International Federation of Information Processing Congress* 2: 506–8.

Sutton-Smith, B. (1997) *The Ambiguity of Play* (London: Harvard University Press).

Taussig, M. (1993) *Mimesis and Alterity: A Particular History of the Senses* (London: Routledge).

Taylor, M.C. (1997) *Hiding* (Chicago: University of Chicago Press).

Thrift, N.J. (2000) 'Afterwords', *Environment and Planning D: Society & Space* 18(1): 213–55.

Thrift, N.J. (2004) 'Summoning life' in P. Cloke, P. Crang and M. Goodwin (eds), *Envisioning Human Geographies* (London: Arnold), pp. 81–103.

Tiao, G. (2004) 'Speaking in Textures, Hearing in Colours: Synaesthesia and the Science of the Senses', *Harvard Science Review*, Winter: 65–7.

Tikka, H. (1994) 'Vision and Dominance: A Critical Look at Interactive Systems', *Proceedings of the ISEA* (International Symposium on Electronic Arts), September, online at http://www.isea.qc.ca/symposium/archives/isea94/pr210. html [Last accessed 30/04/2001].

Tobias, J. (2002) 'Artificial Skin', in E. Lupton (ed.), *Skin: Surface, Substance and Design* (New York: Princeton Architectural Press), pp. 43–53.

Tuer, D. (1998) 'The Second Nature of Simulation: Mirroring the Organic in the Virtual World of Char Davies' Ephémère', *Ephémère* [Exhibition Catalogue] (Ottawa: National Gallery).

Ungar, S. (2000) 'Cognitive Mapping without Visual Experience', in R.K.S. Freundschuh (ed.), *Cognitive Mapping: Past, Present and Future* (London: Routledge).

Van Dongen, E. and Elema, R. (2001) 'The Art of Touching: the Culture of "Body Work" in Nursing', *Anthropology and Medicine* 8(2/3): 149–62.

Vasseleu, C. (1998) *Textures of Light: Vision and Touch in Irigaray, Levinas and Merleau-Ponty* (London: Routledge).

Vischer, R. (1994[1873]) 'On the Optical Sense of Form: A Contribution to Aesthetics', in H.F. Mallgrave and E. Ikonomou (eds), *Empathy, Form, and Space: Problems in German Aesthetics, 1873–1893* (Santa Monica, CA: Getty Center for the History of Art) pp. 89–124.

Voltaire (1967 [1738]) *The Elements of Sir Isaac Newton's Philosophy*, trans. J. Hanna (London: Frank Cass).

Voltaire (1992) 'Eléments de philosophie de Newton', in *Oeuvres complètes*, vol. 15 (Oxford: Alden Press), pp. 183–652.

Von Senden, M. (1960 [1932]) *Space and Sight: The Perception of Space and Shape in the Congenitally Blind Before and After Operation*. trans. P. Heath (London: Methuen).

Wall, S. and Brewster, S. (2006) 'Editorial: Design of Haptic User-interfaces and Applications', *Virtual Reality* 9(2–3): 95–6.

Warren, D.H. (1978) 'Perception by the blind', in E.C. Carterette and M.P. Friedman (eds), *Handbook of Perception*, Vol. 10, *Perceptual Ecology* (London: Academic Press), pp. 65–90.

Warren, D.H. (1982) 'The Development of Haptic Perception', in W Schiff and E. Foulke (eds), *Tactual Perception: A Sourcebook* (Cambridge: Cambridge University Press), pp. 82–129.

Warren, D.H.A. and Rossano, M.J. (1991) 'Intermodality Relations: Vision and Touch', in M.A. Heller and W. Schiff (eds), *The Psychology of Touch* (London: Lawrence Erlbaum).

Weber, E.H. (1978 [1834]) *E H. Weber: The Sense of Touch* [translation of *De Tactu* by E.H. Weber] (New York: Academic Press).

Weiss, Gail (1999) *Body Images: Embodiment as Intercorporeality* (London: Routledge).

Welton, D. (1999) 'Soft, Smooth Hands: Husserl's Phenomenology of the Lived Body', in D. Welton (ed.), *The Body* (Oxford: Blackwell), pp. 38–56.

Whorf, Benjamin Lee (1956) *Language, Thought and Reality: Selected Writings of Benjamin Lee Whorf*, ed. J. Carroll (Cambridge: MIT Press).

Wills, D. (1995) *Prosthesis* (Stanford, CA: Stanford University Press).

Wilson, F.R. (1999) *The Hand: How Its Use Shapes the Brain, Language and Human Culture* (New York: Vintage).

Wyschogrod, E. (1980) 'Doing Before Hearing: On the Primacy of Touch', in F. Laruelle (ed.), *Textes pour Emmanuel Levinas* (Paris: Jean Laplace), pp. 179–203.

Wyschogrod, E. (1981) 'Empathy and Sympathy as Tactile Encounter', *Journal of Medicine and Philosophy* 6: 25–43.

Yelistratov, V., Strauss, W. and Fleischmann, M. (1999) 'Two Approaches for Intuitive Navigation in Virtual Environments', *Proceedings of Graphicon 99, 9th International Conference on Computer Graphics and Vision,* Moscow 1999. Available at http://www.bi.fraunhofer.de/publications/report/0080/Text.pdf [last accessed 28/10/05].

Yolton, J. (1984) *Perceptual Acquaintance from Descartes to Reid* (Minneapolis: University of Minnesota Press).

Yoshida, J. (2005) 'iPod's lesson: please touch', *EE Times Online,* 12/12/05, available at http://www.eetimes.com/showArticle.jhtml?articleID=174909778 [last accessed 23/08/06].

Young, I.M. (1990) *Throwing Like a Girl and Other Essays in Philosophy and Social Theory* (Bloomington: Indiana University Press).

Young, I.M. (1999) 'Pregnant Embodiment' in D. Welton (ed.), *Body and Flesh: A Philosophical Reader* (Oxford: Blackwell), pp. 274–85.

Zaitsev, E.A. (1999) 'The Meaning of Early Modern Geometry: From Euclid and Surveyors' Manuals to Christian Philosophy', *Isis* 90(1): 522–53.

Index